Studies in European Arms and Armor

This publication was supported by grants
from the National Endowment for the Arts, a Federal agency,
and an endowment fund for scholarly publications established by grants
from CIGNA Foundation

Detail of pageant shield, Italian, c. 1535 (see fig. 71).

Studies in European Arms and Armor

THE C. OTTO VON KIENBUSCH COLLECTION
IN THE PHILADELPHIA MUSEUM OF ART

Claude Blair

Lionello G. Boccia

Everett Fahy

Helmut Nickel

A.V. B. Norman

Stuart W. Pyhrr

Donald J. La Rocca

Philadelphia Museum of Art

Cover: Detail of pageant shield, Italian, c.1535 (see fig. 72).

Edited by Jane Watkins

Designed by Greer Allen

Composition by Pagesetters, Inc., Brattleboro, Vermont

Printed in Great Britain by Balding + Mansell, Wisbech, Cambs.

Library of Congress Cataloging-in-Publication Data

Studies in European arms and armor : the C. Otto von Kienbusch collection
   in the Philadelphia Museum of Art / Claude Blair . . . [et al.].
       208 p. cm.
     Includes bibliographical references.
     ISBN 0-8122-7963-8: $49.95 (est.).—ISBN 0-87633-088-X (pb.)
$25.00 (est.)
   1. Armor—Europe.   2. Von Kienbusch, Carl Otto Kretzschmar,
1884–1976—Art collections.   3. Armor—Private collections—
Pennsylvania—Philadelphia.   4. Armor—Pennsylvania—Philadelphia.
5. Philadelphia Museum of Art.   I. Blair, Claude.   II. Philadelphia
Museum of Art.
NK6642.S78   1992
823.4′41′09407474811—dc20   91-47037
                                                              CIP

Contents

Preface

Since 1977, when it was bequeathed to the Museum, the Carl Otto Kretzschmar von Kienbusch Collection of Arms and Armor has been a source of delight to countless visitors to the Philadelphia Museum of Art. This splendid installation, crowning the Museum's monumental staircase, is the first that many people see, and few resist its fascination. Assiduously gathered over a period of seventy years by Mr. von Kienbusch (1884–1976), the collection comprises over fourteen hundred objects, many of remarkable quality, including European armor, edged weapons, and firearms.

The formation of his vast collection inevitably owed much to the particular opportunities afforded in this century, but the caliber of the acquisitions depended equally on Mr. von Kienbusch's impressive connoisseurship and his relentless study of this complex field. What was to be a lifelong passion was first signaled by the purchase of a small group of swords in 1906, the year Kienbusch graduated with honors from Princeton University, where he had demonstrated a lively interest in history and art. After returning to his home in New York City, he entered his family's tobacco business. His true career as an arms and armor collector began in earnest in 1910, when he met Dr. Bashford Dean (1867–1928). The first curator of The Metropolitan Museum of Art's Department of Arms and Armor and a major private collector and gentleman dealer, Dean was the acknowledged head of the American fraternity of arms and armor afficionados. In the years after 1900, during sojourns in Japan, Dean amassed the most encyclopedic collection of Japanese arms and armor ever assembled by a westerner. By 1914 Dean had donated his Japanese collection to the Metropolitan Museum and was devoting himself exclusively to European arms and armor. Following Dean's example, Kienbusch became a serious collector of *tsuba*, Japanese sword-guards. After presenting this collection to Princeton University in 1914, Kienbusch, too, concentrated on European material. During the First World War, Kienbusch was commissioned as a lieutenant and served as Dean's chief assistant in the army's specially created Helmets and Body Armor Division. The two men engaged in the research and development of prototypes of ballistic armor based on their knowledge of historic examples.

After the war, Dean acted as Kienbusch's mentor and regularly purchased modest items on his behalf at overseas auctions; other objects were acquired from auctions held in New York and from a few well-established dealers. In 1923 Kienbusch made his first extended trip to Europe. Traveling for six months, he and his wife Mildred (1887–1968) visited public and private collections and dealers in principal cities from London to Madrid, making purchases along the way. Kienbusch's next large group of acquisitions came as a result of Dean's unexpected death in 1928. While the majority of Dean's collection was bequeathed to the Metropolitan Museum, Kienbusch obtained many important pieces from the hundreds of items remaining in the estate of the connoisseur he so admired.

Kienbusch matured as a collector in the 1930s and 1940s. The aftermath of the Depression and World War II brought arms and armor onto the art market in large numbers, including the holdings of Clarence H. Mackay and William Randolph Hearst, who possessed the two finest private collections then in existence. Along with the Royal Armouries of H. M. Tower of London and the Metropolitan Museum, a principal beneficiary of the dispersal of these treasure troves was Carl Otto von Kienbusch.

By the mid-1950s, Kienbusch was established as the foremost American collector of European arms and armor, and over nine hundred objects filled the armory, which occupied the second floor of his New York townhouse at 12 East 74th Street. Determined to document his holdings, he commissioned a catalogue from a distinguished international team of scholars: Hans Schedelmann, John F. Hayward, Richard H. Randall, and Anita Reinhard. Published in 1963, as a deluxe, cased quarto, now itself a collector's item, *The Kretzschmar von Kienbusch Collection of Armor and Arms* was distributed free to major institutions and libraries around the world.

The catalogue was also an expression of Kienbusch's concern for the eventual disposition of his collection. He had witnessed, and often benefited from, the dispersal of dozens of private arms and armor collections, but he did not wish a similar fate for his own armory. Courted by several museums that hoped to receive the collection as a bequest, the prize was won by the Philadelphia Museum of Art, led in its bid by R. Sturgis Ingersoll, then president of the Museum and, like Kienbusch, a graduate of Princeton. An enlightened Philadelphia city government played a crucial role by agreeing to fund the renovations needed to convert several galleries into a grand armory that Kienbusch simply could not refuse. For the inaugural installation of arms and armor in 1972, Kienbusch lent a selection of more than one hundred of his finest treasures.

By the time of his death in 1976, at the age of ninety-two, Kienbusch had assembled a distinguished and comprehensive collection modeled after the ancestral armories of Europe and the great European and American private collections of the nineteenth and early twentieth centuries. The Kienbusch Collection continues to inspire a wealth of scholarship in the field of arms and armor. To pursue Kienbusch's own practice of encouraging active research, the Museum sought and received funds from the National Endowment for the Arts for the preparation of study storage in 1980 and a grant to host a series of visits by scholars between 1982 and 1986 to study aspects of the collection. Their findings are here presented in five essays. The research for the sixth essay, written by a former member of the Museum staff, was largely supported by a Fellowship for Museum Professionals, also funded by the National Endowment for the Arts, whose support for Kienbusch projects has been invaluable for over a decade.

Dr. Helmut Nickel, author of the first essay in this volume, is Curator Emeritus of the Arms and Armor Department at the Metropolitan Museum. Known for his studies of the iconographic and historical aspects of arms and armor from the migration era through the Renaissance, Dr. Nickel's expertise extends to heraldry and the history of the duchy of Saxony. Kienbusch's own ancestors had emigrated from Saxony to the United States in the 1840s. This family connection and the high quality of the armory of the dukes and later kings of Saxony enlivened Kienbusch's interest in collecting pieces related to the Saxon court. Dr. Nickel, himself a native of Saxony, discusses the personal parade armor of the dukes of Saxony, which are among the finest objects in the Kienbusch Collection.

The second essay is by Dr. Lionello Boccia, Director of the Museo Stibbert in Florence, which possesses an extensive collection formed by a single collector of arms and armor. Dr. Boccia has written extensively about Italian arms and armor from the Middle Ages to the Industrial Revolution. Upon this occasion, he surveys a group of Italian armor from the fifteenth and early sixteenth centuries in the Kienbusch Collection.

A.V.B. Norman, former Master of the Royal Armouries, H. M. Tower of London, is an authority on European swords. His essay focuses on Kienbusch's choice group of court swords and small swords, the last manifestation of the sword worn with civilian dress. Using examples in the collection, Mr. Norman traces the history of the small-sword from about 1650 to 1800 and its evolution from a sturdy fighting weapon to an elaborate costume accessory.

Claude Blair, former Keeper of Metalwork at the Victoria and Albert Museum, London, has written on many aspects of European armor and metalwork from the Middle Ages through the nineteenth century. His essay examines a single helmet, the intriguing history of which sheds much light on collectors and collecting in the late nineteenth and early twentieth centuries.

Stuart W. Pyhrr, Curator of Arms and Armor, The Metropolitan Museum of Art, is noted for his studies of the art-historical aspects of arms and armor. Together with Everett Fahy, The John Pope-Hennessy Chairman of European Paintings at the Metropolitan Museum and an authority on early Italian painting, he discusses a splendid Italian Renaissance painted shield in the Kienbusch Collection and a related group of pageant shields.

It is a particular pleasure to publish a companion essay by a young scholar in the field, Donald J. LaRocca, who served as administrator and then as Assistant Curator of the Kienbusch Collection from 1982 to 1988 and coordinated the visiting scholars program during his tenure. Now Assistant Curator of Arms and Armor at The Metropolitan Museum of Art, Mr. LaRocca explores the decoration of *armes de luxe* as it appears in a series of late seventeenth and early eighteenth-century French pattern books in the Kienbusch Library.

Handsomely designed by Greer Allen, this volume was thoughtfully edited by Jane Watkins, Senior Editor in the Department of Publications at this Museum. A generous grant from the National Endowment for the Arts and the Cigna-Mellon fund for scholarly publications supported its production. These six essays offer individual approaches to the

ANNE D'HARNONCOURT
8

study of arms and armor by leading scholars in the field today. Together, they advance our knowledge of the Kienbusch Collection and underscore the variety of its holdings. No one would have been more interested in these studies than Kienbusch himself. Following his example and celebrating almost two decades of the public display of his treasures, the Philadelphia Museum of Art publishes this volume in the hope that it will, in turn, stimulate a new generation of connoisseurs, scholars, and enthusiasts in this fascinating field.

Anne d'Harnoncourt
The George D. Widener Director

Parade Armor for Three Prince Electors of Saxony in the Kienbusch Collection

HELMUT NICKEL

Among the ancient princely collections of arms and armor still surviving in Europe, one of the most distinguished is that of the Historisches Museum at Dresden. Originally, during the sixteenth through eighteenth centuries, the collection formed the arsenal—*Rüstkammer*—for field, tournament, and parade armor of the court of the dukes and prince electors of Saxony, of the House of Wettin. In 1831 it was turned into a historical museum. The prince electors had become kings of Saxony in 1806, after the dissolution of the Holy Roman Empire by Napoleon Bonaparte; the last king of Saxony abdicated in 1918, at the end of World War I. The Weimar Republic, which followed, nationalized the former royal collections and subsequently held several fundraising sales from the seemingly inexhaustible resources of the Historisches Museum. At the end of World War II the bulk of the celebrated art collections of Dresden, which had been evacuated and thus survived the destruction of the city itself, were transported to the Soviet Union, to be returned piecemeal after 1958. In the 1970s the East German authorities resumed sales from the Historisches Museum. As a result, Saxon arms—without exception always of the highest quality—are to be found in museums and private collections the world over.

One of the American collections particularly rich in arms of this prized Saxon provenance is the Kienbusch Collection of Armor and Arms in the Philadelphia Museum of Art. Its founder, Carl Otto Kretzschmar von Kienbusch, had a special interest in Saxonica because he was a descendant of a Saxon family who owned the *Rittergut*, or "knight's holding" manor estate, of Untermarksgrün in the Vogtland, the westernmost part of the former kingdom of Saxony, now a few miles east of what was until recently the border that separated East from West Germany.

The Saxon arms in the Kienbusch Collection consist of polearms, edged weapons, firearms, and helmets of the various palace guard units—*Trabantengarde*, chevalier guard, Swiss guard, and Janissary guard—which were maintained by the prince electors in their heyday, as well as several outstanding pieces of parade armor made for the prince electors themselves. Among them are four colletins and one half armor of great artistic and historical interest, having been made for three seventeenth-century prince electors, Johann Georg I (reigned 1611–56), Johann Georg II (reigned 1656–81), and Johann Georg III (reigned 1681–93).

Fig. 1. Colletin, German, Saxony, made between 1666 and 1681 for Prince Elector Johann Georg III of Saxony. Decorated with insignia of the Danish Order of the Elephant on the frontplate and the arms of Duke Johann Georg III as heir apparent on the backplate. Steel, etched, and partly silvered and gilt; leather lining edged with green velvet piccadills; 1977-167-220.

The latest of these parade pieces is a richly etched colletin (fig. 1) bearing the insignia of the Danish Order of the Elephant on its frontplate and the full armorial achievement of Duke Johann Georg III as heir apparent on its backplate. It is of steel, lined with leather that is edged with green velvet piccadills (green being one of the livery colors of Saxony). The Order of the Elephant was awarded to Johann Georg III in 1666, on the occasion of his marriage to a Danish princess. According to the surviving inventory of 1689, this colletin was deposited in the Dresden *Rüstkammer* in 1681, when Johann Georg III succeeded as prince elector after his father, Johann Georg II (see fig. 6).

The twenty-one quarterings of the armorial shield on the backplate give a heraldic summary of the complicated history of the dukedom and of the territorial claims and aspirations of the House of Wettin, one of the oldest dynasties in Germany, which can be traced to the ninth century. The counts of Wettin, named after a small castle on the Saale River, were border wardens at the edge of Christendom, in the disputed area between the Holy Roman Empire in the west and Slavic tribal lands to the east. In 928 the border was advanced farther eastward all the way to the river Elbe, into the territory of the Slavic Daleminzians, thus creating the important frontier bastion of the margraviate of Meissen. In 932 another margraviate, Lusatia, was carved out of the lands of the Lusizes, to the north. In 1032, one of the Wettin counts, Dietrich II, lord of Brehna, was put in charge of the margraviate of Lusatia, and in 1089 his grandson, Heinrich, became margrave of Meissen. Confirmed in 1127 as a hereditary fief of the empire to Konrad of Wettin, the margraviate of Meissen remained the heartland of the holdings of the Wettin dynasty for eight hundred years following.

To the north of Meissen, and downriver on the Elbe, was the duchy of Saxony, ruled by the Ascanian dynasty (fig. 2). In 1423, after the death of the last Ascanian duke, the Wettin margrave of Meissen was entrusted with this dukedom by Emperor Sigismund. The dignity of the duke of Saxony was bound to the hereditary office of archmarshal of the empire. The archmarshal was the commander-in-chief of the imperial forces, which office, in turn, made its bearer a member of the council of seven prince electors, whose privilege and duty it was to elect the next emperor.[1] The first Wettin prince elector and archmarshal was the aptly named Friedrich *der Streitbare* (the Battle-Ready). After large territorial inheritances in Thuringia had made the duchy too unwieldy to rule as a unit, his two grandsons, Ernst and Albrecht, divided the country in 1486 into a western and an eastern part, with capitals at Wittenberg and Dresden. The title of prince elector remained with the older brother, Ernst of Saxe-Wittenberg. His descendants held it until 1547, when it was handed over to Duke Moritz of the junior Dresden-Meissen branch, as a reward for services during the wars of religion that shook the empire as an aftermath of the Reformation.[2]

The arms of office of the archmarshal were as follows: per fess (that is, divided horizontally) of black and silver, with two red crossed swords overall. Borne as an inshield, they were reserved for the prince elector himself, and their absence from this colletin indicates unmistakably that the existing arms are those of the heir apparent, used while his father was

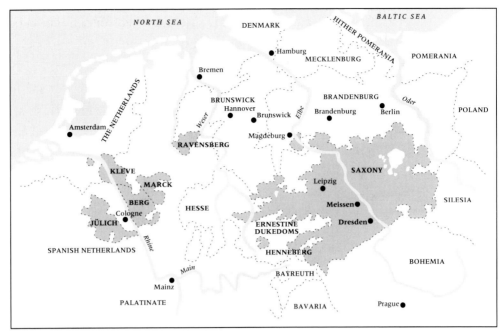

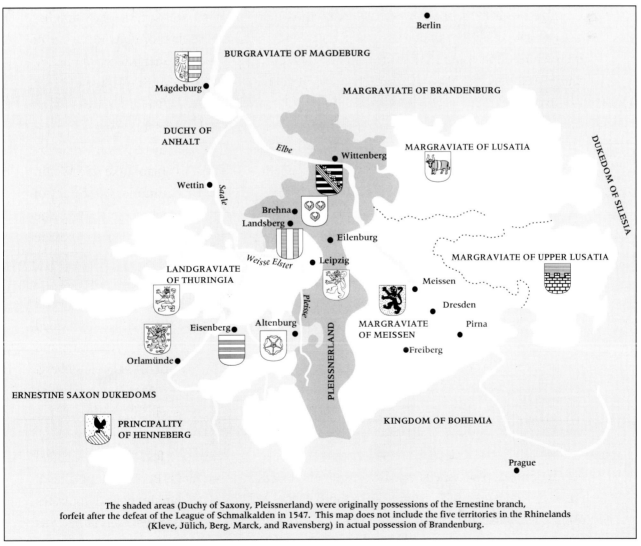

The shaded areas (Duchy of Saxony, Pleissnerland) were originally possessions of the Ernestine branch, forfeit after the defeat of the League of Schmalkalden in 1547. This map does not include the five territories in the Rhinelands (Kleve, Jülich, Berg, Marck, and Ravensberg) in actual possession of Brandenburg.

Fig 2. Above, *Western Europe and the Holy Roman Empire, c. 1650.*
Below, *The Duchy of Saxony and dependent territories with their coats of arms, c. 1650*

3

4

Fig. 3. Colletin, German, Saxony, c.1660, attributed to Prince Elector Johann Georg II, probably made by court armorer Jacob Jöringk. Steel, gilt over a punched ground; leather lining edged with crimson velvet piccadills; 1977-167-219.

Fig. 4. Colletin, German, Saxony, 1654, made for Prince Elector Johann Georg II. Steel, etched, and gilt on blued ground; lining of doeskin edged with red velvet piccadills; 1977-167-222.

Fig. 5. Parade armor, German, Saxony, c.1650–60, made for Prince Elector Johann Georg II. Copper, embossed, and gilt, set with paste jewels; helmet lined with crimson silk, embroidered with gold thread; breast and back lined with doeskin, edged with red velvet piccadills; 1977-167-44.

6a

6b

8

7

Fig. 6. a. Taler of Prince Elector Johann Georg III, 1683. b. Reverse with full arms of Johann Georg III as prince elector. The Metropolitan Museum of Art, New York; Gift of Bashford Dean, 1922; 22.122.33.

Fig. 7. Medal struck by order of Johann Georg II, on Saint George's Day, 1678, to commemorate the seventh anniversary of his election to the Order of the Garter. Silver. The Metropolitan Museum of Art, New York; Gift of Bashford Dean, 1922; 22.122.32.

Fig. 8. Back of parade armor made for Prince Elector Johann Georg II (see fig. 5).

still alive. The quarterings of the shield are as follows, starting in the upper left-hand corner (fig. 1, backplate):

1. In blue, a lion barry (striped horizontally) of red and silver, golden crowned (landgraviate of Thuringia, acquired in 1482).

2. In red, a golden escarbuncle, overlaid with a silver escutcheon (duchy of Kleve, retained in the arms as a claim on territory annexed by Brandenburg in 1610).

3. In silver, a red lion (duchy of Berg, retained as a claim for territory annexed by Brandenburg in 1610, and in possession of Pfalz-Neuburg since 1614).

4. In gold, a black lion (margraviate of Meissen, in possession of the House of Wettin since 1089).

5. Inshield, a barry of black and gold, with a green wreath of rue (*Rautenkranz*) in bend overall (duchy of Saxony, acquired in 1423).

6. In gold, a black lion (duchy of Jülich, retained as a claim, as in quartering number 3). These arms are coincidentally identical to those of Meissen, although as a rule heraldic charges were made as distinctive as possible. However, Jülich is situated in the Rhinelands, more than three hundred miles from Meissen, and at the time these arms were adopted—independently from each other, about 1200—it could not be foreseen that they would one day be united in one shield.

7. In black, a golden eagle (palatinate of Thuringia, acquired in 1482 as an honorific title). Palatinates were imperial fiefs distributed all over the empire, but most had ceased to exist as actual territories by the fifteenth century.

8. In blue, a golden wall with three crenellations (margraviate of Upper Lusatia, acquired in 1635).

9. In blue, a golden eagle (palatinate of Saxony, acquired in 1347).

10. In gold, a red bull with a white stripe around his middle (margraviate of Lusatia, acquired in 1032, lost to Bohemia in 1076, and reacquired in 1635). The red bull seems to have been a tribal totem animal of the Slavic Lusizes, similar to the white horse of the northern Saxons, still surviving as the arms of Hanover and Kent.

11. In a golden field strewn with red hearts, a black lion (county of Orlamünde—from 1342, part of the landgraviate of Thuringia, which was acquired in 1482).

12. In gold, two blue pales (vertical stripes) (county of Landsberg, in possession of the House of Wettin, 1156–1291; reacquired in 1347). This simple blazon was probably derived from the striped fabric of a banner; it is also the family coat of arms of the Wettiners.

13. In blue, a lion divided horizontally of gold and silver (lordship of Pleissnerland, acquired in 1308).

14. In silver, a red rose (lordship of Altenburg, acquired in 1329 and turned over to the Ernestine branch in the treaty of 1554).

15. Divided per pale: in silver, a red demieagle; and barry of silver and red (burgraviate of Magdeburg, acquired in 1538; it was released by the treaty of 1579, but the title claim and arms were maintained).

16. In silver, three red waterlily leaves (county of Brehna, acquired about 1025).

17. In gold, a fess (horizontal stripe) checkered of red and silver (county of Marck, maintained claim on territory annexed by Brandenburg in 1610).

18. In silver, three blue bars (lordship of Eisenberg, acquired in 1547, but released to the Ernestines in 1554).

19. In silver, three red chevrons (county of Ravensberg; maintained claim, but annexed by Brandenburg in 1610).

20. In gold, a black hen on a green mountain (principality of Henneberg, first acquired in the fourteenth century; after several divisions, part of the county was retained in 1583). These are so-called canting arms, representing a rebus on *Henne* (hen) and *Berg* (mountain).

21. Plain red (*Regalienschild*, a mark of sovereignty found only in German heraldry).

German heraldic custom demanded that in an achievement of multiple quarterings the principal charges should be accompanied by their respective helmet crests. This practice was abhorrent to English heraldists, who claimed that more than one helmet surmounting a shield could be used only by a person with more than one head. Nevertheless, it was the rule with all classes of German armigers, and princely houses not uncommonly had more than a dozen crested helmets arrayed above their shields.

The full achievement of the heir apparent on this colletin displays eight such helmets (see fig. 1, backplate):

1. Issuant from a crown, a pair of blue wings, their lower part overlaid by a golden crenellated wall (margraviate of Upper Lusatia).

2. A red bull's head, golden crowned, the crown with a browband checkered red and silver (duchy of Kleve).

3. Issuant from a golden crown, a pair of silver horns, edged with gold rods, spangled with silver linden leaves (landgraviate of Thuringia).

4. Issuant from a golden crown, a conical column barry of black and gold, with a green wreath of rue (*Rautenkranz*) in bend overall; the column topped by a gold coronet sprouting a tuft of peacock feathers (duchy of Saxony).

5. A bearded man's torso, clad in a garment striped white and red, with a pointed cap of the same, styled after the tribal headgear of the Daleminzians (margraviate of Meissen).

6. A golden hound's head, collared chequy red and silver, between two black wings (duchy of Jülich, combined with county of Marck).

7. Issuant from a golden crown, a plume of peacock feathers (duchy of Berg).

8. On top of a red cap with upturned ermine brim, a silver eagle's head (margraviate of Lusatia).

This armorial achievement is placed within a roughly circular medallion frame on a dotted background, surrounded by heavy floral scrollwork of leaves and peony-like flowers. The style of the etching is identical to that on another colletin formerly at the Historisches Museum, Dresden, with the insignia of the Order of the Garter, which was awarded to Prince Elector Johann Georg II in 1671, and also to the decoration on a half armor for foot combat made for the heir apparent Johann Georg III in 1666 by the armorer Jacob Jöringk and the etcher Christian Heroldt.[3]

On the frontplate of the Kienbusch colletin (fig. 1), a central medallion in a Baroque frame encloses the eight-pointed star of the Order of the Elephant on a dotted background. The Order of the Elephant, founded in 1462 by King Christian I of Denmark, is one of three

9

10

Fig. 9. Back of colletin made for Prince Elector Johann Georg II (see fig. 4).
Fig. 10. Interior of colletin attributed to Prince Elector Johann Georg II (see fig. 3).

medieval orders of chivalry surviving today.⁴ Its seemingly strange device of the elephant symbolizes the virtues of magnanimity toward the weak and of nonabuse of power. (The elephant, although the largest land animal, does not prey on others but is a vegetarian, and was thought to use his long trunk to blow ants and other small creatures out of the way, to avoid stepping on them.) The medallion is flanked by two warriors in pseudoclassical armor, holding the ends of a ribbon draped around the lower part of this frame, from which is suspended the badge of the order, a white elephant with a crenellated tower on his back and with a turbaned Moor as mahout. On each side of the neck opening, high in the shoulder area, clusters of weapons and musical instruments are worked into the floral scrollwork.

Colletins such as this were the last vestigial remains of armor, in a period when armor plates, to be bulletproof, had to be made increasingly thicker and thus had become too heavy for comfortable wear. Originally, colletins had been designed as protection for the neck and as support for the shoulder straps of the heavy cuirass. During the first half of the seventeenth century when the cumbersome cuirass was replaced by the lighter and pliable buffcoat, the colletin was retained as a defense for the neck, but even more so as an outward token that its wearer was entitled to wear a knight's full armor.

Parade armor, because of its value as a status symbol and also simply for the romantic showiness of "shining armor," was retained and even cultivated as an important element in the pageantry of Baroque court festivities. The court of the prince electors of Saxony was justly famous for spectacular events. (Tournaments were held fairly regularly even up to World War II in the tiltyard of the castle at Dresden, the *Stallhof*, using armor from the Historisches Museum; they have been resumed after the unification of the two Germanies amidst general rejoicing.) One of the most dazzling examples of such Saxon pageant armor is now in the Kienbusch Collection (figs. 5, 8). The armor consists of a cuirass and a broad-brimmed morion-style helmet. Its material is not steel, as it would be for armor used in battles or tournaments, but gilt copper. Its surface is heavily embossed and studded with paste jewels of colored glass. The crest of the helmet bears the figure of a snarling winged dragon, with triple volutes of copper straps fore and aft curling up from the umbril and neck guard.[5] The helmet bowl is embossed in shallow relief, with a large heraldic rose on each side, surrounded by floral scrollwork, and is lavishly "jeweled." It is especially fortunate that the helmet lining, of crimson silk, is still preserved; the visible parts around its rim are delicately embroidered in gold thread to heighten the sumptuous effect.

The breastplate of the cuirass is embossed with a rampant lion and a scaly dragon clawing at each other in mortal combat; the background is strewn with flowers in the same naturalistic, Baroque style as the etched floral decoration on the colletin of Johann Georg III, previously discussed. Similar flowers, among them daffodils and several types of tulips, are clearly recognizable and are spread over the entire surface of the backplate. With the exception of two pairs of cabochons serving as eyes of the lion and dragon, and others set into the centers of flowers, the "jewels" are scattered rather haphazardly over the background, producing a glittering effect like a starry sky.

The two halves of the cuirass are held together by a pair of metal-studded shoulder straps covered with red velvet and edged in gold, and by a matching belt. Both the shoulder straps and the belt are riveted to the backplate and lap over the breastplate, with the belt to be buckled in front and the shoulder straps to be locked onto studs on the breast. The cuirass is lined with doeskin; the lining of the backplate retains its scalloped piccadills of red velvet. A row of paired eyelets along the lower rim of the cuirass—five on the backplate and four on the breastplate (covered by the belt, when buckled)—indicate that there must have been tassets or a skirt, or both, associated with this cuirass.

The cuirass is of surprisingly small dimensions, even taking into account the fashion of the mid-seventeenth century, when gentlemen in northern Europe, Germany, and the Netherlands wore their belts and sashes extremely high, almost under the armpits, to give the impression of elegant long-leggedness. Cuirasses, if worn at all, had very short breastplates therefore, but disproportionately long and bulky tassets to accommodate voluminous breeches.

When still at Dresden, this parade armor was attributed to Prince Elector Johann Georg II (fig. 12). A parallel can be found in a cuirass of blued steel (HMD29) that once belonged to Johann Georg II. Though missing since World War II, it is documented to have been of similarly small dimensions; its helmet was also of unusual shape, a lobster-tail *chapel-de-fer* with an upturned triangular umbril and a spirally fluted bowl surmounted by a small, spiky crown. Since 1688, when it was transferred to the *Rüstkammer* from the elector's private chapel, the earlier-mentioned Dresden colletin etched with the insignia of the Order of the Garter has been associated with this cuirass, although it is clear from the workmanship and decoration on these two objects that they were not made for each other.[6]

Fig. 11. Detail of a Portrait of Prince Elector Johann Georg II of Saxony, by Johann Fink (German, 1628–1675). Oil on canvas, 57¹/₂ x 46¹/₂" (146 x 118 cm). Historisches Museum, Dresden; HMD199.

Fig. 12. Parade armor (fig. 5) photographed in the collection of the Historisches Museum, Dresden.

Fig. 13. Pageant paraphernalia in the Historisches Museum, Dresden, including the sun mask and scepters for Sol and Luna; N171.

In his illustrated catalogue *Kostbare Waffen aus der Dresdner Rüstkammer* (Leipzig, 1923), Erich Haenel, former director of the Historisches Museum, remarked on the small size of the Dresden cuirass (HMD29): "[It] seems to have been made for a sixteen-year-old boy rather than for a fifty-six-year-old gentleman." This suggests that Haenel was inclined to assume that the small cuirass was made for Johann Georg III when he was a young heir apparent, rather than for his father, Johann Georg II (fig. 11). On plate 23 in Haenel's *Kostbare Waffen* the cuirass HMD29 and the foot combat armor HMD30, made for Johann Georg III in 1666, are illustrated side by side. The foot combat armor shows considerably wider dimensions than the cuirass HMD29, even though the heir apparent was only nineteen years old in 1666. It is known that Johann Georg II was of unusually small body size, and therefore the attribution of the parade armor in the Kienbusch Collection to Johann Georg II can be accepted with confidence. It would have been made for the prince elector's own person, at a time when the Saxon economy had recovered sufficiently from the ravages of the Thirty Years' War (1618–48) to allow the cherished tradition of spectacular court festivities to be resumed.[7]

Particularly sumptuous parades were held at Dresden during the Shrovetide festivals of 1660, 1661, 1662, 1663, and 1665. Also in 1662, the celebration of the wedding of Princess Erdmuthe Sophie to Margrave Ernst Christian of Brandenburg-Bayreuth lasted for three weeks in October and November; highlights were a tilting at the ring in which participants wore costumes of the seven planets, and an opera about the Judgment of Paris and the ensuing Siege of Troy, which tested the audience's endurance for four full days. During spectacles like these, the members of the court society, including the prince elector and his family, participated in competition with each other. The parade armor of the Kienbusch Collection is exactly what such a princely actor would have worn in the role of Achilles or Hector of Troy, or as the planet Mars in the tilt.

In contrast to this dazzling costume party armor, the two colletins in the Kienbusch Collection that are attributed to Johann Georg II are relatively plain. One of them (fig. 3) was constructed with two movable neck lames, as had been the practice for colletins worn as parts of full armor, although it is evident from the size and shape of this colletin that it was intended to be worn by itself. Its entire surface is gilded and covered with scrollwork outlined by a myriad of tiny close-set punches, against a densely stippled background. Following its border and accentuating the center lines of the front and backplate are wide bands filled with scallops interspersed with trefoils and small rosettes somewhat reminiscent of the wreath of rue charge in the Saxon arms. The colletin still retains its buff leather lining (fig. 10), edged with fashionably slashed piccadills of crimson velvet. The delicately punched decoration of this colletin is practically identical to that on four gilded foot-combat armors commissioned by Johann Georg II and made by the earlier-mentioned court armorer Jacob Jöringk in 1654, which are still in the Historisches Museum.[8]

The second colletin attributed to Johann Georg II (fig. 4) was also ordered by him, in 1654, and was delivered to the *Rüstkammer* the same year. It is of steel, lined with leather edged with red velvet. Its frontplate is divided by a central ridge, with an equestrian figure etched on each side; on the backplate are assorted military trophies and cannon (fig. 9). The figures and trophies are gilded and slightly raised above the blued background. Delineated as elegant silhouettes, they have delicately engraved interior details, now much blurred by polishing over the centuries. The right-hand horseman on the frontplate is the hero of classical Roman legend Marcus Curtius; the left-hand figure is Saint George Slaying the Dragon. Saint George was, of course, the namesake and patron of Johann Georg II. The latter's staunch Protestantism notwithstanding, he had a special affinity for this knightly saint, and was so delighted to be made a knight of the Order of the Garter that he had the Garter device of Saint George and the motto *"HONI SOIT QUI MAL Y PENSE"* emblazoned on the company colors of his *Trabantengarde*, and also issued a medal, on the seventh anniversary of his election to the Garter (fig. 7). As for Marcus Curtius, he—together with Gaius Mucius Scaevola[9]—had been standard iconography in the decoration of the black and gold morions (fig. 17) worn by the *Trabantengarde* since at least 1568, the reign of Prince Elector Augustus (ruled 1553–86). Marcus Curtius was the hero who, according to legend, saved Rome when a flaming chasm opened up in the middle of the Forum and the augurs predicted that it would close only after the city's most precious possession had been thrown in. After all material sacrifices had failed, Marcus Curtius declared that Rome's greatest treasure was not gold and jewels but the prowess and courage of her youth. In full armor, he plunged his battle charger into the abyss, which closed over him.

The decoration on the backplate of the colletin (fig. 9) consists of two large cannons facing each other, surrounded by gunners' equipment such as ramrods, linstocks, powder scoops, powder kegs, and priming flasks; higher up in the shoulder sections are groups of bombs, grapeshot, and incendiary arrows. The central neck section bears a trophy composed of a drum, a pipe in its case, two muskets, and a musket fork, between two swags formed from musketeer bandoliers. Although there are innumerable prints and woodcuts of prancing horsemen that could have served as models for the equestrian figures, the arrangements of martial gear on the backplate are clearly adapted from engravings by the Netherlandish artist Jan Vredeman de Vries (1527–1604), published in *Panoplia* in 1572 (fig. 16).

The fourth colletin in the Kienbusch Collection is of gilded copper, overlaid with a sheet of silver, pierced in openwork decorations of medallions, equestrian figures, military trophies, and floral scrolls (fig. 14). On the frontplate four oval medallions with the planetary deities Saturnus, Jupiter, Sol, and Mars are arranged around a fifth, heart-shaped medallion. In this are displayed two sets of military trophies side by side; one is composed of a cuirass, helmet, and weapons in pseudoclassical style, and the other is a half armor for the foot tourney, with a sword in its right gauntlet.

The planetary deities in the medallions are represented as riding in chariots on clouds. Their vehicles are drawn by a variety of animals, corresponding to the astrological nature of each planet, and each chariot has on its backrest—much like a ship's figurehead—the animal's head as a symbolic decoration. Most of the deities bear diadems of rays not unlike that on the Statue of Liberty in New York harbor.

Fig. 14. Colletin, German, Saxony, 1617, probably made for Prince Elector Johann Georg I by the court goldsmith Michael Botza (German, c. 1592–1633). Copper, gilt, and overlaid with pierced and engraved silver sheet; 1977-167-218.

Fig. 15. Portrait of Johann Georg I of Saxony, c. 1647, by Daniel Bretschneider the Younger (German, died 1658). Oil on panel, 7¹/₈ x 4¹/₈" (18.1 x 10.5 cm); 1977-167-1032.

Saturnus (upper left) is shown as a bearded old man, carrying a scythe in his right hand and holding in his upraised left hand an infant dangling by its leg. The latter is a reference to the myth of Cronos/Saturnus, who swallowed his own children because of a prophecy that one of them would overthrow him; Zeus/Jupiter, however, eluded him and fulfilled the prophecy. Saturnus's chariot is drawn by two bat-winged dragons.

Jupiter (upper right) is a bearded man of mature years. As befits the head of the Olympian gods, he wears a crown from which rays burst forth. He holds aloft in his right hand a flaming thunderbolt, and in his left, a scepter. Two eagles are harnessed to his chariot.

Sol (lower left) is represented as a young man, but having the sun's face, encircled by rays alternately wavy and straight. He carries a wand topped with a similarly rayed sun with a human face. His chariot is drawn by two lions.

Mars (lower right) is a fiercely mustachioed soldier in contemporary three-quarter field armor holding a marshal's baton in his right hand. His chariot is loaded with warlike paraphernalia, such as cannon, halberds, a drum, and a fluttering banner; it is hitched to a pair of galloping horses, and a horse's head arches from the backrest.

Surmounting the central medallion with the arms trophies is a large crown encircling a laurel branch and a palm leaf. Above the crown is an assemblage of a smaller crown—this one unmistakably meant to be the imperial crown—with a sword and a scepter crossed and two crossed lances bearing pennons, one engraved with the double-headed eagle of the empire, the other with the fork-tailed lion of Bohemia. Flanking this regal array are two horsemen in three-quarter armor—*Lantzierer*—with their lances couched; below the group of medallions are two *Pistolenreiter* firing their wheel locks.[10] Farther down, at the lowermost tip of the frontplate, is yet another military trophy, composed of Turkish arms, a bow and arrow quiver, a scimitar, a shield, and a Janissary's cap.

On the backplate (fig. 14) are three medallions with the remaining planetary deities Mercury, Luna, and Venus (left to right). On the neck section above them is an arrangement of an oversize bow and arrow quiver, a halberd, a scimitar, and a lance with a pennon, between two diminutive cannons, each with a pile of cannon balls. The spaces below the medallions of Mercury and Venus are filled with two equestrian figures: a sword-wielding armored knight who is charging against a Turkish horseman brandishing a scimitar.

The planet Mercury is represented as a young man and is identified by his winged hat and the caduceus staff in his hand. His chariot is drawn by a pair of roosters.

Luna is a young woman in the short tunic and high buskins of Diana the Huntress; her face is encircled by the crescent moon. In her raised right hand she holds a wand topped by a half-moon with a human profile. Her chariot is drawn by two stags.

Venus is fully clothed in a long peplos-style gown; she is holding a flaming heart in her right hand and is looking with concern backward over her shoulder at a small cupid perched on the chariot's backrest, aiming his arrow at her. Her chariot's draught animals are a pair of peacocks, but in this case there is no animal head on the chariot.

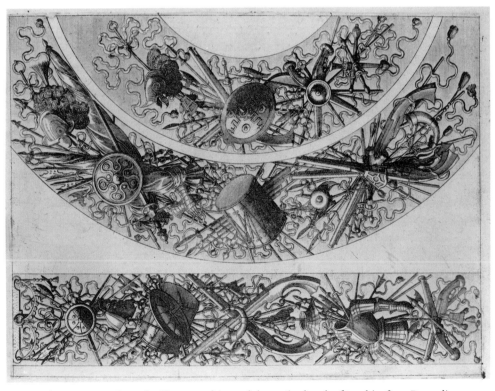

Fig. 16. Engravings of military trophies and decorative bands of trophies from Panoplia
(Antwerp, 1572), by Jan Vredeman de Vries (Netherlandish, 1527–1604).
The Metropolitan Museum of Art, New York; 24.70.4.

There seems to be no direct graphic source for the planetary deities in these medallions, although several series of engravings and woodcuts on the subject were available at the time. Some of the deities, such as Saturnus and Mercury, show a certain similarity to the popular engraving series of about 1550 by Virgil Solis (German, 1514–1562), but the designer of the medallions displays considerable originality in his compositions, particularly in his choice of the animals drawing the chariots. In engravings the chariot of Jupiter, for instance, is usually drawn by peacocks, that of Mars by foxes, Sol's by horses, Venus's by doves, and Luna's by a team of dolphins, the latter presumably an allusion to the moon's influence on the tides.

The theme of the seven planets followed the astronomical interests of Johann Georg I, who in 1612, 1613, and 1617 had ordered telescopes for the scientific section of the famous *Kunstkammer* at Dresden, established by his grandfather, Prince Elector Augustus, in the middle of the sixteenth century as a sort of university museum, and diligently used and enlarged by all his successors. The seven planets were also a popular theme for the pageants, parades, and *Ringrennen* (tilts at the ring) so enthusiastically celebrated at the Dresden court, where they were recorded in the years 1587, 1591, 1607, 1613, 1622, 1662, and 1678. There were presumably many more seven-planets spectacles, which were recorded there only as "et cetera" in events with multiple themes. The positioning of the four planetary deities in the medallions on the frontplate—the upper two riding to the left and the lower two riding to the right—suggests that the designer envisioned them as riding in a circle, as in a parade in the castle courtyard. The three deities on the backplate, too, are all riding the same way, to the left, as in a parade procession.

Up to World War II the Historisches Museum preserved a number of *Inventionsstücke* (pageant paraphernalia). Among them were two scepters, one topped with a sun's face and one surmounted by a half-moon with a human profile, together with a copper-gilt sun mask. The scepters are practically identical to those carried by Sol and Luna, and the face of Sol resembles the sun mask, with its surrounding double circle of short and long rays (fig. 13). These three objects were thought to have been made in the early eighteenth century for the much more famous court extravaganzas staged by Augustus the Strong (reigned 1694–1733). The only surviving object among these, the sun mask, is documented to have been used in 1709 in a parade of the gods of the classical world, but the wands were already registered in the inventory of 1689. It seems likely that they were the actual models for the paraphernalia of Sol and Luna, and were perhaps even created by the designer of the colletin's decoration.

The Dresden goldsmith Michael Botza (German, c. 1592–1633) has been suggested as the master of this colletin, which is unparalleled as a seventeenth-century piece of parade armor. In the Historisches Museum was the scabbard of a hunting trousse (fig. 18) with the initials of Johann Georg I and the ducal arms. Mounted in a sheet of silver, it is pierced in a lacelike technique similar to the openwork on this colletin. The silver mounting is stamped with the Dresden hallmark and Michael Botza's master's mark *MB*; one of the trousse's surviving implements bears the date 1619.

Fig. 17. Morion, German, c. 1575, made for the Trabantengarde *of Prince Elector Augustus I (1553–86); also used by Christian I (1586–91) and Christian II (1601–11); with Marcus Curtius in medallion on the bowl, and arms of the dukes of Saxony on the comb. Steel, etched, and gilt, mounted with brass. The Metropolitan Museum of Art, New York; Gift of William H. Riggs, 1913; 14.25.652.*

Fig. 18. Hunting trousse, dated 1619, made for Johann Georg I by Michael Botza (German, c. 1592–1633). Historisches Museum, Dresden; M262.

18

It is strange, however, that this colletin of the seven planets does not display any of the heraldic devices otherwise ubiquitous on Saxon arms—no crossed swords of the archmarshalship, no wreath of rue for the duchy of Saxony. Instead, it shows the eagle of the empire and the lion of Bohemia on the pennons that wave from the lances crossed behind the assemblage of sword and scepter—the regalia held by the imperial eagle in his claws in full panoply—and crown, recognizably the imperial crown.

The most likely explanation is that this extraordinary piece of gentleman's jewelry was made for a special event. Such an event could have been the state visit paid to Johann Georg I by Emperor Matthias, in July and August 1617. The imperial party, which also included the emperor's brother, Archduke Maximilian, and his cousin Ferdinand, king of Bohemia,[11] came from Prague, traveling down the river Elbe in seven ships sent by Johann Georg, who met his illustrious guests at the Saxon-Bohemian border with nine more ships. The party proceeded downstream at a leisurely pace, stopping twice for sumptuous receptions, banquets, and prearranged hunting parties. At the disembarkation at Dresden and during the grand entry through the city on July 23, 1617, the chronicler mentioned that the prince elector was "bedecked with golden [armor] pieces." This meeting was a last-ditch effort to avert the threatened religious civil war by achieving an understanding between the Catholic faction of the empire, represented by the Imperial Hapsburgs, and the Protestants, whose most conciliatory leader was Johann Georg I of Saxony.[12]

A summit conference like this would have been just the occasion for the perfect host to subtly honor his guests by wearing a piece of personal jewelry in which their armorial devices—the eagle of the empire and the lion of Bohemia—were discretely small but conspicuously placed, and in a decoration of the seven planets, a theme that would also flatter the scholarly bend of the emperor, whose *Kunstkammer* at Prague surpassed even that at Dresden.

In the Kienbusch Collection is a portrait of Johann George I (fig. 15) thirty years later, from about 1647, by Daniel Bretschneider the Younger (German, died 1658). In the portrait the elderly prince elector is dressed in hunting costume, with a hunting trousse and powder flask at his belt; on his left side on a bandolier is a hunting sword, crossed by the bandolier with the hunting horn. The panel at the foot of the painting shows a view of Dresden from the eastern bank of the river Elbe. The turreted building in the lower-left foreground is the *Jägerhof*, where the hunting equipment was stored and the dog kennels were kept. The triple-gabled building just to the right of the tall steeple of the Holy Cross Church in the center, and above the low roof of the white building on top of the city wall, is the *Stallhof*, where the Dresden *Rüstkammer* was located from the sixteenth century until 1945.[13]

NOTES

1 The other six prince electors were the archbishop of Cologne, as the chancellor for Italian affairs; the archbishop of Mainz, as the chancellor for Germany; the archbishop of Trier, as the chancellor for Gaul and the Arelate; the king of Bohemia, as the archbutler; the margrave of Brandenburg, as the archchamberlain; and the count palatinate of the Rhine, as the archsteward.

2 It was to the door of the Castle Church in Wittenberg that Martin Luther nailed his *Ninety-five Theses* on October 31, 1517, launching the Reformation in response to the indulgence-peddling sanctified by Rome. The most notorious agent of the indulgences was the Dominican monk Johann Tetzel, from Pirna, a small town upriver from Dresden. The Wettiners of both branches were supporters of Luther.

3 Colletin associated with cuirass and helmet of blued steel, Historisches Museum, Dresden, HMD 29; half armor for foot combat, HMD 30.

4 The membership of the Order of the Elephant is limited to thirty knights, excepting the king and his sons. According to a constitution drawn up in 1693 by King Christian V, members of the order must be Protestants and at least thirty years old, again excepting the royal princes, who are eligible when twenty years of age.

5 The record photograph (fig. 12) from the Historisches Museum, Dresden, shows the dragon crest facing forward but the helmet bowl rotated by 180 degrees, as compared with its present, presumably correct, arrangement. The volutes of the present neck guard are also attached in a slightly different way.

6 See note 3 for HMD 29. The gauntlets associated with this ensemble bear embossed on their cuffs the badge of the Spanish Order of Santiago, an order that was particularly strict in accepting only qualified Catholics as its members.

7 Erich Haenel, *Kostbare Waffen aus der Dresdner Rüstkammer* (Leipzig, 1923), p. 46. Another indication

of Johann Georg II's effort to increase the pomp and circumstance of his court is that he created six new guard units in addition to the already existing *Trabantengarde* on foot (about 70 men). The new units were a Swiss guard Halberdier company (120 men), a Swiss guard musketeer company (approximately 200 men), a troop of *mousquetons à cheval* (20 "young noblemen"), a company of dragoon guards (about 120 men), a horse guard regiment (335 men), and a horse guard company of Croatians (about 100 men).

8 Historisches Museum, Dresden, HMD 23–26.

9 Gaius Mucius was a legendary noble Roman youth who attempted to assassinate Lars Porsena, the Etruscan king who besieged Rome in the sixth century B.C. Apprehended and threatened with torture to reveal the assassination plot, Mucius thrust his right hand into a burning brazier, as a demonstration of his contempt for pain. Impressed, Porsena released him and lifted the siege; Mucius was afterward known as Scaevola (Left-hand; Livy 2.12–13).

10 Seventeenth-century heavy cavalry—*cuirassiers*—wore three-quarter armor, consisting of cuirasses (breast- and backplates with knee-long tassets, arm defenses, and helmets). They were armed, in addition to swords, with long lances (*Lantzierer*) or with a brace of wheel-lock pistols (*Pistolenreiter*). Lantzierers became obsolete during the first decade of the Thirty Years' War.

11 Bohemia was an elective, not a hereditary, kingdom. King Ferdinand, of the Styrian branch of the Hapsburgs, had just been elected, on June 19, 1617.

12 Large parts of the empire were Protestant, but others were solidly Catholic, and the Counter-Reformation was gaining ground in Bavaria and Austria. The situation was especially dangerous in Bohemia, which was not only divided ethnically into Czechs and Germans but also into Protestants (mostly German and city populations), Catholics (mostly Czech), and Utra-quists, a special rite of Catholicism sanctioned by Rome and embraced by Czech nationalists, who, however, sided with the Protestants. King Ferdinand, of Jesuit upbringing, did his best to further Catholicism and end Protestantism. In 1620 the Protestants elected a counter-king, Friedrich of the Palatinate, and the war that had been brewing since 1618 erupted in full force. Johann George I of Saxony, although the most powerful of the Protestant princes, nevertheless remained on the side of the emperor, trying to preserve the union of the empire. The result was that he was considered a traitor by the Protestants and an unreliable ally by the Catholic imperials, and his country, Saxony, was devastated by both parties.

13 As this article was about to go to press, the author was made aware of a list of objects lost or missing since World War II from the Historisches Museum, Dresden. Numbers 12 and 14–17 published in *Vermisste Kunstwerke des Historischen Museums Dresden* by Dieter Schaal, Jutta Bäumel, Holger Schuckelt, and Elfriede Lieber (Dresden, 1990) are the objects treated in this article. They were acquired on the art market by Mr. Kienbusch in 1953, at a time when the fate of the collections of the Historisches Museum, held strictly incommunicado in the Soviet Union, was still unknown. The Kienbusch pieces are listed among the objects that were evacuated by the Historisches Museum from Dresden to a castle located in the western half of Saxony that in 1945 was originally occupied by American forces, but later was turned over to the Russians. Presumably in an attempt to save them from being confiscated by the Soviet Union, the castle's owner took these objects along when he had to flee to the West.

It was only through the publication in 1963 of the catalogue of the Kienbusch Collection that the Dresden museum became aware that the four colletins were not lost, as previously thought.

SELECTED BIBLIOGRAPHY

Haenel, Erich. *Kostbare Waffen aus der Dresdner Rüstkammer.* Leipzig, 1923.

Reibisch, Friedrich Martin. *Eine Auswahl merkwurdiger Gegenstände aus der Königl. Sächsischen Rüstkammer.* Dresden, 1825.

Schaal, Dieter, Jutta Bäumel, Holger Schuckelt, and Elfriede Lieber. *Vermisste Kunstwerke des Historischen Museums Dresden.* Dresden, 1990.

Seidlitz, Woldemar von. *Die Kunst in Dresden vom Mittelalter bis zur Neuzeit.* Dresden, 1920.

Sponsel, Jean Louis. *Der Zwinger, die Hoffeste und die Schlossbaupläne zu Dresden.* Dresden, 1924.

ACKNOWLEDGMENTS

I would like to express my gratitude to the Philadelphia Museum of Art and the National Endowment for the Arts Visiting Specialists Program for giving me the opportunity to study these objects, and my sincerest thanks for valuable help in the research for this article to Stuart W. Pyhrr and Donald LaRocca, The Metropolitan Museum of Art, New York, and to Dr. Dieter Schaal, Historisches Museum, Dresden.

Fig. 19. Italian cuirass, c. 1510. Steel; 1977-167-150.

Ancient Italian Pieces
in the Kienbusch Collection

LIONELLO G. BOCCIA

Of the arms and armor bequeathed by Carl Otto Kretzschmar von Kienbusch to the Philadelphia Museum of Art, more than a quarter are almost certainly of Italian origin. The Italian group is notable, with some important examples illustrating the history of Italian arms and armor.[1] This paper is concerned only with defensive armor of the fifteenth century and the early years of the sixteenth, and deliberately concentrates on the earlier pieces, which represent a particularly rich and significant segment of European Renaissance arms production.

By the end of the fourteenth century, the long evolution of mixed armor of leather and steel (combining mail with lamellar armor, small plates, splints, and studs) had come almost to an end. Attempts and experiments made in the Germanic lands to improve protection of the wearer's torso, and in the Anglo-French territories to perfect an articulated defense of the limbs, had led to the development of effective armor of large steel plates, which defended the body from head to foot. This is not to say that the various European regions did not seek integral solutions, but to stress that each one developed its own characteristic process. In the fourteenth century, the Italian peninsula was the richest part of Europe, and the most organized both commercially and financially. A great number of important cities and small or not so small city-states contributed to this interlocking structure. During the entire century, following the Peace of Caltabellotta in 1302, innumerable local wars and several international ones were fought, especially by the *compagnie di ventura*, the so-called free companies of mercenaries. These hired soldiers came from every corner of Europe, bringing with them their own traditional armors and weapons, with which they confronted each other in battle. Heavily armed troops and more agile ones, mounted men and companies of foot soldiers; long, wide, and heavy cutting swords against rigid and narrow thrusting swords; armors of mail side by side with those predominantly of leather, and others augmented by specialized steel pieces, various types of fabric coats reinforced with lamellae, splints, or other plates: Italy saw all of these, and Italian armorers were in a position to evaluate the capabilities of the various types. The great centers of arms production—Milan, Venice, Florence—turned out large quantities of work remarkable for its high quality and especially for its creativity.

For defensive armor, the last problems to be resolved were the design of a headpiece more suited than the old helm to new requirements for more maneuverability and an adequate protection for the shoulders. Regarding the torso, solutions had been found about 1370, and for the limbs somewhat earlier. In the years around 1400 the remaining weaknesses were resolved and the new "Italian" armor appeared in its entirety.[2] The head was protected by a new type of helmet (*elmetto*), referred to in English as an armet, an invention claimed by both Tuscany and Lombardy. A very close-fitting headpiece, it consists essentially of three principal plates: a bowl that protects the skull and the back of the neck, and two cheekpieces hinged to the bowl that can be opened and closed, covering the cheeks, and fastened at the chin. To these three pieces may be added a frontal, to strengthen the forehead area, and a fifth plate shaped to defend the face, the visor, which turns on two pivots positioned at the temples. The neck can be protected by a mail collar or metal lames: sometimes a bevor is added, which reinforces the helmet from the nose to the chin or throat. The advance over the helm or basnet is evident—the armet is lighter, less restricting, more anatomical, and more functional. The upper part of the torso (from the neck almost to the waist) is defended by a breastplate and a backplate hinged along the left side; the waist is defended by a shallow, lower-breast and backplate (*panziera* and *guardarene*), which are similarly hinged and overlap the corresponding pieces above them. This structure is intended to permit better articulation of the torso. The pelvis is surrounded by the lames of the fauld and the culet (front and back) formed by overlapping plates (at first wide, then narrower) arranged one over the other, and hinged as usual on the left. Following the armet, the second great novelty of the new Italian armor lay in the construction of the cuirass (torso defense); the arrangement for defending the pelvis had already been in use in the 1330s, especially in German lands. For arms and legs there were no difficulties, because the solutions reached earlier were perfectly adequate. What was lacking was an effective protection for the shoulders; here, also, Italian armorers found a remedy, inventing by the first decade of the fifteenth century large asymmetrical pauldrons or shoulderpieces (with the larger one on the left, the exposed side that always required more protection, unless the wearer was left-handed). Shortly thereafter, these were usually fitted with additional reinforcing plates that were circular in Tuscany, shield-shaped in Venice, and square in Milan.[3]

All these elements underwent modifications during the course of the fifteenth century: the general shape of the armet changed, as did those of its constituent parts; with time the body armor of the *panziera* became higher and wider, doubling the breastplate and becoming an over-breastplate; the number of plates on the fauld and the culet increased to protect the upper parts of the thighs; the pauldrons became even wider behind the shoulders, altering the characteristic silhouette from rectangular to triangular; the forms of arm and leg armor were modified, as were elbow and kneepieces; the reinforcing pieces also changed. In practice, about every five years, from the beginning to the end of the fifteenth century, Italian armor underwent small changes while remaining essentially the same: monumental, smooth and rounded in its forms, robotlike, anthropoid, its surfaces left brilliant from the hardening process. This continual course of development is of great assistance in determining the provenance, as well as the dating, of a piece of armor.

Fig. 20. Armor of Frederick I the Victorious, c.1451, made by the Missaglia workshop, Milan. Steel, Kunsthistorisches Museum, Leibrüstkammer, Vienna; inv. no. A2.

The Kienbusch Collection does not include a complete fifteenth-century Italian suit of armor, which is by no means surprising, since in the whole world not more than a dozen full suits of Italian war armor, plus a few incomplete ones, are known to remain. Of these armors only four, however, are homogeneous and complete (or nearly) in their original components: those of Ulrich von Matsch and of Galeazzo d'Arco at Churburg Castle in Sluderno-Schluderns, of Frederick I the Victorious in Vienna (fig. 20), and another preserved as an ex-voto in the Basilica of Our Lady of the Graces in Udine.[4] There are also three suits of armor *da campo chiuso*, for a specialized form of tournament fought on foot, which date from the period considered: two in the Waffensammlung in Vienna and one in the Royal Armouries, Tower of London.[5]

Thus, since there are no complete armors in the collection, the individual pieces may be considered according to type, and those that now form parts of composite armors are discussed with single pieces of similar type.

The Kienbusch Collection possesses three armets, known in Italian as *elmetto da uomo d'arme*, which completed the armor worn by the most heavily armed mounted warriors. They are of the type already described, the military headpiece of true Italian design. All three belong to what is certainly the largest category of surviving Italian armets, that which protects the face with a small visor, termed *ventaglia*, which covers the face beneath the eyes, as opposed to a larger visor, termed *visiera sana*, which covers the entire face and has vision slits. The Florentine model *a ventaglia* was an improvement over the Milanese *a visiera*, which is poorly documented, even iconographically. There are examples in the *San Romano* of 1412

(Pinacoteca Nazionale, Ferrara), in Pisanello's frescoes of about 1438–40 in the ducal palace in Mantua, and—in an exception for Tuscany—in Piero della Francesca's *Legend of the True Cross* of about 1460–66 in San Francesco at Arezzo. After these dates the Florentine *a ventaglia* design became predominant in Italian production until the end of the century.

The earliest of the three Kienbusch helmets (fig. 21) has a bowl with a high rear profile and a raised comb that has a hole for the crest, which sweeps down behind into a wide neckguard; the rondel and its post at the nape of the neck are later additions.[6] The helmet is marked on the left-hand side with two barely legible initials, perhaps *YO*, beneath a crown, accompanied below by the initials *MA* under a split cross pattée; to the right this latter group is repeated. The frontal, whose lower edge projects somewhat obliquely, has lateral edges that rise toward the rear; they are cut off where they meet the upper concave edge. The cheekpieces have at some time been very much restored. The right-hand one—which comes from a different armet—has been shifted downward and forward; the left-hand one has been cut to allow it to be placed beneath the right-hand one (contrary to the general rule, which was always to better defend the more exposed side). Thus the "triangle" of the facial opening is narrower than it should be. Both cheekpieces are poorly shaped at the neck, and are bordered with a metal strip added to hide and to even off the damaged original edge. The visor *a ventaglia*—with a modern lifting peg—is original, but the alteration of the cheekpieces has left it incorrectly positioned; when closed it barely reaches the lower angle of the facial opening; pushed down, there is too much space between it and the front edge of the bowl.[7] Its beak is somewhat low, and its upper edge projects slightly; on the left the hinge is protected by a ridge, which has been sawn away on the right so as not to interfere with the new cheekpiece on that side. Considering the general shape, the lack of large borders, and the exposed hinges, I am inclined to date this piece to the 1470s. The same marks appear on the armor in the Diocesan Museum in Mantua (B1), but separately: the crowned monogram *YO* marks the helmet, together with *CO* (twice) beneath a split cross; the monogram *MA* under the split cross appears (twice) on the reinforce of the left pauldron. The first mark may possibly be that of Giacomo Cantoni (Jacopo da Cantono, an important armorer documented between 1478 and 1492); for various reasons an attribution to Giovanni Corio and Giovanni Correnti must be disallowed. For the second mark I would surmise the Milanese Giovanni Maffioli, master armorer recorded in 1451, rather than Masino Vimercati, a Milanese who emigrated to Brescia and is documented from 1454 to 1486.[8]

The next armet (fig. 22) is similar in shape, but the well-defined comb has a flattened edge and is extended into the restored neckguard; the rondel and post are modern.[9] The frontal extends well toward the rear. It is less hollowed than the previous piece and its lateral edges are cut into a distinct triangular pattern. The cheekpieces are shaped to form a very pronounced chin and are extended considerably to the rear, almost forming a neckguard; both cheeks bear a riveted metal strip along the lower edge. In contrast to the earlier armet, the facial opening is not triangular but forms a trapezoidal aperture, corresponding to the position

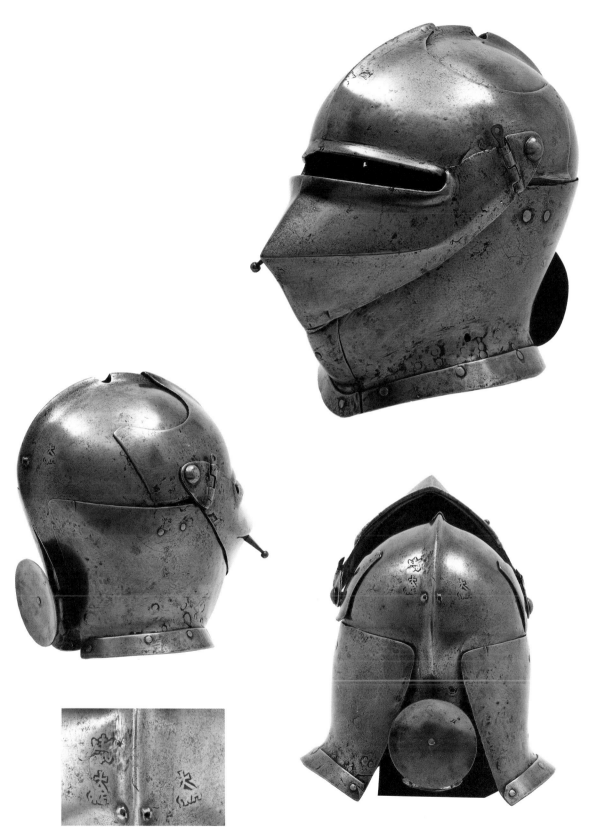

Fig. 21. Italian armet, 1470s. Steel; 1977-167-60. Three views and maker's marks.

Fig. 22. Italian armet, c. 1490. Steel; 1977-167-67. Three views.

of the mouth. This is the third stage in the development of the facial opening in the fifteenth-century Italian armet: at first it was quite large, projecting, U-shaped, and almost at nose height; then it was triangular and tended to be lower; finally we find this sort of opening, which became wider and wider. The beak of the half visor *a ventaglia* rises gently to its upper edge; it seems to me that the lack of alignment between the hinges and the two sides indicates that the half visor did not originally belong to this helmet. In any case, the ventilation slits (two horizontal ones just above the transverse edges of the beak, and five oblique ones to the right) are certainly not original. This headpiece bears no mark, but is undoubtedly of Lombard origin; its general shape indicates a date of 1490 or shortly after.

The third helmet (fig. 23) is the latest of the group. The bowl bears a strong comb of trapezoidal section, which is extended into the narrow neckguard ending in a wedge that engages the rear edges of the cheekpieces (the rondel and the post are, as usual, modern).[10] The frontal is more protective than the two previous examples; it reaches far back, with the lateral edges cut obtusely, and then rises obliquely to form the usual median cusp, being less open at the top. The cheekpieces, too, reach far back to form a neckguard; their rear edges nearly meet and are cut away to accommodate the post of the rondel; the lower rim has a turned edge. The facial opening is arched, has a turned edge at the sides, and is cut in a wide trapezoidal shape in front of the mouth. The visor *a ventaglia* is of advanced design, with concealed hinges, and a raised, protruding lip at its upper edge; the beak is still rather low but the lateral corners rise slightly, bowlike. Its lower edge is not straight or slightly convex as usual, but runs concave from the hinges and then, forming a distinct angle, runs straight to the chin. The lower right-hand side bears eight ventilation holes arranged in a triangle, as well as one hole for the missing lifting peg. This headpiece is also unmarked, but it is Lombard; the shape of the lower edge of the visor betrays some influence from Southern Germany, and an acceptable date would be the last decade of the fifteenth century.

The latest Italian helmet in the Kienbusch Collection that falls within the period under consideration (fig. 24) is not an armet (*elmetto da uomo d'arme*) but is the type known in English as a close-helmet (*elmetto da cavallo*).[11] Instead of the two cheekpieces attaching at the chin, this kind of headpiece has a one-piece chin and cheek defense, or bevor, and a neckguard consisting of plates. This type was used by cavalrymen, intended for warfare but rather less protective than another form of close-helmet known in Italian as *elmetto da incastro* that locked onto and turned on the upper edge of the gorget (the piece that protected the neck and upper shoulders) by means of a coupling formed by a channel inside the lower edge of the helmet and a ridge on the upper edge of the gorget, so as not to interrupt the continuity of the defensive armor. The former type of helmet was less restrictive to wear. The bowl of this example has a crest similar to those on Italian armets of the late fifteenth century (such as the one just discussed), of trapezoidal section. It does not, however, extend farther back than the occiput. Naturally, with this type of helmet there is no napeguard, since the bowl itself covers the posterior part of the skull, and the sides cover a little in front of the ears. The lower edge of

Fig. 23. Italian armet, c. 1490–1500.
Steel; 1977-167-61. Three views.

Fig. 24. Italian close-helmet, c. 1510.
Steel; 1977-167-84. Two views.

the piece is cut at the back in a concave line, and is completed with two small articulated lames. The bevor has a facial opening somewhat ogival beneath. The neck defense consists of two lames, the front one being modern. The one-piece visor is of the "bellows" type, with pronounced edges and a roped border to protect the long vision slit. On the right there are sixteen ventilation holes, four by four, and another hole for the missing lifting peg. This headpiece is strongly influenced by contemporary German design, which made use of the bellows visor for a long period. German armor came into its own during the Italian wars that began in 1494 (and were to last until 1529), and brought new forms of protection for both cavalry and infantry. This helmet is of intermediate type, for cavalry armed more lightly than the man-at-arms (*uomo d'arme*) but more heavily than the light cavalry (*cavalli leggeri*), who were tactically more mobile; it is from about 1510.

The second group of fifteenth-century Italian headpieces in the Kienbusch Collection comprises the type known in Italian as *celata*, and in English variously as a *sallet* or *barbute*. The term *celata* is used to describe a design that leaves the face exposed, at least from the mouth downward, or one that does so when the visor is raised; in the latter case the *celata* is distinguished from the helmet by its lack of an integral bevor, and from the old basnet because it has no mail aventail.[12] This sort of head protection was much easier to wear, and was preferred by foot soldiers. Mounted troops usually used a version with a visor and completed it with a separately attached bevor, which protected the mouth, chin, and throat. Thus, adequate protection was combined with the advantages of a comfortable and solid head-covering.

The earliest example in the Kienbusch Collection (fig. 25) is of the simplest kind, an old form, very compact in shape (it is only 8½ inches high), and was certainly worn by a foot soldier.[13] It is markedly ovoid, and has a slight ridge down the center extending to the nape of the neck. The vertical edges bordering the facial opening protrude forward a bit then shift abruptly, forming along the lower edge a sweeping arc that is slightly concave in profile. The bowl narrows slightly, following the contours of the skull, and then spreads out at the ears, protruding very little at the sides but much more to the rear so as to form a short, curved neckguard. Around the bowl is a line of small, drilled holes for fixing the padding inside. Sallets similar to this one are frequently portrayed in paintings of the period: for example, in Paolo Uccello's *Battle of San Romano*, 1436–40 (fig. 26). Examples of similarly compact shapes are, however, very rare (I have not so far found a counterpart to this particular shape: the Italian sallets that are closest to this piece have a narrower facial opening, and are sometimes rounded behind; they spread out more completely on the neck).[14] The Kienbusch sallet, which is unmarked, may be dated to the second quarter of the fifteenth century and was made in Northern Italy.

The next example (fig. 27) comes from the celebrated cache of armor discovered in 1840 at Xalkìs, the Latin Chalcis, more famous in the Middle Ages by its Venetian name of Negroponte: the strategic key to the Serenissima's Mediterranean-Aegean empire as early as 1205. The fortress was destroyed by the Turks in 1470. The remarkable hoard of armor that came to light when a wall collapsed during renovations in 1840 consisted of more than two hundred and fifty pieces, including headpieces and armor parts, much of it datable to the first seventy years of the fifteenth century.[15] Apart from some minor dispersions, the greater part of this cache, so important for the history of Italian armor, is today divided between the Ethnikon Istorikon Mouseion in Athens and the Metropolitan Museum of Art in New York. In the former there are only five pieces of torso armor from brigandines with large plates (*corazzine a grandi piastre*; three right-hand half-breastplates, one left-hand one, one backpiece), and only two vambraces, for defense of the forearms. On the other hand, there are a great many helmets of Northern Italian or Venetian Adriatic-Aegean origin: sixty-eight in all, counting complete pieces and fragments.[16] The opposite situation exists in the Metropolitan Museum of Art, where there are very few head-coverings but a large number of other defensive pieces: respectively, ten helmets (and eleven helmet fragments), and one hundred and thirty elements of body armor, together with the fragmentary brigandine (29.150.105) and the pieces that were used to compose the suit of armor (29.154.3) with its brigandine, and other armors.[17]

The material from Negroponte—I use this name to emphasize the historical Venetian connection—that is preserved outside of these two great collections is extremely rare, and the Venetian-style sallet in the Kienbusch Collection (fig. 27) is, moreover, of a type without counterpart.[18] Unusual among those formed from two pieces (a bowl riveted onto a base, which surrounds the lower part of the head, leaving a Y-shaped aperture in front for the eyes, nose, and mouth), this one not only has an almost spherical bowl, slightly ribbed and rather pointed, but is also of quite compact shape with very short sides. Also, the line of the opening above the eyes is wider and better modeled than usual, following the arches of the eyebrows and the bridge of the nose. The base is slightly wider at the bottom, and at the nape of the neck turns out to form a small neckguard. Three holes in the forehead must have been used to attach some sort of decoration, but not a frontal, since this type of helmet never had one and there is nothing to fix it at the sides. It is extremely difficult to date pieces like this, but the most likely possibility is the second third of the fifteenth century. While we can be certain that the piece's geographical provenance is Negroponte, its place of production remains uncertain. Some of the helmets with this two-piece construction are of ascertained Lombard (or Venetian-Brescian) origin, as can be seen from the marks on surviving examples, such as the great helmet in the Museo delle Armi L. Marzoli in Brescia (272), or the Metropolitan Museum's great sallet (29.158.42). After 1427, Brescia was part of the Venetian dominions *di terraferma*, and was indeed the Serenissima's most important arms-production center, but we should not discount the dominions *da mar* and the large area under Venetian hegemony. For example, a Ragusan source of arms production has been identified. Ragusa (Dubrovnik) was in the extreme south of Venetian Dalmatia, to which it was united until 1358 before passing to Hungary. In 1410 it obtained independence, which it preserved until 1526, when it placed itself under the protection of Suleiman the Magnificent. Fourteenth-century Ragusan

Fig. 25. Italian sallet,
second quarter of the fifteenth century.
Steel; 1977-167-54.

Fig. 26. Detail of the Battle of San Romano,
1436–40, by Paolo Uccello (Italian, 1396/97–
1475). Panel, The National Gallery, London.

Fig. 27. Venetian sallet from Negroponte, c. 1430–60. Steel; 1977-167-52.

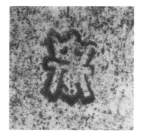

Fig. 28. Venetian sallet, 1450s. Steel; 1977-167-55. Maker's mark.

production is well documented, including its exports; and there is no reason to suppose that it ceased thereafter, although we lack specific studies. Two figures sculpted on the facade of a building in Sebenico (Sibenik, in Northern Dalmatia, which was voluntarily Venetian from 1322 to 1357, and again from 1412 until the fall of the Serenissima in 1797) are from the mid-fifteenth century; they wear great helmets or sallets of the type noted.[19] Furthermore, there must have been immigrant armorers in the Venetian dominions *da mar*, with all their fortresses, as well as some local workshops. The Byzantine influence should not be overlooked, especially in pointed and countercurved headpieces. These types of headpieces were easy to manufacture (possibly with bowls imported from the Venetian *terraferma*), and they seem to have been used only in the Adriatic-Aegean area.[20]

The Venetian-style sallet (fig. 28), whose facial opening recalls the previous piece, is on the other hand almost certainly Brescian.[21] It is a typical model with a T-shaped facial opening, the crest recurved and the neckguard extending well back. In profile the protection of the cheeks protrudes a little beyond the forehead, the upper corners of the cheeks rise slightly, and the opening widens somewhat at the base. The opening is protected by a riveted border, or stop-rib, of rectangular section. There are two holes on each side for the chinstrap, and smaller holes for the padded lining. The piece is marked at the nape of the neck, once on each side, with a crowned *A* containing an *S*. Headpieces with similar facial openings and riveted stop-ribs are to be found in the Poldi Pezzoli Museum in Milan, in the Museo delle Armi L. Marzoli in Brescia, in the Tower of London, in the Art Gallery and Museum in Glasgow (from Churburg Castle of Sluderno-Schluderns), and in the Gwynn Collection in Epsom.[22] I do not think that the mark has an exact counterpart, although two other ones have similar traits. The first appears twice on the neckguard of a bevor in Churburg: an *A*, shaped like the Kienbusch one but surmounted by a little cross, containing an *S*. The second similar mark is an *A* like the Kienbusch one (without anything on top), but containing an *O* or a cursive *D*, and is found once on each side near the lower edge of a sallet also in Churburg.[23] The shape of the *A* is not Milanese but Brescian, and in this context the cross that surmounts it on the neckguard plate is interesting because together with the upper transverse stroke of the *A* it forms a patriarchal cross, which was very often used by Brescian armorers, possibly because it recalled the highly venerated reliquary known as the *stauroteca*, containing fragments of the True Cross, which is in the Cathedral Treasury of Brescia and is in the form of a patriarchal cross. I should therefore conclude that we are dealing with a product of Lombardy, possibly Brescian, datable to the 1450s.

The next Venetian-style sallet (fig. 30) has a facial opening almost intermediate between the usual type and those in the form of a T.[24] Its lateral edges, joined with a curve to the frontal edge, come closer together to cover the cheeks as well, and then diverge to curve gently into the lower edge. The bowl is high, with a countercurved comb; it draws in toward the nape of the neck and then spreads to form the neckguard. It has rivets at the sides for the chinstrap, and others to hold the padding around the skull. It is marked at the nape, once each side, with

Fig. 29. Italian sallet, 1480–90. Steel; 1977-167-2a. Maker's mark.

Fig. 30. Venetian sallet, 1470–80. Steel; 1977-167-56. Maker's mark.

the letters *BA* under an abbreviation sign. The shape is not very common, but other very similar examples are in the Museo delle Armi L. Marzoli in Brescia. Another related piece in the Wallace Collection, London, is extremely interesting because—as in some of the Negroponte headpieces—a part of the cheekpiece is hinged on the right.[25] The mark reappears on a Venetian barbute in the Poldi Pezzoli Museum in Milan, and on another in the Royal Armory in Turin. The Kienbusch piece is Lombard and may be dated about 1470–80.[26]

Another Venetian-style sallet (fig. 32) was similar to the preceding one, but has been considerably altered by cutting away the upper part of the lateral protection.[27] The bowl, which has an ogee crest, is scarcely modeled at the nape but projects strongly to form the neckguard. The frontal edge is somewhat pointed, and at one time a noseguard was attached; the holes for the padding were enlarged (and have since been made small again by Kienbusch). The outline shape of the bowl to the neckguard and the widening of the cheeks are similar to a barbute in the Odescalchi Collection, Rome, and two Marzoli ones.[28] This piece has no mark and is datable to about 1480.

The Venetian-style sallet mounted to complete a composite suit of armor (fig. 29) has a facial opening of the usual upside-down U shape.[29] The bowl is tipped backward and ribbed, without countercurving, and the neckguard is very prominent. The facial opening is narrow, with lateral edges that run slightly obliquely inward; at the top and at the extremities are four holes for fixing a stop-rib. The holes for the chinstrap have been filled; others for the padding follow the contour of the cranium. It is marked, on the right and the left, with two crowned

Fig. 31. Italian visored sallet, fifteenth century. Steel; 1977-167-1a.

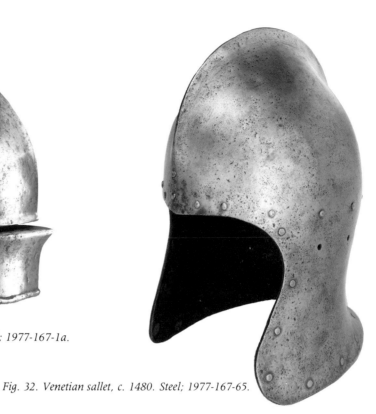

Fig. 32. Venetian sallet, c. 1480. Steel; 1977-167-65.

initials: the first is illegible and the second is an *O*. The piece is probably Milanese and can be dated between 1480 and 1490.

The last of the fifteenth-century headpieces to be considered here is a visored sallet (fig. 31), which has also been mounted as part of a composite suit of armor.[30] The original design is typically German, with its long, pointed neckguard and a visor, which pivots at the temples. The bowl of this example is well modeled at the nape of the neck, countercurved to form a low crest with a flattened edge. The facial opening is low, its frontal edge somewhat oblique and its lateral ones convex until they meet the lower edge, which has an outward turned border. The visor is ribbed down the middle, and has an uninterrupted opening for vision, which is protected by a little ridge formed of its upper edge. On the right there is a spring-clasp. Nine large rivet-heads follow the contour of the cranium, and there are two more on the nape (where perhaps there was a plume-holder). In Italy the preferred light type of head defense was the close-fitting sallet *alla Veneziana* or—later, toward the end of the century—*alla Italiana*, which was shaped gently at the sides (to give known examples, IV.453 and IV.424 in the Royal Armouries, Tower of London).[31] There are examples, such as this, of sallets *alla tedesca* (in the German style), some quite early, made in Lombardy. They were possibly preferred for export (for example, Royal Armouries, Tower of London, II.168).[32] The Philadelphia sallet has no marks and is datable to the third quarter of the fifteenth century. However, the absence of a pointed projection under the vision slit, characteristic of Italian examples, leaves some room for doubt as to the Italian origin of this piece.

The first separate armor element to be considered here is a visor (fig. 34) that comes from Negroponte and was once part of a great Venetian-style helmet.[33] It is ribbed down the middle, slightly inclined toward the apex at the center of the front edge, very slightly countercurved lower down. The lateral edges are very concave, forming the narrow extremities pierced for the pivots; the lower edge comes to an obtuse angle, with slightly convex lines. The visor is equipped with two slits for vision, lipped for reinforcement and protection. Similar visors are to be found on large *alla Veneziana* helmets that have come down to us. One in the Metropolitan Museum of Art (on helmet 29.158.46) is, however, of more compact shape, with the eye-slit almost at mid-point. One in the Museo delle Armi L. Marzoli, Brescia (272), is somewhat closer to the Kienbusch one but also has the eye-slits lower down, and its lateral edges form an obtuse angle before coming together. Although very similar to the Metropolitan Museum's visor, one in Athens at the Ethnikon Istorikon Mouseion (B 17) is remarkable because its right part is cut away directly under the eye-slit, and the left side is better covered and complete. Other visors or parts of visors are to be found in New York and Athens, but none is exactly similar to the Kienbusch example; all are datable to about the second third of the fifteenth century.[34]

I should like to discuss the Kienbusch lower reinforcing bevor, which consists of a protection for the chin, riveted to a neck lame that was originally from another bevor (fig. 33).[35] The piece is important because of its marks: on the right of the bevor are a crowned *M* and two crossed keys (twice) with the wards turned downward and inward, and on the neck lame is the monogram *IH* crowned. The first group of marks appears on a suit of armor in the Diocesan Museum of Mantua (B 1; left pauldron and its reinforce), as well as on another bevor in the Royal Armouries, Tower of London (II.168, formerly Churburg 23). The two keys with wards inward, without the crown, appear on the cuisses (twice) and the greaves (once) of the suit of armor (Churburg 19) that belonged to Ulrich von Matsch; they are the marks of one of the Barini, known as Negroli, possibly Giovanni. In support of this identification is the *IH* on the neck lame of the Kienbusch bevor, which could be read as Iohannes, but the question must remain open for anagraphic reasons; and in any case it is clear that the bevor and the neck lame do not belong together. There has been some lateral adjustment between the two plates, and from the front they are seen not to fit well. Regarding the crowned *M*, I have suggested as a working hypothesis an attribution to the Meraviglias.[36] The bevor may be dated to around 1460, and the neck lame to the third quarter of the fifteenth century. As for the armorers, the bevor can be attributed to Giovanni Barini, working for one of the Meraviglias, although for the present no certain identification can be made in respect to the neck lame, which must have been part of an important suit, since the crown on the monogram indicates the mark of a master armorer.

This piece concludes my survey of fifteenth-century Italian headpieces and their parts or attachments. It seems to me that the bevor (1977-167-182) that is marked and was previously published as Italian is, rather, Spanish, or at any rate transalpine.[37]

33

34

35

Fig. 33. Bevor, c. 1460, Milanese. Steel; 1977-167-184. Maker's mark.

Fig. 34. Italian visor from Negroponte, c. 1430–60. Steel; 1977-167-177.

Fig. 35. Italian plackart, 1480–90. Steel; 1977-167-193.

*Fig. 36. Detail and back
of Italian cuirass (see fig. 19).*

*Fig. 37. Italian breastplate, c.1500.
Steel; 1977-167-132.*

The Kienbusch Collection does not possess a great many separate pieces of Italian body armor that come within the period under study, but each one is in its own way interesting. Chronologically first is the plackart (*panziera*) that is part of a foot-soldier's breastplate *alla tedesca* (in the German style; fig. 35), which is not in the 1963 Kienbusch catalogue. It is sharply pointed at the top in a triangle, with holes at the apex and sides for fixing the upper part of the breastplate that completed it; it has a pronounced ridge down the middle, formed like a crest, and at the bottom turns outward to accommodate the plates of the fauld. The German influence began to be felt in Italy, as we have seen, in the last years of the fifteenth century. Italian protection for the chest and stomach remained the same, consisting of two pieces of which the plackart is the lower, but in these infantry models the shape of the plackart is always triangular and rising (whereas the shape of the heavy cavalry model during the same period was modified to become truly a double-breastplate). Of this type there are many complete examples, especially of Brescian manufacture.[38] I should say that the Kienbusch piece, although it is unmarked, is also Brescian, and from between 1480 and 1490.

Unlike the preceding piece, the next breastplate (fig. 37) is to be worn on horseback, as is clear from the attachments for a lance-rest on the right. (This piece is also not in the 1963 Kienbusch catalogue.)[39] It is very slim and slightly curved and ribbed; the lip at the bottom has three pairs of holes for attaching the fauld. The neckline is bordered by a boldly turned boxed edge modeled as a triangle with the front surface flattened at the apex. The arm openings are cut somewhat obliquely and are bordered like the neckline. On the right side of the chest are four holes for attaching the lance-rest; at present these are filled by four blocks riveted in place. The piece is certainly Italian and datable to around 1500. It is closely related to the breastplate of a suit (B 5) in the Diocesan Museum of Mantua, to two others in Cleveland, and to others— one of which is engraved with foliage—in the Metropolitan Museum of Art.[40]

The cuirass complete with gorget, breastplate with fauld, and backplate with culet (figs. 19, 36)[41] was part of a suit of cavalry armor *alla leggera*, as is clear from the high neckline, very similar to the corselets *da cavallo leggero*, and *da fante a piede* (infantry) in the German style. In Italy a distinction has always been made between the armor *alla leggera*, used by what we would today call cavalry-of-the-line, but which was less heavy and cumbersome than that worn by men-at-arms, and the armor *da cavallo leggero*, used by the lighter and more agile cavalry, or light cavalry, who had different tactical functions. The gorget is in two parts, but only the rearplate retains its articulated neck lame.[42] The breastplate is very globular, with an extremely robust, turned border, which runs along the horizontal neckline, and articulated gussets (the left one is modern). The lance-rest is of German type, with a half-moon baseplate. From the waist a single articulated lame supports the four lames of the fauld, which is embossed with a shallow triangular portion in the center. The backplate has a simpler shallow border at the neck and armpits; it is well modeled and has a culet of three plates that widens toward the flanks. The waistplate is shaped at the ends with swallowtail contours that fit around tongues on the backplate, helping to hold the two together when they are secured by a belt. The whole cuirass is etched. On the gorget the motif consists of bands filled with stylized spirals on a ground of oblique hatching—the classic Italian foliate motif. The treatment of the ground is also typical for this period. On the breastplate are three similar decorative bands. At the top of the center band is a coat-of-arms: barry of six, a light alternating with a dark tincture. On the left there is the letter *M*, the meaning of which is uncertain. Above, as on many Milanese cuirasses of this period, is a wide frieze divided into three panels showing (from left to right) Saint Anthony Abbot (fig. 36) with his symbolic attributes (flame, crutch, bell, and pig), the Virgin and Child, and Saint Bernardine of Siena restraining a devil. Beneath runs the misspelt inscription: *"OS NON CHOMINVETIS EX EO"* ("You shall not break a bone of him," John XIX:36), invoked here to confer invulnerability. On the backplate there are also three decorative bands, the flanking ones engraved with the spiral motif and the center one with a candelabra. Above, quite exceptionally, there is another frieze divided into three panels, showing Saint Sebastian, Saint Christopher with the Christ Child, and Saint Barbara. On the triangle embossed in the center of the fauld lames is another candelabra motif, while the lames of the fauld and the culet are bordered by etched bands bearing the usual spiral designs. In public and private collections there are a great many Italian suits of armor and cuirasses etched similarly; many of them are smooth, like the Kienbusch cuirass, but others have embossed surfaces. To discuss them all here is impossible, and I refer the interested reader to the literature.[43] The Kienbusch cuirass is one of the most remarkable of all, especially for the unusual decoration on the backplate; the nearest piece is the cuirass in Churburg (69). I would date it to 1510 or a little earlier.

The last cuirass (fig. 38) considered here is discussed together with the cavalry helmet (fig. 39) attached to it when acquired by Kienbusch.[44] The extremely heavy cuirass (it weighs 6.5 kilograms) is formed of a breastplate and backplate hinged together at the left side, fastened by a stud on the right side and held at the shoulders by metal shoulder straps that are fastened by turning pins on the breastplate. At the waist hangs a single waist lame and a fauld of two lames. The breastplate is curved but not globular, with a semicircular neckline not very low, and has no gussets. There are two holes for the lance-rest. Near the left shoulder a spacer in the form of a post protrudes obliquely (30 mm); and a little higher and to the left a bolt sticks out (50 mm), attached to a plate riveted on the inside. The backplate is gently modeled, the neckline cut as on the breastplate, the waist cut straight. The whole is painted black. The cavalry helmet has a bowl going well back, and a trapezoidal crest flanked by concave grooves. The neck curves inward and terminates in a throat defense of three lames. To the left and right of the skull are a series of ventilation holes, and farther down is a vertical rectangular slot, probably for a leather strap. There are also several holes on each side near the nape, some of which have been blocked up. The bevor has a neckguard of one lame. The one-piece visor (*visiera sana*) has a continuous vision slit and is of the bellows type, with four rows of ventilation holes on the right and two on the left; on the right is the lifting peg. Like the cuirass, this helmet is painted black. These pieces raise a few problems, because it is clear that although they were not originally together, they have been reworked to match: it is sufficient to note the

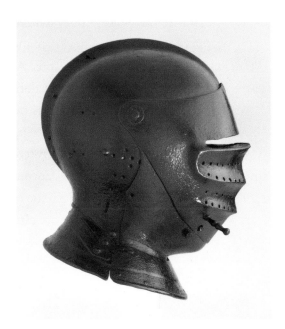

*Fig. 39. Italian
cavalry helmet, c. 1510.
Steel; 1977-167-83.*

*Fig. 38. Italian cuirass, c. 1520.
Steel; 1977-167-149.*

width of the neck lames in relation to the cuirass. Whereas the cuirass was plainly intended for the joust, as one can tell from its protruding spacer and bolt, the helmet is not adapted for such a purpose, with its vulnerable continuous vision slit, which on a true jousting helmet would have been quite different; and yet the holes are arranged as though for attaching a padded jousting cap, which one does not expect to find in a helmet of this type. It is an Italian helmet made under German influence about 1510, whereas the cuirass, also Italian, could be dated some years later. Dating is difficult for lack of similar pieces for comparison; spacers near the shoulder had a long life in Italy. The Kienbusch piece is the oldest known to me that has one, but spacers are found on armor in the Civic Museum in Bologna, on a breastplate datable to about 1520 (inv. 3451), and in the same museum on a breastplate of a tilting armor (inv. 9) from about 1560. At Ravenna, in the Museo Nazionale, there is one from the 1570s (inv. 1725). The Kienbusch breastplate has a single central bolt (to carry a large targe fixed in front), and is therefore closer to breastplates worn in the tournament known as the *carriera* than to breastplates worn for the joust (which in Italy generally have three bolts). The breastplate is already very heavy and seems to me an improbable support for extra weight. The cuirass is probably an early example of one intended for the tilt (in which a lengthwise barrier separated the opponents) to which a helmet was added later, possibly for use in training—for example, for running at the quintain (*al facchino*), a swiveling target.

Among the loose pieces, two vambraces (fig. 40), at present mounted into a composite suit of armor, are not a pair.[45] The right vambrace has a tapered upper arm-cannon, marked with the letters *AM*, apparently surmounted by a poorly stamped heraldic lily, accompanied (twice) by the initials *BI* under a split cross with bifurcated arms, and the remains of a similar cross between these two. The elbow-guard is formed from four plates, from the second of which springs a large asymmetrical wing, which is unusual. The lower arm-cannon turns inside the elbow-guard and is slightly modeled at the wrist. The swiveling joint between the lower cannon and elbow-guard is of an early type but the elbow-guard itself—somewhat ogival, pointed—suggests a date around 1460. The same marks are found on a right pauldron once in the Pauilhac Collection; the first monogram by itself is on a headpiece (IV. 425) in the Royal Armouries, Tower of London, coming from Rhodes, datable to about 1470–80; the second group is found also marked twice on a pair of cuisses on an armor (B 4) in the Diocesan Museum in Mantua, datable to the 1480s. I can make no comment on the first mark, except to note that the lily is quite exceptional among Italian marks and may indicate a piece for export; regarding the second, in the context of Mantuan armor I have advanced some hypotheses, which, however, bear no relation to the present case.[46]

The left vambrace is more wide open at the top than the right one, and is marked with a crowned monogram: *B* and a second, illegible letter, which might be *C, E,* or *G*. The elbow-guard has four plates, with the second one forming a barely ogival but pointed cup; the wing is asymmetrical, with a hole for a detachable reinforce. The well-modeled lower cannon turns, like the other one, inside the elbow-guard. Dating is the same as the other vambrace, or

Fig. 40. Italian vambraces, left and right, c. 1460 or later. Steel; 1977-167-1b, 1c. Two views.

Maker's mark for right vambrace.

Maker's mark for left vambrace.

possibly a little later. Interpreting the monogram is impossible; if the second letter were definitely E after the B, one might think of Bernardino da Carnago.[47]

The manifer (tournament reinforce for the left gauntlet; fig. 42) that has been considered to be German[48] consists of only two plates, a flared piece, which is pierced for a reinforcing rondel, and another, which forms the mitten. In my view this gauntlet is Italian rather than German, and I would compare it with a similar one in the Civic Museum in Bologna (inv. 23), complete with rondel, which may be dated to about 1500.[49]

The right legpiece, or cuisse (fig. 41), has also been mounted onto a composite suit of armor.[50] The top consists of three articulated lames, with a turned border at the uppermost edge and rising toward the outside of the thigh, marked with a small C under a split cross pattée surmounted by a crown. The main plate has a concave upper edge with a turned border and a hinged sideplate. It is embossed with radiating flutes. I do not think that the kneepiece is original. On the turned border of the main plate are palmettes in a delicate pointillé technique. These also appear on the adjacent lame, which bears the invocation AUE (for "Ave," which would have corresponded to "Maria" on the left one). The piece is datable, in as much as it is original, to the 1460s. The same armorer's mark is found on the elements of two vambraces (inv. 842–843) in the Hôtel de Ville Museum at Le Landeron, Switzerland; on the Venetian-style sallet (B 12) from Negroponte in the Ethnikon Istorikon Mouseion in Athens; and on one (A 76) in the Wallace Collection, London; as well as at the Metropolitan Museum of Art, New York, on a helmet (29.150.7), on the left legpiece (29.158.270) and on the left greave (29.158.279b), both also from Negroponte; and also on an armor (HA 3) formerly in the Zeughaus, Berlin. Without the crown it appears on another Venetian-style sallet also in the Metropolitan Museum of Art (14.25.581). As pure speculation, these marks could be linked to Cattaneo Cattanei, a Milanese armorer and merchant of those years.[51]

The last pieces of fifteenth-century Italian defensive armor in the Kienbusch Collection are a pair of greaves (fig. 43), which are not in the 1963 catalogue. The front plate is ribbed along all its length, and there is a row of holes at the instep to attach the mail shoe. The calf plates are well modeled, ribbed along all their length and equipped with keepers at the top for a kneestrap. There are holes that appear to have been used to attach kneepieces and shoes, which did not belong. The greaves are marked at the top, in front, with (twice) GI under a cross whose three upper limbs end in two knobs. Both pieces are datable to the 1440s: the marks, which are well known, are those of the Milanese Giovanni da Garavalle, a specialist in making leg armor who also worked for the Corios. These marks appear on the cuisses and greaves of the famous Avant armor (formerly Churburg 20; now 39–65e in the Glasgow Art Gallery and Museum).[52]

The remaining pieces I should like to mention are elements of horse armor. The chanfron (fig. 45)[53] is of slim proportions, not too large, ribbed in the middle and countercurved to halfway down the nose; other embossed ribs run from the top to the eye-sockets, and from these to the nostrils. The lower portion, contemporary with the rest, is riveted and its upper edge is

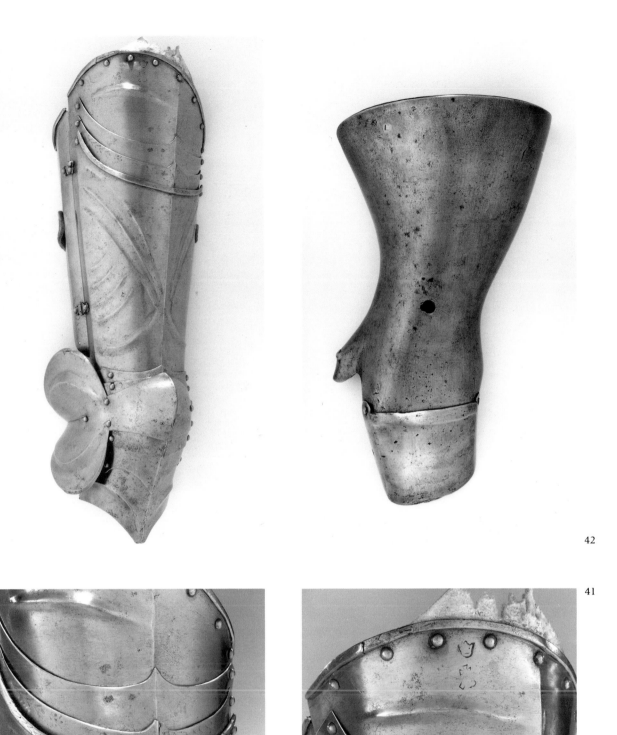

41

42

41

41

Fig. 41. Italian cuisse and detail of decoration, 1460s. Steel; 1977-167-2b. Maker's mark.
Fig. 42. Italian manifer, early sixteenth century. Steel; 1977-167-165.

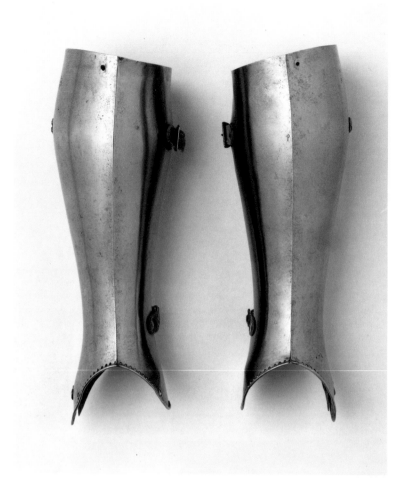

Fig. 43. Pair of greaves, 1440s, made by Giovanni da Garavalle (Milanese). Steel, 1977-167-192.
Maker's mark.

cusped seven times; it may originally have been articulated at the sides, given the way it has been cut obliquely. It is marked at the top on the right (twice) with the monogram *AP* (the second letter not certain) within a mandorla, surmounted by a rounded bifurcated cross. These two crosses are linked together by a split cross. The same mark appears on another chanfron in the Fitzwilliam Museum in Cambridge. This type of mark may very possibly be Tuscan; and the piece may be dated to about 1460–80.[54]

Another chanfron (fig. 44) is unmarked.[55] A central ridge runs vertically as far as the forehead, where the missing escutcheon was. The lower half is counter-curved. The eye-sockets are crisp and simply cut; embossed flutes, some above the eye-sockets and five radiating from each side of the nose, enliven the surface. At the top is a riveted clasp of worked brass. The rivets are in all probability modern: the shape of the outer edges shows that the piece has been heavily cut back, probably to eliminate damage on one or both sides. It was made about 1480.

This overview of the subject is certainly not an exhaustive treatment. The pieces

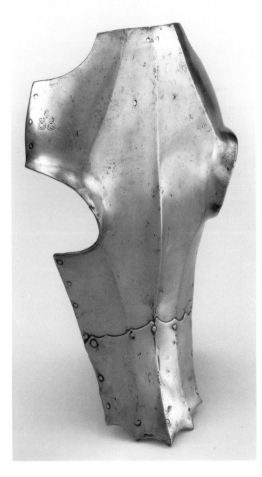

Fig. 44. Italian chanfron,
c. 1480. Steel; 1977-167-266.

Fig. 45. Italian chanfron, 1460–80. Steel; 1977-167-264. Maker's marks.

described as Italian in the 1963 Kienbusch catalogue and not mentioned here have been judged extraneous, or else too problematic in terms of their location of production; other pieces I have rejected because they seem to me highly dubious or certainly modern. I confine this observation to those pieces that would have fallen within my period.[56] In any case, the Kienbusch Collection can assuredly be proud of its Italian defensive material—not only of the early pieces, which are examined here, but also of the later ones.

NOTES

1 My *Gli esemplari italiani nell'Armeria Kienbusch del Phil-adelphia Museum of Art* (Florence, 1988) brings together observations on the whole group of Italian arms from defensive armor to firearms and comprises the first results of research carried out in 1983. A manuscript version, "Introduzione alle armi italiane nella Armeria Kienbusch," is on deposit at the Museum. At this distance of time, I would modify certain conclusions.

2 For this general tendency, see Claude Blair, *European Armour, circa 1066 to circa 1700* (London, 1958; reprint 1972), pp. 37–76. For Italy, see Ortwin Gamber, "Harnischstudien: V. Stilgeschichte des Plattenhar-nisches von den Anfängen bis um 1440," *Jahrbuch der Kunsthistorischen Sammlungen in Wien*, vol. 50 (1953), pp. 53–92; Ortwin Gamber, "Harnischstudien: VI. Stilgeschichte des Plattenharnisches von 1440–1510," *Jahrbuch der Kunsthistorischen Sammlungen in*

Wien, vol. 51 (1955), pp. 31–102; Bruno Thomas and Ortwin Gamber, "L'Arte milanese dell'armatura," *Storia di Milano*, vol. 11 (1958), pp. 697–841; Lionello G. Boccia and E.T. Coelho, "L'Armamento di cuoio e ferro nel Trecento italiano," *L'Illustrazione Italiana*, vol. 1, no. 2 (1974), pt. 2, pp. 24–37; and Lionello G. Boccia, "L'antica produzione di armi in Lombardia" and "L'armatura lombarda tra il xiv e il xvii secolo" in Lionello G. Boccia, Francesco Rossi, and Marco Morin, *Armi e armature Lombarde* (Milan, 1979), pp. 5–77. For more specific aspects see Bengt Thordeman, *Armour from the Battle of Wisby, 1361* (Uppsala, 1939), vol. 1, esp. pp. 211–25, 264–328.

3 As typical examples one could cite at least two warriors on the Saliceti arch of 1403 in the Museo Civico Medievale in Bologna, the *San Romano* of 1412 in the Pinacoteca Nazionale in Ferrara, the tomb of Marino Cossa (died 1417) in the Musée du Louvre, the tomb of Lodovico degli Obizzi (died 1424) from a design by Ghiberti (Italian, 1378–1455) in the church of Santa Croce in Florence, and the Saint George in Gentile da Fabriano's Quaratesi polyptych of 1425 in the Uffizi Gallery, Florence. For these and contemporary armors, see Boccia 1979, esp. pp. 17–22 and figs. 1–28; and Lionello G. Boccia, "Materiali iconografici sull'armamento quattrocentesco d'ambiente toscano," *Antichità Viva*, vol. 26, no. 3 (1988), pp. 37–53 (first given as a lecture "II Convegno sulla civiltà della arti minori in Toscana," Arezzo, 1973).

4 The list includes: in Mantua, the Diocesan Museum, the composite suit of armor B 1, with pieces by the Milanese Antonio Missaglia and, perhaps, Giacomo Cantoni, Giovanni Maffioli, and Giovanni Negroli for the Meraviglias, and Master Biagio for Giovanni Spanzotti, as well as perhaps the Brescian Paolino da Milano, the whole c. 1450–60; armor B 2, with pieces by the Brescian Pietro de Castello, and perhaps by the Milanese Bernardino Cantoni, Giovanni da Castello, Cristoforo Capelli, and other masters, the whole c. 1460–80; armor B 3, with pieces by Antonio Missaglia and Giovanni Antonio dalle Fibbie, and perhaps by the Brescian Antonio de Osma and other masters, the whole c. 1470–90; and armor B 5, with pieces by the Brescian Pietro Giacomo da Castello and other masters, possibly Milanese, the whole c. 1480–1500. To these one could add armor B 6, perhaps Milanese, c. 1510, which is the most representative group, although of varied composition. At Churburg Castle in Sluderno-Schluderns there are the following: the composite suit of armor 18, c. 1410–15, to which was added a helmet (now in the Gwynn Collection in Epsom, England) possibly by the Milanese Petrolo da Fagnano, c. 1410–20; the armor 19, which belonged to Ulrich von Matsch, by the Milanese Pier Innocenzo da Faerno, Antonio Missaglia, and Giovanni Negroli, c. 1445–50; the armor 21, which belonged to Galeazzo d'Arco, by the Milanese Tommaso Negroni (Missaglia), the only one that has come down to us signed by a single maker, c. 1450. For historical reasons one could group with these the composite armor formerly Churburg 20 and now in the Glasgow Museum and Art Gallery, AGM 39–65e, known as the Avant armor from the motto it bears, by the Milanese Giovanni, Ambrogio, Bellino, and Dionisio Corio,

with Giovanni da Garavalle, c. 1440–45. In Vienna, in the Leibrüstkammer, are the suit of armor A 2 (fig. 20), which belonged to Frederick I the Victorious, elector of the Palatinate, by the Milanese Tommaso Negroni (Missaglia), Pier Innocenzo da Faerno, and Antonio Missaglia, c. 1451; and armor A 3, owned by Roberto Sanseverino, Count of Caiazzo, with pieces by the Milanese Giovan Pietro and Bernardino Cantoni, Giovanni Salimbeni, Antonio Missaglia, and perhaps the Brescians Zanetto Ferrari and Albertino Vimercate, working in Venice c. 1480–85. The one in Udine, in the basilica of Our Lady of the Graces, has pieces perhaps by the Milanese Bernardino Cantoni, Giovanni Pampuri, Giovanni Antonio d'Albairate, and others, c. 1485–90. The most important incomplete suits are as follows: in the Reale Armería, Turin (B 19); Bernisches Historisches Museum, Bern (SBZ 102); Rathaus, Historisches Museum, Lucerne (HM 11); Musée de l'Hôtel de Ville, Landeron, Switzerland (HV 837–840); Schweizerisches Landesmuseum, Zurich (LM 4955); Leibrüstkammer des Kunsthistorisches Museum, Vienna (A 111, of Gianfrancesco Gonzaga); Schwäbisch-Gmünd, in the Heiligenkreuzkirche (SML 47–76); Toledo, in the Capilla de los Reyes Nuevos in the cathedral, belonging to the Portuguese Duarte de Almeida (died 1476). The suit of armor from the Bashford Dean Collection in the Metropolitan Museum of Art in New York, 29.154.3, is composed almost entirely of pieces coming from the famous Negroponte-Xalkis hoard. It is composed of pieces that are similar but do not actually belong together; although the result of antiquarian reconstruction, it is not unrepresentative. See Lionello G. Boccia, *Le armature di S. Maria delle Grazie di Curtatone di Mantova e l'armatura Lombarda del '400* (Busto Arsizio, 1982), *passim*; and Stephen V. Grancsay, *The Bashford Dean Collection of Arms and Armor in the Metropolitan Museum of Art* (Portland, Me., 1933), pls. I, III, IX.

5 I refer to the suit B 33 of Claude de Vaudrey, datable to 1495–1500, by Damiano II Missaglia and the da Merates, and to the suit B 71 of Maximilian of Austria, made by Francesco de Merate in the early years of the sixteenth century (both in the Leibrüstkammer, Vienna), as well as to the suit II.5 made by Filippo Grampi and Giovanni Angelo Litta around 1514–15 and decorated by Paul van Vrelant, for Henry VIII of England, now in the Royal Armouries of the Tower of London. See Lionello G. Boccia and E. T. Coelho, *L'Arte dell'armatura in Italia* (Milan, 1967), pp. 153, 154, and 181–87; and Boccia 1982, p. 292, nn. 146–48, with a modified attribution.

6 C. Otto von Kienbusch, *The Kretzschmar von Kienbusch Collection of Armor and Arms* (Princeton, N.J., 1963), p. 56, no. 54, pl. XLII. It comes from the Bashford Dean Collection, where it was claimed to have come from the Doge's Palace in Venice, along with other fifteenth-century armors, helmets, and sallets, which seems to me unlikely. In the 1963 Kienbusch catalogue the first mark is also read as "*YO* (?) crowned"; the monogram is very badly preserved, especially its first letter.

7 The object file for the helmet in the Kienbusch archives declares that (apart from the rondel and its post,

which Kienbusch had added), "the present headpiece is homogeneous and unrestored," but this observation certainly does not refer to the old attempts at restoration, evidence for which is clear in the different shapes and dimensions of the two cheekpieces, and the replacement of the rivets.

8 The group YO crowned plus CO (twice) under a split cross appears also on the helmet A152 in the Wallace Collection, London; on the helmet (formerly G.PO 672 Pauilhac Collection) in the Musée de l'Armée in Paris; and on the breastplate of the suit belonging to Duarte de Almeida in Toledo; and perhaps also, slightly differently, on the barbute A5603 in the Bayerisches Armeemuseum in Ingolstadt. See Boccia 1982, pp. 284–85, with another bibliography.

9 Kienbusch 1963, p. 57, no. 55, pl. XLII. It comes from the William Randolph Hearst Collection. A frontal of similar shape is on the helmet A152 in the Wallace Collection, London; see James G. Mann, *Wallace Collection Catalogues: European Arms and Armour* (London, 1962), vol. 1, p. 129, pl. 68.

10 Kienbusch 1963, p. 56, no. 53, pl. XLII. It comes from the William Randolph Hearst Collection.

11 Kienbusch 1963, p. 61, no. 64, pl. XLIV. It comes from the Sir Guy F. Laking, Henry G. Keasbey, and Bashford Dean collections. The new necklame was added by Dean about 1923–25. In 1950 Kienbusch had the piece cleaned, eliminating its dark coloring (not that this was necessarily the original burnishing; J.F. Hayward and Hans Schedelmann, two of the authors of the 1963 Kienbusch catalogue, refer only to the "former black color," and Dean in the 1925 sale catalogue described its "blackened surface").

12 In the sixteenth century the terminology changed, because the word *celata* was applied to every kind of headpiece, qualified so as to distinguish between types: thus, *celata da cavallo* (for the cavalry helmet), or *celata da piede* (for the burgonet), and so on. In English the terms *barbute* and *barbuta* are often used for the Italian *celata*, though in Italian *barbuta* is to be used solely for the fourteenth-century headpiece without visor and with a mail aventail (which becomes a *bacinetto* with the addition of a visor).

13 Kienbusch 1963, p. 52, no. 42, pl. XXXIX. It comes from the Frank Gair Macomber Collection.

14 Among these low sallets one could cite IV.20 in the Royal Armouries in the Tower of London, with the receding line of its cheekpieces (A.R. Dufty, *European Armour in the Tower of London* [London, 1968], pl. LXXVII), and 724 in the Odescalchi Collection, Rome, of somewhat less pronounced lateral form but with a very prominent neckguard (Nolfo di Carpegna, *Antiche armi dal sec. IX al XVIII già Collezione Odescalchi* [Rome, 1969], p. 8, no. 26, repro.). Both are much later, however, and it would seem that the outline of the compact shape of the low sallet became progressively more streamlined.

15 In 1841 the discovery was published by J. A. Buchon, "Archéologie," *Courier Grec*, February 27, 1841, which was historically unsatisfactory but republished by him without alteration two years later as *La Grèce continentale et la Morée: Voyage, séjour et études historiques en 1840 et 1841* (Paris, 1843). Almost immediately, iconographic evidence was provided by Jacob

Heinrich von Hefner-Alteneck (*Costume du moyen-âge chrétien d'après des monumens contemporains* [Mannheim, 1840–54], vol. 1, pp. 90–91, vol. 2, pl. 63) in a plate that inaccurately depicts eight headpieces, wrongly dated to the thirteenth century; another plate that was announced as forthcoming never appeared. In Italy, a few lines were penned by Cesare Cantù on the subject; they are worth recalling, since they have been ignored by historians (*Storia Universale* [Turin, 1857], p. 429, paragraph 72; "Armerie"): "Buchon, who traveled to Greece in 1840, searching for the vestiges of the French domination in the Middle Ages, speaks of a collection of ancient arms and armor at Athens, very curious, which explains the *gasigan* mentioned by Henri of Valenciennes as being iron plates somewhat concave and extremely light, adapted to the habits of the knights, who in those hot climates did not wish to be weighed down. And an enormous pile of arms from the Middle Ages was brought to light, with very many headpieces and legpieces marked with an *M*, which perhaps means 'made in Milan,' considering the reputation of the armor made in that city, known also as the city 'of the wolf.' " Apart from this last observation, which is erroneous, it is interesting that both historians compare this material to the Islamic *kazaghand* (which, however, bore protection of mail and not of plates), and that Cantù had proposed a Milanese solution for the *M*. The first description in the literature is by Charles J. ffoulkes ("On Italian Armour from Chalcis in the Ethnological Museum at Athens," *Archaeologia*, vol. 12 (1911), pp. 381–90; a first (and incorrect) reconstruction of the events of the discovery—and of the dispersal due to Bashford Dean—is by Konstantinos N. Rados, "Ta ek Xalkidos krani tou Istorikon kai Ethnologikou Mouseiou" (The Helmets from Chalcis in the Historical and Ethnological Museum), *Deltion Istorikis kai Ethnologikis Etaireias*, vol. 8 (1923), pp. 606–13. In recent years the subject has been treated by this author in a lecture on the occasion of the 9th Congress of the International Association of Museums of Arms and Military History, in New York, "The Xalkìs Finds in Athens and New York," 1981; and Claude Blair, "Notes on Armour from Chalcis," *Arms & Armour at the Dorchester* (London, 1982), pp. 7–14 (with a full bibliography and new information). The Athens pieces have been catalogued by A.V.B. Norman (unpublished).

16 In detail (applying the provisional numbering adopted by the author in Athens, distinguished by the initial *B* in front of the numbers [Boccia 1981]): armet 59 and bowl of helmet 60; barbute 1; Venetian-style sallets 8–15; Venetian-style great sallets 2–5, 7, and 24–26, with the remains 6 and the bowls 32–39; the Venetian-style great helmets 16–23 (16 and 17 complete with visors) with the bowls 27–30; the sallet 46; *ribalda*s 44–45; light sallets 40–43; the sallet with frontal 47, with the remains 48; and the bowls 49–53 and 56–57 with the remains of the bowl 58; the bowls of the sallets with neckguards 54–55 and of the skullcap 31; the skullcap 68; the visor of the great Venetian-style helmet 61 and the visor of the helmet 62; the remains of the bevors 63–65; the neckguard 66 and the remains 67. The parts of chest armor are the right half-breastplates 70–72, the left half-

breastplate 73, the backplate 74; and two left vambraces 75 and 76. The Ethnikon Istorikon Mouseion also conserves the Turkish domed helmets 77–80 with the remains 81, and the conical helmet 82, with the remains 83–85. In addition there are the morion 69 and the burgonet 95, which are much later, and various hafted arms 87–94, other fragments, shafts and tips of arrows, and thirty-five caltrops.

17 In the suit of armor 29.154.3 in the Metropolitan Museum of Art, New York, the basnet is not from Negroponte, and the right shoulderpiece, the right cuisse, the left greave, and some other plates are modern; the brigandine is partly homogeneous and partly completed by pieces also from Negroponte. The headpieces are: the helmets 29.158.5, 29.150.7, 29.158.22, and 29.158.45; the Venetian-style great helmet with visor 29.158.46; the barbute 29.158.43; the Venetian-style great helmets without visors 29.158.42 and 29.158.47; the sallets 29.158.39 and 29.158.41; the little sallet 29.158.3a is of uncertain provenance. The loose pieces are as follows: four lower halves for Venetian-style great helmets, and seven visors; thirty half-breastplates, rights and lefts; fifteen backplates, and seven other plates of chest-armor; two shoulderpieces, four armlets, two gauntlets, four legpieces, and four backplates; and sixty-two protective pieces for the arms, including upper and lower vambraces, elbowpieces, and their parts. See Grancsay 1933, *passim*, and esp. pls. III, IV, V, X, XII, XIII; there are, as well, the pieces in the composite suits 29.150.7, 29.150.5, and 29.156.66 (and in the two groups already noted), the elbowpiece with vambrace 29.150.22, and the vambraces 29.150.33, .19, .29, .32, .40; the rest is in the museum's storage.

18 Kienbusch 1963, no. 40, p. 52, pl. XXXIX. It comes from the Bashford Dean Collection. None of the three examples that the catalogue cites as parallels has the slightest resemblance to it: neither the Venetian-style great helmet 29.158.42 in the Metropolitan Museum of Art, which is much higher, with its cusped bowl and narrower facial opening; nor the basnet B1 in the Cleveland Museum of Art, composed of an ogival Venetian-style helmet and a visor that does not seem to me to be from Negroponte; nor the Venetian-style great helmet in the Museo delle Armi L. Marzoli in Brescia, inv. 272, marked with a crowned *P* and a crowned *N* (twice). See Grancsay 1933, pl. III, no. 27; Helen Ives Gilchrist, *A Catalogue of the Collection of Arms & Armor Presented to The Cleveland Museum of Art by Mr. and Mrs. John Long Severance, 1916–1923* (Cleveland, 1924), pl. VII, B1; and Francesco Rossi and Nolfo di Carpegna, *Armi antiche dal Museo Civico L. Marzoli* (Milan, 1969), no. 63.

19 D. Petrović, *Dubrovacko Oruzje u XIV veku* (Belgrade, 1976), in particular pp. 135–44 and 276–82; Blair 1982, pp. 11–13. Sebenico Cathedral was rebuilt by Venetian masters from 1431; from 1441 work was carried out by Giorgio Orsini da Zara, who until then had been working in Venice with the Bon. The reliefs are connected with the Venetian figurative sources.

20 I assigned the headpieces of the figures 37, 38, and 39 to Lombardy including Brescia, which was politically Venetian (Boccia 1979). My research undertaken later in Athens and New York in 1981 did not modify this

specific attribution; there are "Adriatic-Aegean" pieces (as regards use and type) with "Lombard" marks (as regards production), and very probably there are headpieces of this "Adriatic-Aegean" type that are of local production.

21 Kienbusch 1963, p. 52, no. 41, pl. XXXIX. It comes from the Bashford Dean Collection. The catalogue records that it was earlier in Casa Vendramin-Calergi in Venice, but the archive entry makes no mention of this. The mark is not the usual Milanese type.

22 See Lionello G. Boccia and José A. Godoy, *Museo Poldi Pezzoli, Milan*, vol. 1, *Armería I* (Milan, 1985), p. 85, no. 25, pl. 38; Rossi and di Carpegna 1969, inv. 270, no. 73, repro.; Dufty 1968, no. IV. 17, pl. LXXIV; Oswald Graf Trapp, *The Armoury of the Castle of Churburg* (London, 1929), no. 58, pl. XXXIX. A similar helmet in the Wallace Collection in London, A76, has lost its riveted strip but the traces of it are clearly visible; another, with the very narrow facial opening intermediate between T and Y, with a strip surround, is in Turin, Royal Armory E9; another similar one is in London, Wallace Collection A78. See Mann 1962, vol. 1, pp. 97–98, pl. 55; Giorgio Dondi, Marisa Cartesegna, et al. *L'Armería Reale di Torino* (Busto Arsizio, 1982), p. 343, no. 63, pl. V.

23 See Trapp 1929, no. 56, and (formerly) no. 60, pl. XXVI, b. The mark of a more elegant *A* (without crown or cross), which seems as though it might contain another letter, is on the right greave of the Sanseverino suit, A 3, in the Leibrüstkammer, Vienna, which, however, is a substitute and much older; see Boccia 1982, p. 287, no. 77. According to some scholars, the mark on Churburg 56 appears also on seals and could be that of a juridical person.

24 Kienbusch 1963, p. 53, no. 43, pl. XXXIX. It comes from the Bashford Dean Collection.

25 Rossi and di Carpegna 1969, pp. 37–38, inv. 201, no. 66, repro; p. 43, inv. 288, no. 81, repro., with the convexity of the cheeks cut away; p. 43, inv. 289, no. 82, repro., later equipped with crimson velvet (now lost) and gilded decoration, as a gift—accompanied by a sword–to some captain of the Venetian mainland territories; Mann 1962, vol. 1, A 77, pp. 97–98, pl. 55 (it is possible that there was also a visor; see A.V.B. Norman, *Wallace Collection Catalogues: European Arms and Armour Supplement* [London, 1986], p. 42).

26 Boccia and Godoy 1985, vol. 1, p. 85, no. 25, pl. 38; Dondi and Cartesegna 1982, p. 342, no. 62, E7.

27 Not in the Kienbusch 1963 catalogue, even though it was acquired in 1961. It comes from the William Randolph Hearst and Hollander collections.

28 See di Carpegna 1969, p. 8, inv. 732, no. 25, repro., coming from the Bardini Collection, via Samuel Whawell; adorned with gilded brass, like the one mentioned in note 25. See also Rossi and di Carpegna 1969, pp. 37–38, inv. 201, no. 66, and p. 43, inv. 288, no. 81, mentioned above in note 25, and p. 41, inv. 296, no. 76, repro., reworked at the facial opening.

29 Kienbusch 1963, pp. 14–15, no. 2, pl. II. It comes from the Echaurren Valeiro, Henry G. Keasbey, and George D. Pratt collections. The Lombard marks with *O* for the second letter are too many for an attribution, even a hypothetical one, to be attempted.

30 Kienbusch 1963, pp. 13–14, no. 1, pl. I. It comes from

the arsenal in Constantinople and from the Bashford Dean Collection (private communication with Stuart W. Pyhrr).

31 Dufty 1968, pl. LXXVII. In my view the first is earlier than the second and may be dated about 1480–90; the second would be about 1500.

32 Formerly Churburg 61; Trapp 1929, pp. 98–99, pl. XXXI; Dufty 1968, pl. LXXVI.

33 Kienbusch 1963, p. 107, no. 181, pl. LXX. It comes from the Negroponte cache and from the Bashford Dean Collection. The Museum's archive entry records that Dean mounted the visor on the Venetian sallet 1977-167-56 in one of his "puttings together," as Kienbusch called them, for which Dean was "a bit overenthusiastic." Kienbusch rightly separated the pieces.

34 See Grancsay 1933, no. 29, pl. III; Boccia 1979, fig. 39; Boccia 1981, pl. B, fig. 17. The shapes of this type of visor vary considerably: to consider those in the Metropolitan Museum of Art, New York, only 29.158.544 has separate vision slits, but it is small, strangely shaped at the top and pointed at the bottom; the closest to the Kienbusch piece, 29.158.547, has a continuous vision slit that is lower, almost no molding, and countercurved lateral edges; two others, 29.158.547 and 29.158.552, are strongly cusped in the center of the upper edge; the others are also different, and more compact than the Philadelphia one.

35 Kienbusch 1963, pp. 79–80, no. 111, pl. LIV. It comes from the Madrid Opera House, and from the Don Juan Vera, Mariano Fortuny, Baron Charles Alexandre de Cosson, and William Randolph Hearst collections. See Charles A. de Cosson and William Burges, "Catalogue of the Exhibition of Ancient Helmets and Examples of Mail," *The Archaeological Journal*, vol. 37 (1880), pp. 501–3, no. 23, pl. II, fig. 20.

36 For this complicated and still-open discussion, see Boccia 1982, pp. 282–83 (mark 10) and pp. 284–85 (group 35–36). The crowned *M* is often accompanied (twice) by an *M* surmounted by a cross; very important among pieces thus marked is the visored sallet *alla francese* A2334 in the Leibrüstkammer, Vienna, which exemplifies a type intended for export, with the cusped bowl raised in countercurve (Bruno Thomas and Ortwin Gamber, *Kunsthistorisches Museum, Wien, Waffensammlung: Katalog der Leibrüstkammer*, vol. 1, *Teil, Der Zeitraum von 500 bis 1530* [Vienna, 1976], pp. 84–85, fig. 28). The keys with their wards turned upwards appear accompanied by a split cross on the breastplate 35152, in the armory of the Duke of Medinaceli in the Museo del Ejercito in Madrid, and also in Madrid on the gorget of the armor A6 in the Real Armería (Juan Crooke y Navarrot, de Valencia de Don Juan, *Catálogo histórico-descriptivo de la Real Armería de Madrid* [Madrid, 1898], p.6), but this variant may not be Italian. Keys with their wards turned downwards, but crowned, are found on the breastplate C3 in the Cleveland Museum of Art, on the sallet IV.424 in the Royal Armouries, Tower of London, on the sallets D12 and D13 also in the Real Armería, on the jousting helmet I 230 in the Hermitage, Leningrad, and elsewhere (Gilchrist 1924, p. 61, pl. XII; Dufty 1968, pl. LXXVII; de Valencia 1898, pp. 141–43, pl. XX; Eduard von Lenz, *Imperatorskiy Ermitazh. Sobranie oruzhiya*

[St. Petersburg, 1908], vol. 1, pp. 164–65, illustrated in Florent Gille and A. Rockstühl, *Musée de Tzarskoe—Selo, ou collection d'armes de Sa Majesté l'Empereur de toutes les Russies* [St. Petersburg and Karlsruhe, 1835–53], pl. CXII). The jousting helmet is of the type *alla spagnola*. All these pieces could be attributed, at different dates but nevertheless within the period under discussion, to the Barini-Negroli workshops.

37 Its mark, possibly two *C*s back-to-back under a crown, reappears on the bevor H7 formerly in the Zeughaus in Berlin. Two other Kienbusch bevors, 1977-167-186 and 1977-167-178, are not considered here because they are heavily restored (the second, which I do not think is Italian, has "patched up" plates).

38 See, for example, B15 in the Diocesan Museum in Mantua; Churburg 38; and the Royal Armouries, Tower of London, III.1282 (also from Churburg), these last two by the Brescian Zanetto Ferrari; all with identical plackarts; Boccia 1982, figs. 157, 492; Dufty 1968, pl. CIX.

39 It comes from the Bashford Dean Collection. According to the Museum's archive entry, the buckles are "almost certainly remade"; I should say that they are genuine, but not the original ones.

40 Boccia 1982, figs. 360, and 364–67; Gilchrist 1924, p. 61, C1 and C3, pl. XII (the second of which is marked with the crowned keys; see note 36); and Grancsay 1933, no. 64, pl. XXXVI, with other references to similar pieces in the Metropolitan Museum of Art, New York.

41 Kienbusch 1963, pp. 83–84, no. 122, pl. LVI. It comes from the Robert Curzon, Baron Zouche, and Edward H. Litchfield collections.

42 The headpiece to complete the armor ought to have been a sallet with a bellows visor, which seems to have been the preferred type in Italy for this kind of armor; see, for example, the famous one in the Musée de l'Armée, Paris, G8, with headpiece by Giovan Angelo Missaglia. A variant of this type, with the addition of two bevor plates attaching at the chin, formed a helmet (such as the Carrand C1635 in the Bargello in Florence). The presence of robust bordering on the upper neckplate of the Kienbusch piece would have permitted this latter solution. See Boccia and Coelho 1967, figs. 159–62 and 198–203.

43 See Trapp 1929, pp. 111–15, nos. 69–70, pls. XLII–XLIV; James G. Mann, "Notes on the Armour of the Maximilian Period and the Italian Wars," *Archaeologia*, vol. 79 (1929), esp. pp. 221–31; Thomas and Gamber 1958, pp. 753–56; Boccia and Coelho 1967, pp. 184–204, 211–36; and Lionello G. Boccia, "I corsaletti 'alla leggera' del Santuario di Curtatone," in *Scritti di storia dell'arte in onore di Ugo Procacci*, 2 vols. (Milan, 1977), vol. 2, pp. 333–39; Boccia 1979, pp. 17–18, figs. 97–98 and 102–7; Boccia 1982, pp. 121–22, no. B10; Helmut Nickel, Stuart W. Pyhrr, and Leonid Tarassuk, *The Art of Chivalry: European Arms and Armor from The Metropolitan Museum of Art* (New York, 1982), pp. 34 and 36–38. This last example, in the Metropolitan Museum of Art, New York, 14.25.716, formerly in the Uboldo Collection in Milan, is the most complete of this kind in an American collection. Smooth corselets engraved like this one are in the Diocesan Museum in Mantua, B10;

Churburg 69 and 70; in the Stibbert Museum in Florence, 3146; and in the Historisches Museum in Dresden, M8. The inscription on the Kienbusch cuirass may be compared with Churburg Castle 69, the Dresden piece M8, and the breastplate 2 in the Zeughaus, Solothurn, Switzerland (Rudolf Wegeli, *Katalog der Waffen-Sammlung im Zeughause zu Solothurn* [Solothurn, 1905], p. 2, pl. II).

44 Kienbusch 1963, p. 35, no. 20, pl. XXI; Stephen V. Grancsay, *The Metropolitan Museum of Art: Loan Exhibition of European Arms and Armor* (New York, 1931), no. 32 (only the cuirass); Boccia and Godoy 1985, p. 75. The pieces were bought by Kienbusch in 1921, and the dealer who sold them asserted that the previous owner had acquired them in Italy.

45 Kienbusch 1963, pp. 13–14, no. 1, pl. I. According to the Museum's archive entry, they came from the Negroponte cache; formerly in the Clarence H. Mackay Collection.

46 Dufty 1968, pl. LXXVII; Boccia 1982, p. 287, no. 89. An interesting hypothesis would be to regard Ambrogio da Binago, documented at Lyon between 1458 and 1483, as the armorer and engraver. This would be reversing the usual order of the monograms, taking the main one (*AM*) for the given name and the secondary one (*BI*) for the surname (a rare but possible circumstance). See N. Rondot, "Les Artistes et les maîtres de métier étrangers ayant travaillé à Lyon," *Gazette des Beaux-Arts*, 1883, pp. 157–69; recorded by E. Chicco, "I maestri d'arte italiani a Lione dal XV al XVII secolo," *Bollettino del Ministero degli Affari Esteri*, 1900; and Thomas and Gamber 1958, p. 711.

47 Compare war hat KZ3700 and backplate KZ1922 in the Schweizerisches Landesmuseum in Zurich; cuirass *da uomo d'arme* HM11 in the Historisches Museum in Lucerne; right cuisse of the Sanseverino suit of armor A3 in the Leibrüstkammer, Vienna; Venetian-style sallet (with Y-shaped opening) 42.50.14 in the Metropolitan Museum of Art; all theses pieces are datable roughly between 1465 and 1485. See Boccia 1982, pp. 284, no. 28, p. 287, no. 73, p. 290, no. 128.

48 Kienbusch 1963, p. 102, no. 167, pl. LXVI. It comes from the Bourgeois and Hans C. Leiden collections, which were both in Cologne. The 1963 Kienbusch catalogue assigns it to the "last quarter of the XVI century," and compares it to II.80 in the Royal Armouries, Tower of London (Dufty 1968, pl. LII), which seems to me to have no possible connection with this one.

49 Boccia 1979, fig. 96. In this piece, however, the mitten is of two plates.

50 Kienbusch 1963, p. 15, no. 2, pl. II. It comes from the Clarence H. Mackay Collection.

51 See H. Schneider et al., *Waffen als Freiburg in den Bund der Eidgenossen trat* (Freiburg, 1981), p. 51, 1g–1h, with the initial read as *A* rather than *C*; Boccia 1981, p. 9, repro.; Mann 1962, vol. 1, p. 97, pl. 55; Norman 1986, p. 42; Grancsay 1933, no. 2, pl. I; and Boccia 1982, p. 291, nos. 132–33.

52 Boccia 1982, p. 282, no. 7.

53 Kienbusch 1963, p. 117, no. 211, pl. LXXVI. It comes from the John Newton Mappin, Samuel Whawell, E. W. Stead, and William Randolph Hearst collections.

54 A similar mark but with only the *A*, repeated twice but without the chevron, was on another chanfron that came on the market in 1972.

55 Kienbusch 1963, p. 117, no. 210, pl. LXXVI. It comes from the Rhodes arsenal and Bashford Dean collections.

56 A comment needs to be made on the gauntlets 1977-167-159 (Kienbusch 1963, p. 97, no. 153, pl. LXVI), which were considered to be Italian of the second quarter of the fifteenth century, and—rightly—"one of the earliest surviving pairs of gauntlets" of that period. The Kienbusch catalogue cites examples that do not seem to me to fit the facts, however; only the Churburg gauntlet 19 and those appearing in the Van Eyck altarpiece in Ghent seem comparable to the Kienbusch pair, which in my opinion is German.

SELECTED BIBLIOGRAPHY

Blair, Claude. *European Armour, circa 1066 to circa 1700.* London, 1958; reprint 1972.

Blair, Claude. "Notes on Armour from Chalcis." In *Arms & Armour at the Dorchester.* London, 1982, pp. 7–14.

Boccia, Lionello G. "Materiali iconografici sull'armamento quattrocentesco d'ambiente toscano." *Antichità Viva*, vol. 26, no. 3 (1988), pp. 37–53 (given as a lecture "II Convegno sulla civiltà delle arti minori in Toscana," Arezzo, 1973).

Boccia, Lionello G. "I corsaletti 'alla leggera' del Santuario di Curtatone." In *Scritti di storia dell'arte in onore di Ugo Procacci.* 2 vols. Milan, 1977; vol. 2, pp. 331–39.

Boccia, Lionello G. "L'antica produzione di armi in Lombardia" and "L'armatura lombarda tra il xiv e il xvii secolo." In Lionello G. Boccia, Francesco Rossi, and Marco Morin, *Armi e armature Lombarde.* Milan, 1979.

Boccia, Lionello G. "The Xalkìs Finds in Athens and New York." Lecture on the occasion of the 9th Congress of the International Association of Museums of Arms and Military History, New York, 1981; reprint, Florence, 1988.

Boccia, Lionello G. *Le armature di S. Maria delle Grazie di Curtatone di Mantova e l'armatura Lombarda del '400.* Busto Arsizio, 1982.

Boccia, Lionello G., and E. T. Coelho. *L'Arte dell'armatura in Italia.* Milan, 1967.

Boccia, Lionello G., and E. T. Coelho. "L'Armamento di cuoio e ferro nel Trecento italiano." *L'Illustrazione Italiana*, vol. 1, no. 2 (1974), pp. 24–37.

Boccia, Lionello G., and José A. Godoy. *Museo Poldi Pezzoli, Milan.* Vol. 1, *Armería I.* Milan, 1985. Vol. 2, *Armería II.* Milan, 1986.

Buchon, J. A. "Archéologie." *Courier Grec*, February 27, 1841 (reprinted in *La Grèce continentale et la Morée*, Paris, 1843).

Cantù, Cesare. *Storia Universale.* Turin, 1857.

di Carpegna, Nolfo. *Antiche armi dal sec. IX al XVIII già Collezione Odescalchi.* Rome, 1969.

Chicco, E. "I maestri d'arte italiani a Lione dal XV al XVII secolo." *Bollettino del Ministero degli Affari Esteri* (1900).

de Cosson, Charles A., and William Burges. "Catalogue of the Exhibition of Ancient Helmets and Examples of Mail." *The Archaeological Journal*, vol. 37 (1880), pp. 455–594.

Dondi, Giorgio, Marisa Cartesegna, et al. *L'Armería Reale di Torino.* Busto Arsizio, 1982.

Dufty, A.R. *European Armour in the Tower of London,* with introduction by William Reid. London, 1968.

ffoulkes, Charles J. "On Italian Armour from Chalcis in the Ethnological Museum at Athens." *Archaeologia*, vol. 12 (1911), pp. 381–90.

Gamber, Ortwin. "Harnischstudien: V. Stilgeschichte des Plattenharnisches von den Anfängen bis um 1440." *Jahrbuch der Kunsthistorischen Sammlungen in Wien*, vol. 50 (1953), pp. 53–92.

Gamber, Ortwin. "Harnischstudien: VI. Stilgeschichte des Plattenharnisches von 1440–1510." *Jahrbuch der Kunsthistorischen Sammlungen in Wien*, vol. 51 (1955), pp. 31–102.

Gilchrist, Helen Ives. *A Catalogue of the Collection of Arms & Armor Presented to The Cleveland Museum of Art by Mr. and Mrs. John Long Severance, 1916–1923.* Cleveland, 1924.

Gille, Florent, and A. Rockstühl. *Musée de Tzarskoe-Selo, ou collection d'armes de Sa Majesté l'Empereur de toutes les Russies.* 3 vols. in 1. St. Petersburg and Karlsruhe, 1835–53.

Grancsay, Stephen V. *The Metropolitan Museum of Art: Loan Exhibition of European Arms and Armor.* New York, 1931.

Grancsay, Stephen V. *The Bashford Dean Collection of Arms and Armor in the Metropolitan Museum of Art.* Portland, Me., 1933.

Hefner-Alteneck, Jacob Heinrich von. *Costume du moyen-âge chrétien d'après des monumens contemporains.* 3 vols. Mannheim, 1840–54.

Lenz, Eduard von. *Imperatorskiy Ermitazh. Sobranie oruzhiya.* St. Petersburg, 1908.

Mann, James G. "Notes on the Armour of the Maximilian Period and the Italian Wars." *Archaeologia*, vol. 79 (1929), pp. 217–44.

Mann, James G. *Wallace Collection Catalogues: European Arms and Armour.* London, 1962.

Nickel, Helmut, Stuart W. Pyhrr, and Leonid Tarassuk. *The Art of Chivalry: European Arms and Armor from The Metropolitan Museum of Art.* New York, 1982.

Norman, A.V.B. *Wallace Collection Catalogues: European Arms and Armour Supplement.* London, 1986.

Petrović, D. *Dubrovacko Oruzje u XIV veku.* Belgrade, 1976.

Rados, Konstantinos N. "Ta ek Xalkidos krani tou Istorikon kai Ethnologikou Mouseiou" (The Helmets from Chalcis in the Historical and Ethnological Museum). *Deltion Istorikis kai Ethnologikis Etaireias*, vol. 8 (1923), pp. 606–13.

Rondot, N. "Les Artistes et les maîtres de métier étrangers ayant travaillé à Lyon." *Gazette des Beaux-Arts*, 1883, pp. 157–69.

Rossi, Francesco, and Nolfo di Carpegna. *Armi antiche dal Museo Civico L. Marzoli.* Milan, 1969.

Schneider, Hugo, et al. *Waffen als Freiburg in den Bund der Eidgenossen trat.* Freiburg, 1981.

Thomas, Bruno, and Ortwin Gamber. "L'Arte milanese dell'armatura." *Storia di Milano*, vol. 11 (1958), pp. 697–841 (revised in Bruno Thomas, *Gesammelte Schriften*, Graz, 1977, pp. 971–1098).

Thomas, Bruno, and Ortwin Gamber. *Kunsthistorisches Museum, Wien, Waffensammlung: Katalog der Leibrüstkammer.* Vol. l, *Teil, Der Zeitraum von 500 bis 1530.* Vienna, 1976.

Thordeman, Bengt. *Armour from the Battle of Wisby, 1361.* 2 vols. Uppsala, 1939.

Trapp, Oswald Graf. *The Armoury of the Castle of Churburg.* Translated by James Gow Mann. London, 1929.

de Valencia de Don Juan, Juan Crooke y Navarrot. *Catálogo histórico-descriptivo de la Real Armería de Madrid.* Madrid, 1898.

Wegeli, Rudolf. *Katalog der Waffen-Sammlung im Zeughause zu Solothurn.* Solothurn, 1905.

Wilbrand, W. "Die hundert Helme von Negroponte." *Zeitschrift für Historische Waffen-und Kostümkunde*, vol. 8 (1918), p. 30.

Small-Swords and Court-Swords
in the Kienbusch Collection

A.V.B. NORMAN

The Kienbusch Collection of Armor and Arms is probably most renowned for its many examples of fine armor, and only a little less noted for its series of sixteenth- and seventeenth-century swords of the highest quality from the old Saxon Electoral Armory in Dresden. The collection's many fine examples of later swords designed for civilian wear tend to be overshadowed by the romance and glamour of the earlier pieces.

The 1963 catalogue of the Kienbusch Collection contained nine complete swords and seven detached sword hilts of the sort intended for wear with one's best clothes in town or at court, as fashionable costume jewelry rather than to defend one's person.[1] These expensive hilts were intended to dazzle with their elegance, to make the eyes of one's beloved sparkle, and to turn one's rival green with envy.[2]

During the 1630s it had become fashionable for civilians in Northern Europe to wear a lighter version of the military sword with a smaller hilt.[3] The newly developed French style of swordsmanship required a relatively short blade designed purely for thrusting. The method of parrying thrusts by means of the blade and a supple wrist meant that large and complicated hilts were no longer necessary to protect the hand. By the 1640s a simple hilt developed consisting of a pommel, to act as a counterweight to the blade; a pair of shells in front of the hand, formed of a single plate with one lobe inside the hilt and the other outside; and a pair of cross-guards made in one with the sleeve, through which the tang of the blade passed. This sleeve also supported on each side a short C-shaped guard, the vestigial arms of the hilt found on earlier rapier hilts. Only tyros still used such guards to protect the fingers, according to Sir William Hope of Balcombie, the seventeenth-century authority on the use of the sword.[4] This is the characteristic form of hilt found on weapons known today as small-swords or court-swords.

From about 1640 onward, the practical use of the sword ceased to have much effect on the design of this sort of hilt. Although steel hilts remained popular, those of softer metals such as brass and silver were common, as they were more easily worked with elaborate decoration. Both could be cast, and thereafter required only chasing to perfect the details of even the most intricate decoration. Latterly, the brightly polished steel hilts particularly fashionable in Great Britain were made of metal so hard that the guards frequently snapped with only a relatively light knock. In the last decade of the eighteenth century it became fashionable to wear, when

Fig. 46. Left, Small-sword, English, London, 1798–99, hilt by James Morisset (active c. 1766–c. 1800).
Silver cast and gilt and set with enamel plaques; 1977-167-648. Right, Small-sword,
English, London, 1806–7, hilt by John Ray and James Montague (active c. 1800–c. 1816). Cast gold; 1977-167-654.

in mourning, a hilt made entirely of faceted jet beads set in a light frame of metal or strung on wires. A few hilts were made of similar glass beads in many colors.

Some, but by no means all, early hilts of small-swords had one end of the cross-guard extended to form a knuckle-guard, its end either screwed to the pommel or plugged into it. In a few cases hilts originally made without a knuckle-guard had one added, once this sort of guard became *de rigueur*. An outstanding example of this sort of adapted hilt is in the Old Imperial Armory in Vienna.[5]

The earliest datable examples of the small-sword hilt are two swords ordered in Paris in preparation for the coronation of Charles X of Sweden in 1654.[6] They are exquisitely chiseled with tiny equestrian figures in high relief amid cartilaginous decoration and human terminal figures; one of the hilts is in steel and the other in silver gilt. The work on these swords was no doubt done by the leading Parisian medalists. The Kienbusch Collection includes the pommel and guard of a somewhat similarly decorated cross-hilt (fig. 49, left) and a second, comparable pommel of exceptional quality chiseled with men in classical dress on prancing horses flanked by allegorical figures, all amid strapwork (fig. 49, right). Unfortunately, it has not yet been possible to identify this pommel's original guards; the zeal of nineteenth-century collectors of pommels has left many fine swords bereft. A comparable hilt chiseled with extraordinary virtuosity, now in the British Royal Collection at Windsor, was traditionally thought to have been presented to the 1st Duke of Marlborough (1650–1722) by Emperor Charles VI.[7] If this tradition is correct, the weapon must have been quite old at the time. A comparable hilt appears in the *Antique Dealer*, painted by Jan de Herdt (born 1646/47) in 1667, now at Karlsruhe.[8]

Presumably only the wealthiest could afford hilts so exquisitely decorated as these, and only about a dozen such hilts have survived. A group of hilts apparently of slightly later date, and of mediocre quality, chiseled all over with cavalry battles, presumably catered to those of middle rank who followed the fashions of the nobility at one remove. A typical example is the Northern European small-sword of about 1660–70, in the Kienbusch Collection (fig. 48). Judging by this and other surviving specimens, at least a dozen different chiselers of widely varying skill were engaged in making such hilts. An example dated 1662 on the guards is in a Dutch private collection.[9] The hilt referred to in an advertisement for a lost sword in the *London Gazette* of February 28–March 3, 1697, was probably of this type: "Lost . . . a wrought Steel Sword, representing a Horse Fight, with a black Ribbon tied to it."[10]

After the publication of the Kienbusch catalogue in 1963, Kienbusch added to the collection a number of early small-swords illustrating different styles of decoration. The earliest of these (fig. 47, right) has a hilt of steel encrusted all over with rows of small silver studs outlining panels containing bunches of silver flowers in the larger areas, and a single flower head flanked on each side by a leaf in the more confined spaces. The background was probably originally fire-gilt. The center of the outer edge of each shell is drawn out and curled toward the pommel, a feature common in depictions of swords in Dutch paintings of the

47

Fig. 47. Left, *Small-sword, Northern European, possibly Dutch, c.1650–60. Steel, counterfeit-damascened with gold; 1977-167-628.* Right, *Small-sword, Northern European, possibly Dutch, c.1650. Steel encrusted with silver; 1977-167-636.*

Fig. 48. *Small-sword, Northern European, possibly Dutch, c.1660–70. Chiseled steel; 1977-167-633.*

Fig. 49. Left, *Pommel and matching guard, French, possibly Paris, c.1660, Chiseled steel; 1977-167-727.* Right, *Pommel, French, possibly Paris, c.1660. Chiseled steel; 1977-167-726.*

48

49

Fig. 50. Left, *Cross-hilted sword, probably North Italian, c.1650. Chiseled steel. Philadelphia Museum of Art, Purchased Bloomfield Moore Fund; 21-68-5.* Right, *Sword, possibly North Italian, c.1650–60. Pierced and chiseled steel, silvered and parcel gilt; 1977-167-627.*

1640s and 1650s, for instance, *Parental Admonition* of about 1654 by Gerard ter Borch (1617– 1681) in the Rijksmuseum, Amsterdam.[11]

Another early hilt (fig. 47, left) added to the Kienbusch Collection after 1963 is damascened in gold with flowers, foliage scrolls, and swags. It belongs to a group of hilts in which the knuckle-guard and rear quillon and the broad, raised rims of the shell guards are of rectangular cross-section with slightly hollowed faces. This hilt has no knuckle-guard and an unusual pommel, pear-shaped in profile but rectangular in section. For some reason the arms of the hilt, which must always have been very small, have been cut off. An example of this type of hilt, with a more conventional pommel and a knuckle-guard in addition, is illustrated in the portrait of Cornelius van Aerssen painted by Adriaen Hanneman (Netherlandish, c. 1601– 1671) in 1658.[12] The hilt of a sword in the Royal Armouries in the Tower of London, very like that in the portrait, is traditionally that of Major General Charles Worsley, who died in 1656.[13] The two-edged blade, which is dated 1651, fits the scabbard, the locket of which is decorated to match the hilt. Another comparable hilt, in the Badisches Landesmuseum, Karlsruhe, is identified with a sword described in the 1680 Inventory of the Margraves of Baden as having been worn by Margrave Carl Magnus, who died in 1658.[14]

The conventional small-sword hilt was not yet the only kind worn by civilians in their best clothes. Some fashionable swords still had only a simple cross-hilt. The Philadelphia Museum of Art has a very fine example (fig. 50, left), mounted on a blade dated 1655, chiseled to look as though its pommel, quillon-ends, and the center of the steel grip were all made of graduated washers fitted over a central core, an exceptionally rare technique.[15] The rest of the quillons and the grip are shaped like balusters clasped by acanthus calyxes and chiseled with scalework. The quillon-block is chiseled in very shallow relief with symmetrical foliage scrolls in a style more common on gun mounts. Although it is never safe to assume that the date on a blade also indicates the age of the mounts, unless the original scabbard survives, a mid-century date would certainly be acceptable for this elegant hilt. The straight two-edged blade has a high central rib on each face to stiffen it without adding too much to its weight.

Some of these simple hilts with short cross-guards had an open side-ring on the quillon-block outside the hand, in the manner of sixteenth-century arming swords. Side-rings were originally intended to stop an opponent's weapon from sliding down the blade onto the hand, but it is doubtful whether these light swords were ever actually meant for combat. Another late acquisition by Kienbusch (fig. 50, right) has a large bun-shaped pommel and matching ends to its very short quillons of the type characteristic of the period 1645 to 1670.[16] The pommel and quillon ends are pierced and chiseled with lush foliage and flowers, and, in the center of the C-shaped side-ring is a stout and scantily clad horsewoman. The surface of the steel is hatched with silver and parcel gilt. The pretty grip, woven with silver wire, appears to be original. The blade of this sword, which bears traces of etched foliage, birds, and mottoes, is of a stiffened form similar to that of the blade just described. A comparable hilt can be seen in the *Portrait of a Young Commander*, thought to represent Alfonso IV d'Este, painted between 1649 and 1654, now in the Isabella Stuart Gardner Museum, Boston.[17]

The Kienbusch Collection unfortunately lacks one of the characteristic English small-swords of the last quarter of the seventeenth century, with hilts cast in relief with small figures and rows of tips of very stylized acanthus leaves. However, it does contain an unusually fine English horseman's sword with a silver hilt decorated in this manner (fig. 51). The main motifs are Saint George and the Dragon, in some places represented separately and elsewhere together. The fillings of the side-shells contain finely chiseled and pierced foliate scrolls and an oval panel containing Saint George Slaying the Dragon. The Kienbusch hilt bears only the mark of an unidentified maker, the capital letters IW within a shield, but no hallmark or date-letter. This hilt can, however, be dated by comparison with a very similar example by the same maker, recently acquired by the Metropolitan Museum of Art, New York, which bears London silver marks and the date-letter f, for 1683/84.[18]

The Kienbusch hilt, which retains the original mount for the mouth of the scabbard, has had an extended life. Some years after it was made, an extra guard was added on each side of the hand by an inferior smith. There is a mysterious inscription on the top mount of the scabbard in what appears to be a late-eighteenth-century hand: "*Colonel/W. H. Maxwell/10th Regt. Infty.*" The pommel is also engraved in script with Colonel Maxwell's initials, WHM. The mystery lies in the fact that the British army did not refer to regiments by number until the middle of the eighteenth century, long after this hilt would have been out of fashion. Furthermore, infantry regiments in the British service were known as "Regiments of Foot" rather than "of Infantry." On the other hand, regiments in the service of the Honourable East India Company were known as "Infantry," but normally the title included the name of the Presidency, for instance, the 4th Regiment of Madras Native Infantry. So far, no record of any officer of this name has been found in the British service connected with any regiment numbered ten.

The relatively narrow, straight, two-edged blade has a central fuller stamped on the outside "DEAIALAE," and is struck with a king's head in an open crown viewed from his left. On the inside is "DETOMAS" and again the king's head mark. Also on the inside is an incised stylized animal, presumably representing the wolf of Solingen.[19] A great variety of kings' heads were used as marks by members of the Wundes family in Solingen. This is a German forgery of a blade by one of the Toledo sword cutlers called Thomàs de Ayala.[20]

Probably the next earliest small-sword in the Kienbusch Collection is one with a rather large hilt of cast brass (fig. 52). The decoration is in low relief, with the background pierced through the pommel, sleeve, and shells. There are cherubic heads at the top of the pommel, at the center of the ribbed knuckle-guard, on the end of the rear quillon, on the sleeve, and at the center of the rim of each shell. Groups of crudely cast and chiseled naked figures disport themselves in grotesque Bacchic scenes on the main areas of the pommel, sleeve, and shells. The grip is a recent and inaccurate replacement. The blade, which is of flattened-hexagonal section, is etched in line and gilt to the tip with candelabra ornament, including panels of strapwork flanking a sunburst, a six-pointed spur-rowel, a fleur-de-lis, a cross pattée, and an electoral bonnet over a military trophy with a heart at its center.

Very little dating material survives for the hilts of early small-swords such as this, because so few fully marked silver ones have survived, it being customary to give an old hilt in part-exchange when buying a new one. The nearest parallel to this particular hilt is one salvaged from a shipwreck believed to be the *Stirling Castle*, which sank in 1703 on Ramsgate Sands, off the Kent coast.[21]

The decoration of hilts depended on the vagaries of fashion, and certainly for the first three-quarters of the eighteenth century differed not at all from the decoration of such things as snuffboxes, etuis, and watch cases. Frequently the same sources, such as the engravings of works by Jean-Baptiste Oudry (French, 1686–1755) and François Boucher (French, 1703–1770) and of their many imitators, were used by box-makers and hilt-makers alike. Indeed, in some cases they were the same men. The British Royal Collection includes an exceptionally elegant Neoclassical gold hilt enameled in blue and white and bearing the mark of the Parisian goldsmith Joseph-Etienne Blerzy, the most prestigious maker of gold boxes of his day.[22] The Kienbusch Collection has two especially splendid English sword hilts, one by James Morisset (fig. 46, left) and the other by his successors John Ray and James Montague (fig. 46, right), all of whom also made very grand presentation boxes.[23]

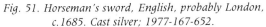

Fig. 51. Horseman's sword, English, probably London, c.1685. Cast silver; 1977-167-652.

Fig. 52. Small-sword, Northern European, possibly Dutch or German, c.1690. Cast brass; 1977-167-626.

The advertisements of the Parisian *marchand merciers*, such as Charles-Raymond Grancher "au Petit Dunkerque," indicate that fashions in the decoration of both hilts and gold boxes changed with the seasons and that taste was as fickle and restless then as now.[24] In France in the early eighteenth century the rather ponderous and serious style of the reign of Louis XIV began to yield to a lighter and more frivolous fashion, the precursor of the Rococo. This style, known today as *Régence*, spread out from France to inspire designers and craftsmen all over Europe. By about 1720 the *Régence* style was all the rage in both Britain and the German lands. The Kienbusch Collection contains a very pretty silver-hilted small-sword decorated in precisely this way (fig. 54), with trophies of classical arms and armor flanked by broken scrolls in typical *Régence* fashion. The shells are marked out in diverging rays as on a cockleshell, between which the trophies are arranged. A design by Georg Daniel Neumann (active 1715–59), the Nuremberg engraver and architect, illustrates a hilt for a hunting sword with very similar decoration.[25] Although the Kienbusch hilt may perhaps owe something to German design, it bears partly illegible London silver marks, as well as an unidentified maker's mark, PR (fig. 55). Since this hilt was made about 1730, it unfortunately falls into the period when the records of the smallworkers of the London Goldsmiths' Company are missing. It would not be at all surprising to find the decoration of its shells repeated on the lid of a snuffbox; indeed, a very similar design for a box, probably made in the first decade of the eighteenth century, is illustrated in a series of engravings by Paul Decker (1677–1713), another Nuremberg engraver and architect.[26] The makers of tortoiseshell boxes, or perhaps their clients, seem to have particularly favored these shell-like designs. Clare Le Corbeiller illustrates two examples in her book *European and American Snuff Boxes*—one *piqué* in silver and the other, an English box in gold, of about 1720.[27] Extraordinary as it may seem, a few sword hilts are known that are decorated with plaques of tortoiseshell inlaid with precious metal.[28]

The light and largely symmetrical *Régence* style was followed by the Rococo style. In this new mode, all decorum and seriousness in decoration were cast aside, and surfaces were covered with a riot of asymmetrical C-scrolls, sprays of casually arranged blossoms and branches, clumps of bullrushes, and shell-like features often merging into large cabbage-like leaves sometimes pierced with rows of oval holes of graduated size, as though attacked by a plague of caterpillars. Amid this bizarre asymmetrical jungle, tumbled and played the figures of innumerable enchanting, scantily draped children, sometimes framing scenes from classical mythology treated with an abandon characteristic of the works of Boucher. Ruins and waterfalls were favorite backgrounds for *fêtes-champêtres*, or romantic scenes of infant shepherds and shepherdesses neglecting their flocks. Charm, innocence, and sensibility were the principal criteria; the leitmotiv of the Rococo style was the giving of pleasure. The earliest datable objects in the new style, now alas lost, were the gold sword hilts designed and perhaps made by Juste-Aurèle Meissonnier (1695?–1750), the great Parisian goldsmith-designer, as presents for the Polish gentlemen at the marriage of Louis XV in 1725.[29]

The craze for asymmetry affected the hilts and mounts of swords less than one might have expected. It is rare to find a hilt in which the decoration, however riotous, actually distorts the conventional outline. In a very few cases the hilt is made to resemble a trophy of classical armor, an archer's bow forming the knuckle-guard and a Roman cuirass forming the sleeve, with a sword thrust through its armholes to act as the quillon. An example in steel is in the Musée des Arts Décoratifs, Paris. Another, in silver, made in Paris in 1767/68, was formerly in the Carrington-Peirce Collection.[30] Most hilts of this period, however, retain the conventional shape and are decorated in low relief with small naked children amid swirling foliage and swags, little sprays of flowers, and the characteristic asymmetrical scrolls and shells

Fig. 53. Small-sword hilt, Dutch, Amsterdam, c.1750–60.
Cast silver; 1977-167-666.

Fig. 54. Small-sword, English, London, c.1730.
Cast silver; 1977-167-665.

Fig. 55. Maker's mark PR and London hallmarks (illegible)
on small-sword (fig. 54).

54

55

of Rococo decoration. A few, for example, a superb gold hilt in the National Museum of Ireland, made in Paris in 1750/51, have scenes from classical mythology framed in Rococo ornament on each of the broader areas, all chiseled in exquisite relief.[31]

The impact of Rococo, however, does seem to have encouraged the use of a small-sword hilt with a heart-shaped guard in place of the usual bilobate shells. In 1965 a beautiful silver hilt of this type was added to the Kienbusch Collection (fig. 53). Decorated with softly writhen flutes in a restrained Rococo style, it bears the town mark of Amsterdam, as well as a partially defaced maker's mark, almost certainly that of Gerrit Hoying. In common with many Dutch hilts, the knuckle-guard is screwed to the pommel instead of being plugged into it, as on the conventional hilt. The reason that so many hilts made in Japan for the European market have screwed knuckle-guards is probably that Holland was the principal market.

It is rather surprising to find this elegant hilt mounted on a short, curved, single-edged blade. If the blade is not a later replacement, the explanation may be that the original owner was an officer in a light infantry unit or a grenadier company, in both of which short, curved swords were fashionable. The hilt can be dated by its very close resemblance to another hilt also by Hoying, which bears the Amsterdam date-letter w, for 1756.[32]

The taste for exotic materials and designs led to the importation of hilts made in the East in the current European form, but with Oriental decoration. Japanese hilts presumably accompanied a taste for lacquers, whereas an Indian hilt might have set off a coat of the latest sprigged fabric imported from Calcutta. The Kienbusch Collection includes a fine Japanese hilt in the alloy of copper and gold known as *shakudo* (fig. 57). It is decorated with gilded plum blossom and birds against a mat black ground, and its grip, in a slightly different style, has golden animals racing though a spiral of pierced black foliage. The dating of such hilts is extremely difficult, because one cannot presume that they necessarily reflect the minute changes in the form of the European hilt as it developed. A few Japanese hilts are known that were made for the European market in the most advanced Rococo style, indicating a date not earlier than the 1750s.[33] Claude Blair has shown that such hilts almost certainly came to Europe via the Dutch East India Company factory at Deshima.[34]

The Kienbusch Collection also includes a small-sword with mounts made or decorated at a thus far unidentified place in North India for export to Europe (fig. 56). Judging by its form, the sword dates from the early eighteenth century, and appears, in fact, to be one of the earliest surviving Indian export swords. The decoration, in a rather thin gold damascening, of a type known as *koftgari*, includes somewhat stylized representations of irises and lilies elegantly displayed against the fire-blue of the steel. The design is reminiscent of the low-relief panels on the kiosk of Shah Jahan in the fort at Agra, but with less attention given to botanical detail. It differs not at all from what might be found on a contemporary Indian native weapon. Contemporary paintings showing these Indian-made hilts are rare, but such a hilt is clearly shown in the full-length portrait of Field Marshal, the Marquess Townsend painted by Sir Joshua Reynolds (British, 1723–1792) in 1779.[35]

The blade of the Kienbusch sword is of triangular section, with hollow faces to give it as much rigidity as possible without making it too heavy. The part near the hilt, the forte, is considerably broader than the remainder, so that in parrying, a relatively slight movement of the wrist would deflect an opponent's blade much more than the same movement with a conventional narrow blade. The presence of the original scabbard with its matching mounts proves that the blade is the one originally mounted in this hilt; it is of a type known at the time as a Königsberg or Coningsmark.

Two silver hilts in the Kienbusch Collection clearly demonstrate the changes in the fashion of the hilt that occurred in Britain in the early 1760s. Both are decorated in the latest fashion, with pierced and chiseled trophies of arms, both military and naval, in a mild Rococo style. On both hilts the arms and knuckle-guards are decorated with a row of small pyramidal studs in imitation of jewels, a mode that was destined to dominate the decoration of small-sword hilts well into the nineteenth century. One of these hilts (fig. 63, right) is conventional in form, with relatively large arms of the hilt and bilobate shells much as small-swords had been for the past century.[36] It bears London silver marks and a Gothic G, the date-letter for 1762/63. The other hilt (fig. 63, left) must be one of the first made in the new fashion with an additional forward quillon, very small clawlike arms and a single oval shell, through the center of which the tang of the blade passes.[37] With a nod to the past, this shell is chiseled to look like a conventional bilobate shell with the inlets between the lobes filled with a fanlike spray of diverging flutes. It bears London silver marks and the same date-letter G for 1762/63.

The first of these hilts was made by John Carman the Younger, "at the Ewer & Swords, Near Bartlett's Building, Holborn." Carman was active from about 1743 until his death about 1764 and was one of the most prolific of all the hilt-makers of this period.[38] According to the inscription on the silver mouth of the scabbard, this sword was retailed by "Kentish/Ye corner of/Popes head Alley/Cornhill." His shop sign was a star.[39] The second hilt bears a slightly defaced mark, apparently GF, presumably that of the well-known hilt-maker George Fayle, although his name has not yet been found in the records before 1767, when he registered his mark at Goldsmiths' Hall. He was then living in "Gillats Court, Little Old Bailey."[40]

Apart from silver hilts, which their makers were obliged to mark by guild regulations, signed hilts are rare in any period. It is therefore remarkable that three steel hilts for small-swords in the Kienbusch Collection are signed. All the signatures appear in places where they can be seen only when the hilts are dismounted. No doubt many other hilts are signed in this way, but happily have never been taken apart.

The first of these (fig. 59, left), a steel hilt of about 1740–50, is chiseled in relief with rather overfussy Rococo scrolls, foliage, and trophies symbolic of the sciences, the liberal arts, the chase, love, war, and husbandry. It is engraved on the underside of the washer with the name "A. Beraud," the A and B conjoined (fig. 60). A hilt with a similar signature is reported to be in the Walters Art Gallery, Baltimore.[41] This is probably the *fourbisseur* of this name who was working in the rue Saint Martin in Paris, recorded in the *Almanach de Paris* for 1789.[42]

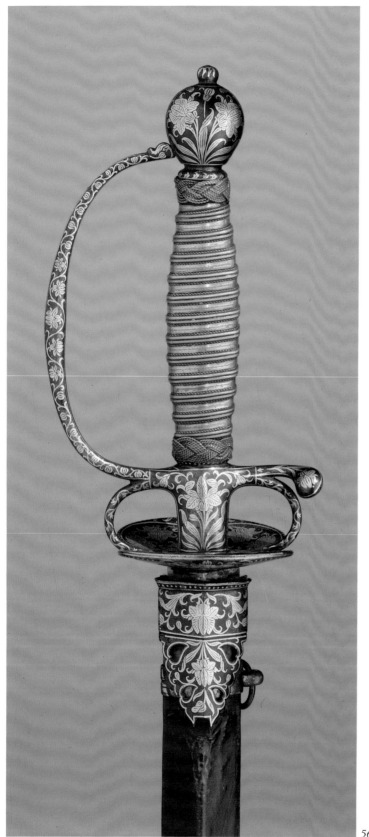

56

57

58

Fig. 56. Small-sword hilt, Northern Indian for the European market, c.1700–1725. Blued steel damascened with gold; 1977-167-643.

Fig. 57. Elements of a small-sword hilt, Japanese for the European market, c.1750–75. Shakudo (copper and gold alloy), blackened and parcel gilt; 1977-167-724.

Fig. 58. Left, Small-sword, English, London, c.1800, hilt possibly by Thomas Gray or William Gray. Steel; 1977-167-653. Right, Small-sword, French, Paris, 1809–19. Cast silver; 1977-167-647.

59

60

61

62

Fig. 59. Left, *Elements of a small-sword hilt, French, Paris, c.1740–50, signed* A. BERAUD. *Chiseled and parcel-gilt steel; 1977-167-720.* Center, *Elements of a small-sword hilt, probably French, c.1750, signed* CHALEIER. *Chiseled steel; 1977-167-722.* Right, *Elements of a small-sword hilt, French, c.1780, signed* PER. *Chiseled and parcel-gilt steel; 1977-167-723.*

Fig. 60. *Maker's signature* A. BERAUD *on small-sword washer (fig. 59, left).*

Fig. 61. *Maker's signature* CHALEIER *on small-sword pommel (fig. 59, center).*

Fig. 62. *Maker's signature* PER *on small-sword guard (fig. 59, right).*

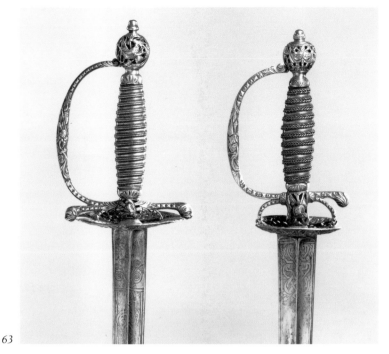

63

64

The second of these (fig. 59, center), a hilt of about 1750, chiseled in relief with trophies symbolic of music, war, and the chase, all amid lush Rococo foliate scrolls and sprays of flowers, is stamped under the stand of the pommel with the name "CHALEIER" (fig. 61). Nothing appears to be known about this man, but another pommel signed by him is in the Bayerisches Nationalmuseum, Munich.⁴³ The name suggests that the maker was French.

The third of these three (fig. 59, right), a hilt of about 1780, chiseled in relief against a ground overlaid with gold, with panels containing pendant trophies symbolic of music, war, and husbandry, is engraved on the part of the sleeve that fits into the central hole in the shells with the enigmatic letters "PER" (fig. 62).

Since a small-sword was probably a relatively poor deterrent against footpads in a poorly lit street at night, swords were occasionally fitted with a small pistol that fired along the flat of the blade. Very few of these combined weapons that one sees today are genuine; it is only too easy to make a rather uninteresting sword more desirable to the unwary collector by attaching to it a pocket-sized pistol. A chiseled and pierced small-sword hilt of about 1770 in the Kienbusch Collection (fig. 64) is quite exceptional in that its hilt was actually designed from the beginning to accommodate the trigger mechanism of the small flintlock pocket pistol attached to the forte of the blade. The hilt, which is chiseled and pierced with fine foliate scrolls, has a bilobate shell and only one small clawlike arm of the hilt at the rear. The place of the forward arm is taken by a block on which pivots the firing-lever, which is itself connected by a short bar transmitting its movement to the actual trigger. This lever passes through the outer shell via a specially made rectangular aperture, around which the decoration skirts.

In the 1770s a wave of revulsion against the frivolity of Rococo ornament swept Europe, except at the French court itself. The swags and sprays of flowers and the rioting scrolls, shell-like ornaments, all asymmetrical, and playful children, were banished, to be replaced once more by symmetry, dignity, and decorum. Attenuated and severe Neoclassical motifs were everywhere predominant in the decoration of swords, as in the architecture of the period, for example, that of the Adam brothers, Robert and James.

A rather elegant hilt sparingly engraved with swags and paterae in the Kienbusch Collection admirably demonstrates the new style (fig. 65).[44] It has the fashionable vase-shaped pommel, the tiny claws in place of the arms of the hilt, and the oval patera-like guard, through the center of which the blade passes. It bears London hallmarks, the date-letter for 1781/82, and the maker's mark of the most successful hilt maker of the day, William Kinman of 9 New Street Square.[45] The inscription on the back of the top locket indicates that it was retailed by "Drury/Cutler to His Majesty/Strand," referring to Dru Drury the Younger, the goldsmith and hilt maker working at that time at the corner of the Strand and Villiers Street.[46]

This sword still retains its gold lace sword-knot with its stylish spangled bullion tassel. Originally the loop of the knot was slipped over the wrist to prevent the sword from being lost in action. By this date the knot had become purely decorative and as much at the mercy of the caprice of fashion as was the hilt itself. An elegant knot in the latest fashion was considered to be a suitable present for a lady to give to her admirer.

In England, technical improvements in steel making, later described by the Birmingham manufacturer Thomas Gill, coincided with this new wave of classicism. Brightly polished steel, faceted to catch the light, was set with hundreds of tiny twinkling faceted beads and nailheads to make sword mounts for a nation where good taste eschewed expensive display. The collection of the future King George IV at Carlton House included a number of these, now at Windsor Castle.[47] Even the sword-knot was sometimes made of numerous strings of tiny beads on silken threads. When additional decoration was present, it usually consisted only of gold sparingly encrusted in paterae and swags of laurel foliage in Neoclassical taste on a brightly blued steel ground. In a few cases, plaques of blue and white china from Josiah Wedgwood's Etruria Works were set into hilts. A particularly graceful example is in the Metropolitan Museum of Art, New York.[48] Wedgwood's partner, Matthew Boulton, illustrated many examples of cut-steel hilts in his pattern book, preserved in the Reference Library in Birmingham, England.[49]

A few of these shiny steel hilts, perhaps intended for wear in mourning, were colored a deep and lustrous blue. This style was also copied in blue and other colored glass beads. Few of

Fig. 65. Small-sword with sword-knot, English, London, 1781–82, hilt by William Kinman (active 1759–82?). Cast silver, gilt, and engraved; 1977-167-646.

Fig. 66. Left, Elements of a small-sword hilt, French, c.1785. Chiseled and parcel-gilt steel; 1977-167-721. Right, Elements of a small-sword hilt and scabbard locket, French, c.1760. Chiseled steel, blued, parcel-gilt and encrusted with gold; 1977-167-725.

67

68

Fig. 67. Small-sword with sword-knot, German, Munich, c.1825, hilt by Johann Stroblberger. Cast brass, blackened and polished; 1977-167-662.

Fig. 68. Rapier in seventeenth-century style with sword-knot, German, Munich, c.1825– 50, hilt by Johann Stroblberger. Cast brass, parcel-gilt and blackened; 1977-167-661.

Fig. 69. Small-sword with sword-knot, English, London or Birmingham, c.1850. Cast brass; 1977-167-660.

69

the multicolored glass hilts once in the Prince Regent's collection are now at Windsor Castle, but a brilliant blue one described in the prince's inventory as "a very handsome Mourning Sword" is still there.[50]

By this time the production of sword mounts was no longer the prerogative of sword cutlers. They were sold by a class of tradesmen known as "toy makers," who also sold gold boxes, jewels, tie-pins, cuff-links, tooth-pick cases, and all those little costly trinkets the very rich found so essential. The firm of Yardley of London, now famous for perfumes and fine toilet soaps, started as buckle makers and sword cutlers, then developed into "toy makers" or "suppliers of fancy goods," and finally became perfumiers. Thomas Gray of Sackville Street, who was patronized by the Prince Regent, the future George IV, was just such a man. A number of splendidly twinkly beaded hilts by Gray are still at Windsor Castle,[51] and the Kienbusch Collection may contain an example of his work. It is impossible to identify with certainty the maker of one of these cut-steel hilts, unless the hilt is accompanied by its original scabbard with the maker's name on the top-locket. The hilt of the sword just mentioned (fig. 58, left) could, however, be by Thomas Gray or his rival William Gray of Bond Street. A scabbard signed "Thos Gray/Sackville/Strt" on a small-sword with a cut-steel hilt is in the Kienbusch Collection, but almost certainly does not belong to it.

Until about 1800 the French were apparently unable to make steel of the quality required to produce cut and faceted decoration in the English style, although this was much sought after in a country where the aristocracy were markedly anglophile and where English fashions were all the rage. Ready-made hilts were therefore imported from England, or pieces of faceted and highly polished steel were brought in for mounting locally. In 1772 the advertisements of the Parisian *marchand mercier* Grancher, "au Petit Dunkerque," included "Nouvelles épées dorées faîtes à Paris, avec pieces de rapport d'acier poli d'Angleterre."[52] Others were made of silver that took a polish comparable to that of English steel hilts. An example of the second kind with inlaid faceted steel buttons is in the Metropolitan Museum of Art, New York.[53] The Kienbusch Collection includes a very late example of the first type in silver (fig. 58, right). Like many late-eighteenth-century French hilts, it has an oval shell and tiny claws in the English fashion. The decoration consists of panels of tiny foliate scrolls alternating with rows of small, highly polished pyramids in imitation of cut-steel studs. It bears the mark of an unknown hilt maker with the initials I.J. and the Paris marks for 1809–19. It was made, therefore, at least twenty years after the outbreak of the French Revolution. The straight slender blade of triangular section, which still retains all but the tip of its fragile scabbard with its white fishskin cover, is etched, blued, and gilt, and signed I.G.B. All the best French swords of this time were mounted with blades made in Solingen, in the Rhineland not far from Dusseldorf, but unfortunately this combination of letters does not appear among the surviving records of the Solingen cutlers.[54]

The Kienbusch Collection also has two very charming French small-sword hilts of the period immediately before the outbreak of the Revolution in 1789, both unfortunately detached from their original blades (fig. 66). They still have conventional bilobate shells, and the arms, which are quite small, are still much more tightly curved than the clawlike type found in Britain by this date. The olive-shaped pommels are narrower and taller than earlier examples. On both hilts the main features of the chiseled decoration are oval panels containing bunches of flowers. On the slightly earlier of the two (fig. 66, right), the background is mostly covered with narrow flutes all fire-blued and set with tiny encrusted gold flower heads in the hollows. The edges and some other parts are chiseled with laurel wreaths and are fire gilded. The background of the sprays of flowers is pierced to accentuate the relief chiseling. On the later of these two hilts (fig. 66, left), the background is covered with panels formed with late Rococo scrolls, some enclosing sprays of flowers and others bridged by zigzags of ribbons, all against a ground covered with fine sheet gold, attached by means of matting with a variety of differently faced tools. This hilt can be dated to the period around 1785 by comparison with similar silver hilts that are marked, for example, a sword in the Metropolitan Museum of Art, New York, with Paris marks for 1785/86.[55] In most other countries Neoclassical taste had by now entirely swept away all traces of the Rococo, whereas in France, and particularly in court circles, Rococo survived, at least in the decoration of sword hilts, until the end of the monarchy.

During the second half of the eighteenth century it became increasingly fashionable for governments or groups of admirers to present successful naval or military commanders with specially designed swords that were mounted in gold, or at least silver-gilt, and were elaborately decorated in the latest style. The young republic of the United States presented a number of its heroes of the War of Independence with small-swords fitted with particularly elegant silver-gilt hilts specially commissioned in Paris by Colonel David Humphreys, Secretary of the Paris legation. They were purchased from one of the most fashionable sword cutlers, Liger, who described himself as "fourbisseur De S. As. le Duc de Chartre & Comte de Clermond, rue Coquilliere à Paris."[56] Although the Kienbusch Collection does not contain an example of this type, it does have two of the elaborately decorated presentation small-swords fashionable in Britain during the French revolutionary wars and the subsequent Napoleonic Wars. These were either gold or silver gilt and were usually set with panels of delicately painted enamel commemorating the deed for which they were awarded; sometimes they were set off with precious stones.

The Kienbusch Collection includes a silver-gilt example with enamel plaques (fig. 46, left), but without the diamonds and the battle scenes found on the more elaborate specimens.[57] In keeping with British taste, it has an oval shell, and in place of the arms, two small laurel wreaths. The metal is cast and chased in late Neoclassical taste with swags of husks, laurel wreaths bound with fillets, and stylized acanthus foliage in low relief. The sleeve and the centers of the knuckle-guard and grip are inlet with enamel panels painted with trophies of arms on a deep blue translucent ground. On the outside of the globular pommel is an oval enamel bearing the crowned harp of Ireland. On the inner face of the pommel is the monogram *H.J.* on an oval plaque. The frames of the ovals on the grip and the edge of the shell nearer the hand are decorated with bands of shamrock leaves cast and chased in low relief. The face of the shell toward the hand is pierced and chased with an elaborate trophy of arms and flags against a ground of translucent blue enamel. The face of the shell toward the blade is polished bright, except around the edge, where the chiseled laurel wreath is bound at intervals with fillets, and set between two flutes. It is engraved: "TO /*MAJOR GENERAL HENRY JOHNSON*/ *from the Associated Gentlemen of the*/BARONY OF IDA/*in the County of Kilkenny*/In grateful Testimony of the Signal Services/*effected by his conduct and valour*/in the BATTLE of Ross on the 15th June 1798/*for all Ireland/and in particular for that*/BARONY." The numeral five of the date has been cut after gilding, replacing a two. The battle actually took place on June 5.

On the knuckle-guard the hilt bears the following silver marks: a leopard, the sterling mark; the leopard's head, the London assay mark; the letter C in a shield, the London date-letter for 1798/99; and the king's head facing right, the duty mark. On the side of the shell toward the blade is the same sterling mark accompanied by the maker's mark, I.M., whom Claude Blair has shown to be James Morisset, a London goldsmith, probably of French or Swiss extraction, who worked at 11, Denmark Street, Soho. Morisset worked at first in partnership with his brother-in-law, the jeweler Louis Toussaint,[58] but by the time this sword was made, he was in partnership with the brothers Robert and Charles Lukin. The leopard and the date-letter also occur on the end of the grip. The washer between the sleeve and the shell bears the sterling mark. The straight blade, which is of hollow-ground triangular section, is etched in line with foliated scrollwork, and is blued and gilded.

The wooden scabbard, which has been re-covered in black leather, has top- and mid-lockets of silver gilt decorated *en suite* with the hilt. The top-locket is engraved on the reverse, "*R. Makepiece/London*." The chape is a later replacement in plain silver. Both lockets bear the sterling mark, the London assay mark, and the maker's mark, I.M. The retailer was the jeweler Robert Makepiece, who was also employed by the Corporation of the City of London to supply swords valued at two hundred guineas for military or naval officers whom the city wished to honor. An example not unlike that under discussion was presented by the City to Admiral Sir John Jervis, later Earl St. Vincent, on February 14, 1797. It is now on loan to the National Maritime Museum in Greenwich.[59] In place of the small wreaths acting as the arms of the hilt are tiny anchors, in acknowledgment of the naval connection. Jervis's sword was also made by James Morisset.

Henry Johnson (1748–1835), recipient of the Kienbusch Collection sword just discussed, was the second son of Allen Johnson of Kilternan, County Dublin, and his wife Olivia, daughter of John Walsh of Ballykilearn, Queen's County. He was gazetted ensign in the 28th Regiment of Foot in 1761. By 1775 he had risen to the rank of major and was sent to North America, where he commanded a provisional battalion of light infantry and, in 1778, was appointed lieutenant-colonel of the 17th Regiment of Foot, commanding operations in the Jerseys and afterwards, under Lord Cornwallis, in Virginia and the Carolinas. After the

Fig. 70. Small-sword, English, London, 1806–7, hilt by John Ray
and James Montague (active c.1800–c.1816). Cast gold;
1977-167-654 (see fig. 46, right).

surrender of Yorktown in 1781, he returned home and served in Nova Scotia and Newfoundland.

At the outbreak of war with France in 1789, he was appointed Inspector-General of recruiting for the English Establishment in Ireland. During the Irish Rebellion in the same year, Johnson defended the important river crossing at Ross, ten miles northeast of Waterford, in what was to prove the hardest fought action of the insurrection. His force consisted largely of Irish militia regiments, whose men might well have been expected to sympathize with the rebels. His only cavalry units consisted of detachments from the 5th Dragoons, a regular regiment, and the Midlothian Fencible Cavalry, a home-defense unit. On June 5, 1798, the town was furiously attacked by Bagenal Hervey and Father Roche with a considerable force of insurgents. They were driven off by Johnson's forces only after ten hours of fierce fighting. Johnson was later appointed colonel of the 81st Foot in 1798, lieutenant-general in 1799, and a full general in 1809. On December 1, 1818, he was created a baronet. He died on March 18, 1835, in Bath, where a memorial to him was erected in the cathedral.[60] Incidentally, this is not the only enameled small-sword presented to an officer for this campaign. The sword given to the Honourable William Wellesley-Pole, the future 3rd Earl of Mornington, the brother of the Iron Duke, the Duke of Wellington, victor of Waterloo, is still in the possession of his family.

A second sword of this type entered the Kienbusch Collection in 1968 (figs. 46, right; 70). Although generally resembling the one just described, it differs in certain important details. In place of the enamels on the pommel, grip, and sleeve are oval plaques containing whorls of acanthus foliage in low relief. Those on the outside are made separately of a softer gold and are set into oval openings, in which they are held by a series of tags around their inner edges. These plaques are of inferior workmanship; Claude Blair has suggested that they might be of Indian manufacture to replace damaged enamels.[61]

The knuckle-guard, which has no central feature, is cast in low relief and chased with alternating diagonals of laurel leaves and flowers and leaves, except at the ends which, like the quillon, are in the form of lush stylized acanthus scrolls. The arms also consist of recurved scrolls of stylized foliage. The grip is decorated along each side with laurel wreaths, and at both ends of each face with laurel sprays tied with fillets and clasping the central oval plaques. The shell-guard is bilobate. Each face is made separately; the one toward the blade includes the low rim into which the other face fits. The very unusually shaped lobes are in the form of the Greek shield known as a *pelta*. Small oval plaques, on which the ends of the arms rest, fill the inlets between the scrolled corners of the lobes. The shell is decorated toward the hand with a series of diverging rays comprised of acanthus tips in low relief to resemble a cockleshell. The other face is engine-turned with a wavy pattern also resembling a cockle.

On the shell are the following marks: the crowned leopard's head; the king's head mark; the letter L in a shield, the London date-letter for 1806/7; a closed crown; the numeral eighteen, indicating that the metal is 18-carat gold; and the letters IR over IM in a single rectangular punch, the maker's mark registered on May 4, 1800, by the partnership of John

Ray and James Montague, goldworkers of Denmark Street in Soho, London.[62] They were Morisset's successors and produced works very similar to his. On the sleeve are marks of the closed crown, the numeral eighteen, and the maker's mark IR over IM.

The straight blade, which is of hollow-ground triangular section, is etched in relief (what in the trade is called "embossing") with foliate scrolls bright against a frosted ground. The wooden scabbard, which is covered in black fishskin, has three gold mounts *en suite* with the hilt, both lockets with loose split-rings for suspension. The back of the top-locket is engraved: "*Rundell Bridge & Rundell*/Jewellers to Their Majesties/*& all the Royal Family*/LONDON."

The top- and mid-lockets each bear the marks of a crowned leopard's head, a closed crown, and the numeral eighteen. The chape bears the numeral eighteen and other marks defaced by the rivet securing it to the scabbard.

The retailer of this sword, Rundell Bridge and Rundell, was one of the most prestigious London jewelers of this period. Among the artists they employed to design their grander pieces of plate were a number of Royal Academicians: John Flaxman (1755–1826), Edward Hodges Bailey (1788–1867), and Thomas Stothard (1755–1834), for example. The client would have ordered the sword from Rundell, who would then have subcontracted the work to John Ray and James Montague.[63]

There is no inscription anywhere on this sword to indicate who commissioned it, but its red morocco leather traveling case is inscribed in gold letters, "COL. BOWIE." No officer of this rank and name is recorded as serving in the British army at this date, but a Robert Bowie served in the East India Company's army on the Bengal Establishment from 1778 until his death at Agra in 1814.[64] He became a cadet in the Bengal army in 1778, rose to the rank of lieutenant-colonel of the 22nd Bengal Native Infantry, and became brevet-colonel on June 4, 1813. He was present on detachment to the Madras army at the siege of Seringapatam in 1799, for which he received the gold medal. The date of the sword, if indeed it was Bowie's, suggests that it might have been presented to him for command of the successful operation against the Rana of Gohad in 1806. It could have been presented to him while on home leave from 1806 to 1809, when he returned to Britain and married.

Toward the end of the eighteenth century a final development occurred in the small-sword hilt. The arms of the hilt, already very small, finally withered away altogether with the sleeve from which they grew. The outer shell, which was now mounted on the root of the knuckle-guard and the quillon, was bent toward the blade, in extreme cases so that it lay parallel to the plane of the blade. The inner shell disappeared altogether. The shell could be oval, or shaped like a *pelta* (Greek shield) or, if it was a descendant of a boat-shell hilt, asymmetrical. The latter type appears to have been known to contemporaries as "*à clavier*," presumably because the asymmetrical shell was thought to resemble the top of the musical instrument of that name.

The Kienbusch Collection contains a very unusual example of a small-sword with an oval shell turned toward the blade (fig. 67). It is mounted in brass partly blackened, partly bright, the guards made up of seaweed-like scrolls and its grip cast with a spiral of similar vegetation around it. In the center of the pommel are the distinctive lozengy arms of Bavaria, and at the center of the knuckle-guard is the Bavarian rampant lion in an oval with pearled edge. In the center of the foliate curls making up the shell is a cartouche cast in relief with a monogram consisting of two crossed *A*s under a crown. The gold lace sword-knot has a bullion tassle with the same monogram embroidered upon it. The straight blade, which is of flattened-hexagonal section near the hilt and almond section thereafter, is etched in line and blued and gilded with trophies of arms. This sword retains its black leather scabbard mounted *en suite*. The top-locket is engraved on the reverse: *"Johann/Stroblberger/München."* So far no details of Stroblberger's career as a sword cutler have been published. The Bayerisches Armeemuseum, Ingolstadt, the Bayerisches Nationalmuseum, and the Stadtmuseum of Munich all have examples of his work, mostly from the second quarter of the nineteenth century.[65]

It is difficult to find a suitable Bavarian candidate for the double-*A* monogram on the shell of this sword. It is possible, however, that it stands for Augusta-Amelia von Bayern, the daughter of Maximilian-Joseph, King of Bavaria, and his first wife Maria-Wilhelmina-Augusta von Hesse-Darmstadt. Augusta-Amelia was born in 1788, and on January 14, 1806, she married Eugène-Pierre de Beauharnais, called Prince Eugène, the adopted son of Napoleon I, and Viceroy of Italy. She became a widow in 1824 and died in 1851. It may be that this sword was worn by one of her court officials.

While on the subject of Bavarian court swords, one of the most remarkable weapons in the Kienbusch Collection bears mention (fig. 68). It is not a small-sword, but a fancy-dress sword imitating an older weapon. The partly blackened, partly gilt-brass hilt is also the work of Stroblberger, and is based on that of a rapier of about 1600, except that the quillons have been moved several inches forward and the arms of the hilt dispensed with altogether. The pommel is a very beautiful winged head entwined with snakes, a rather eccentric combination of Medusa and Perseus. The frontally symmetrical guards consist of a pair of straight quillons, ending in grotesque dragon heads, which support on each side a side-ring at right angles to the plane of the blade, and a second larger side-ring inclined toward the pommel and linked to the knuckle-guard by a short loop-guard. The guards are all cast and chased with seaweed-like vegetation in high relief. The grip is spirally writhen and bound with fine steel wire and with a twist of gilt wire flanked on each side by a plain wire that follows the spiral twist of the grip. The smaller side-ring outside the hand is bound with a sword-knot of gold lace of an unusual Greek-key pattern with a bullion tassel. The straight blade, of flattened-almond section with a central fuller running to within five and one-half inches from the tip, is etched in relief with elaborate foliate scrolls against a fire-gilt ground. The blade is struck near the hilt outside the hand with a small outline of a king's head in profile seen from his left, the mark of the Solingen firm of Weyersberg.[66] The steel scabbard has brass mounts cast in relief with laurel sprays centered on quatrefoils, and still retains its smart red morocco waistbelt and slings, overlaid with gold lace of a Greek-key pattern, with its lion mask and snake clasp. A very similar sword was sold in Lucerne in 1976.[67] Yet another, but with an ivory grip of octagonal section, sold in Zurich in 1981, had a scabbard covered in blue velvet, with brass mounts designed to be worn in a baldric.[68]

Old rapiers or rapiers made in older styles were occasionally worn in the nineteenth century as a result of various romantic revivals. The costumes designed for state occasions by George IV, both before and after he ascended the throne, were somewhat Tudor in character, and, accordingly, when he was being painted in Garter robes, he wore an early sword from his own collection. This sword is still at Windsor Castle.[69] The Knights of the Bavarian Order of Saint George seem also to have worn swords in an older style. In a portrait by Erich Correns, painted in 1856, Prince Adalbert of Bavaria is shown wearing a hilt of a type fashionable around 1600, which may be an old-fashioned sword.[70] On the other hand, however, a hilt of chiseled and enameled steel encrusted with precious stones, on the London art market in 1981, was clearly made during the romantic revival in Bavaria.[71] This sword may indeed have been intended to be worn by the king with the robes of his order. At least one other archaizing hilt survives.[72] It was based on an elaborately chiseled steel hilt that was perhaps formerly in the Bavarian ducal collection and is now in the Stadtmuseum of Munich.[73]

The latest small-sword in the Kienbusch Collection has a most unusual brass hilt "*à clavier*," with a lively dragon over a blank scroll on the shell, and a scaly beast, apparently a crocodile, but probably standing in for a dragon on this occasion, forming the grip, its tail acting as the rear quillon and its head as the pommel (fig. 69). The edges of the shell and the knuckle-guard, which is largely concealed by the gold lace sword-knot, are decorated with laurel leaves in low relief. The straight blade of flattened-almond section is etched in relief, bright against a frosted ground, with foliage and a dragon on both sides, and with the addition inside of the inscription "*H./POOLE/& Co./Savile/Row/LONDON.*" The firm of Henry Poole, tailors, which still has premises in Savile Row today, changed its name from James Poole about 1847.[74] The scabbard is engraved at the mouth and tip with stylized foliage and is fitted with a leaf-shaped button for wear in a frog attached to a shoulder-belt concealed by the uniform coat. The tip of the scabbard is guarded by a little cast dragon curled around its end. It has been suggested that this was one of the swords given to officers of the Royal Navy who had served under Admiral Horatio Nelson at the Battle of the Nile (1798).[75] The dragon on the shell, however, is an adaptation of an existing design based on the badge of one of the British regiments that had taken part in the war with China in 1840–42, with the inscription of the scroll obliterated before casting. It certainly indicates a connection not with Egypt but with China. In fact a very similar, but not identical, sword in the National Army Museum, Chelsea, also by Poole, has the word "China" in relief on the scroll.[76] This type of sword, which dates from the middle of the nineteenth century, was probably intended for some minor Chinese official, probably in the consular service. The crocodile forming the grip may also be an adaptation, and was perhaps originally intended for use on a sword for the Egyptian service.

Here one sees the beginning of a practice common today. Whenever a special new pattern of sword is required nowadays, there is usually no question of a designer producing a fresh idea. An old pattern for which the molds still exist is simply adapted by replacing the old badge or device with the new one. The blades are usually etched by means of a transfer originally produced in the reign of Queen Victoria and modified, if at all, with no concession to modern taste. Only the swords produced for members of the French Academy on their appointment still show originality of design. In such a case the hilt is invariably decorated with motifs relevant to the wearer's career, and, indeed, the form of the guards is often governed by the desire to shape them into the principal symbolic motif. Only France, the original home of the small-sword, has kept alive the traditional combination of patron, artist, and specialist craftsman to produce new weapons in the mainstream of modern design and genius.

NOTES

1 C. Otto von Kienbusch, *The Kretzschmar von Kienbusch Collection of Armor and Arms* (Princeton, N.J., 1963).

2 See A.V.B. Norman and C. M. Barne, *The Rapier and Small-Sword, 1460–1820* (London, 1980).

3 Ibid., p. 47.

4 Sir William Hope, *The Scots Fencing Master* (Edinburgh, 1687), pp. 11–12.

5 Waffensammlung, Kunsthistorisches Museum, Vienna, inv. no. A1605; see Heribert Seitz, *Blankwaffen II . . .* (Brunswick, 1968), pl. 106.

6 Livrustkammaren, Stockholm, inv. nos. 10729 and 10784; see Lena Nordström, *White Arms of the Royal Armoury* (Stockholm, 1984), nos. 99 and 100.

7 Sir Guy Francis Laking, *The Armoury of Windsor Castle* (London, 1904), cat. no. 59, which erroneously gave the donor as Charles XII of Sweden.

8 Staatliche Kunsthalle, Karlsruhe, inv. no. 189.

9 Exhibited Stedelijk Museum, Leiden, *Nederlandse Vuurwapens uit de 17e en 18e eeuw*, 1978, cat. no. 206, repro.

10 See A.V.B. Norman, "Some References to Arms, Sword Cutlers, and Gunsmiths in English Newspapers, 1660–1727," *Journal of the Arms & Armour Society*, vol. 8, no. 6 (December, 1976), p. 368.

11 Rijksmuseum, Amsterdam, inv. no. A404; S. J. Gudlaugsson, *Geraert ter Borch*, vol. 1 (The Hague, 1959), no. 110, I.

12 Rijksmuseum, Amsterdam, inv. no. 1104.

13 Royal Armouries, London, inv. no. IX.1428; purchased from the Worsley family with this tradition.

14 Badisches Landesmuseum, Karlsruhe, inv. no. G. 122; 1680 inv. no. 52.

15 Norman and Barne 1980, pp. 375–76.

16 Ibid., pp. 269–70.

17 See Lisa Goldenberg Stoppato, "Suttermans' *Young Commander* Identified," *Fenway Court, 1982* (Boston, 1983), pp. 28–35.

18 The Metropolitan Museum of Art, New York, acc. no. 1985.259.1; sale, Christie's, London, November 13, 1985, lot 31, repro.

19 A. Weyersberg, *Soligen Schwertschmiede des 16. und 17. Jahrhunderts und ihre Erzeugnisse* (Solingen, 1926), pp. 57–62, marks nos. 140–55.

20 A.V.B. Norman, *Wallace Collection Catalogues: European Arms and Armour, Supplement* (London, 1986), under cat. no. A567, pp. 132–33.

21 I am very grateful to my old friend H. L. Blackmore, formerly Deputy Master of the Tower of London Armouries, for most kindly drawing my attention to this hilt.

22 Laking 1904, cat. no. 609.

23 Claude Blair, *Three Presentation Swords in the Victoria and Albert Museum, and a Group of English Enamels* (London, 1972).

24 Norman and Barne 1980, pp. 301, 314, 347, and 391.

25 For example, Victoria and Albert Museum, London, Department of Prints and Drawings, reg. no. E1410-1908.

26 A. Kenneth Snowman, *Eighteenth-Century Gold Boxes of Europe* (London, 1966), pl. 25.

27 Clare Le Corbeiller, *European and American Snuff Boxes, 1730–1830* (New York, 1966), pls. 618 and 619.

28 Norman and Barne 1980, p. 367.

29 Denis Diderot and J. le Rond d'Alembert, *Encyclopédie . . .* (Paris, 1771), pl. II, figs. 12 and 13.

30 Respectively, M. Louis Metman, *Le Musée des Arts Décoratifs, Palais du Louvre, Pavillon de Marsan, Le Métal* (Paris, n.d.), no. 1276, pl. CXV; and no. 29, in the manuscript catalogue in the library of the Department of Metalwork, Victoria and Albert Museum, London.

31 National Museum of Ireland, Dublin, reg. no. 1065-1888.

32 Nederlands Leger en Wapenmuseum, Delft, inv. no. 744 EA-148; see J. P. Puype, *Blanke Wapens: Nederlandse slag- en steekwapens sinds 1600 . . .* (Lochem-Poperinge, 1981), no. 45.

33 For instance, Victoria and Albert Museum, London, reg. no. 1736-1888; see Anthony North, *An Introduction to European Swords* (London, 1982), fig. 61.

34 Claude Blair, *European & American Arms, c. 1100–1850* (London, 1962), p. 86.

35 Art Gallery of Ontario, Toronto, acc. no. 48/6.

A . V . B .   N O R M A N

36 Formerly P. Carrington-Peirce Collection; sale, Sotheby's, London, April 4, 1960, lot 56; Norman and Barne 1980, p. 206.

37 Formerly P. Carrington-Peirce Collection; sale, Sotheby's, London, April 4, 1960, lot 54, repro.; Norman and Barne 1980, p. 206, but with the inaccurate reading of the date-letter given in Carrington-Peirce's own manuscript catalogue in the library of the Department of Metalwork, Victoria and Albert Museum, London.

38 Commander W. E. May and P.G.W. Annis, *Swords for Sea Service* (London, 1970), vol. 2, p. 272; Arthur G. Grimwade, *London Goldsmiths, 1697–1837* . . . (London, 1975), pp. 458-59, no. 1204.

39 May and Annis 1970, p. 289; Grimwade 1975, p. 569, no. 3648.

40 May and Annis 1970, p. 277; Grimwade 1975, p. 507, no. 797.

41 Walters Art Gallery, Baltimore, acc. no. 51.1368.

42 In Norman and Barne 1980, pp. 333–34.

43 Bayerisches Nationalmuseum, Munich, inv. no. W2760.

44 Formerly P. Carrington-Peirce Collection; sale, Sotheby's, London, April 4, 1960, lot 62.

45 May and Annis 1970, p. 290; Grimwade 1975, p. 572, no. 3210.

46 May and Annis 1970, p. 275; Grimwade 1975, p. 495, no. 458.

47 Laking 1904, cat. nos. 519–22.

48 The Metropolitan Museum of Art, New York, acc. no. 42.50.46.

49 For instance, Norman and Barne 1980, pls. 137 and 151.

50 Laking 1904, cat. no. 594.

51 Ibid., cat. nos. 511, 512, 519, 521, and 540.

52 *L'Avant-Coureur*, Paris (no. 48), November 30, 1772.

53 The Metropolitan Museum of Art, New York, acc. no. 26.145.267; see Bashford Dean, *Catalogue of European Court Swords and Hunting Swords* . . . (New York, 1929), no. 96, pl. LXXIII.

54 Letter of Dr. Hanns-Ulrich Haedeke to author, January 19, 1987.

55 The Metropolitan Museum of Art, New York, acc. no. 26.145.321; see Dean 1929, no. 79, pl. LIX.

56 J. B. Brown, *Swords Voted to Officers of the Revolution by the Continental Congress, 1775–1784* (Washington, D.C., 1965).

57 I am extremely grateful to Claude Blair for his customary, but nevertheless much appreciated, kindness and generosity in allowing me to use his notes on this and the next sword, and also for reading this article with insight and sympathy.

58 Blair 1972, pp. 4–6.

59 Reg. no. 493; Blair 1972, p. 11, pl. 5. In his discussion of Morisset's surviving output of both swords and presentation boxes, Blair included the Kienbusch sword (1977-167-648) as his number 20.

60 Sir Sidney Lee, ed., *The Dictionary of National Biography*, s.v. "Henry Johnson"; H. W. Maxwell, *History of the Irish Rebellion* (London, 1845), pp. 116–20.

61 Accession files, Kienbusch Collection of Armor and Arms, Philadelphia Museum of Art.

62 Blair 1972, pp. 16–17.

63 Shirley Bury, "The Lengthening Shadow of Rundell's. Part 1: Rundell's and Their Silversmiths," *Connoisseur*, vol. 161 (February 1966), pp. 79–85.

64 Robert Bowie's years of army service are recorded in V. C. Hodson's *List of Officers of the Bengal Army, 1758–1834* (London, 1927–47).

65 I am very grateful to Dr. Michael Gordon for his most helpful suggestions about this particular Kienbusch sword in his letters to me of March 12, 1986, and April 20, 1987.

66 R. Cronau, *Geschichte der Solinger Klingenindustrie* (Stuttgart, 1885), mark no. 168.

67 Sale, Fischer's, Lucerne, November 24, 1976, lot 282, repro. I would like to express my gratitude to Donald LaRocca, formerly Assistant Curator of the Kienbusch Collection, for drawing my attention to this sword, and for his help in the preparation of this article.

68 Sale, Auktionhaus Peter Ineichen, Zurich, October 30, 1981, lot 541, pl. 17.

69 Laking 1904, cat. no. 34.

70 Exhibited Residenz, Munich, *Der Bayerische Hausritterorden vom Heiligen George, 1729–1979*, April 21–June 24, 1979, no. 62, fig. 12.

71 W. Herman and E. L. Wagner, *Alte Waffen* (Munich, 1979), p. 140, fig. 210.

72 Recently on the London art market.

73 Inv. no. Z1688; see Rudolf H. Wackernagel, *Das münchner Zeughaus* (Munich, 1983), cat. no. 72, pl. 25a.

74 May and Annis 1970, p. 299.

75 Accession files, Kienbusch Collection of Armor and Arms, Philadelphia Museum of Art.

76 National Army Museum, Chelsea, reg. no. 8305-59.

A Renaissance Painted Shield
Attributed to Girolamo da Treviso

STUART W. PYHRR AND EVERETT FAHY

PART I · BY STUART W. PYHRR

The Kienbusch Shield and Related Examples

The sixteenth-century pageant shield that forms the subject of this study is one of the most unusual and intriguing objects in the Kienbusch Collection (figs. 71, 72, 74–77). Unlike most of the arms, it is made of painted wood rather than steel, and it is the work of a painter rather than an armorer. Despite the originality and quality of its painting, the shield has attracted little scholarly attention. The description in the 1963 catalogue raisonné of the Kienbusch Collection offered little more than a physical description of the piece.[1] The scene on the front of the shield was described as the storming of a castle, and the two scenes on the back as a battle between horsemen and horsemen leaving camp. No attempt was made to identify the subject matter further. Referring to "a tradition of the Este family," the shield was attributed to Pordenone (Giovanni Antonio Licinio, 1483–1539), a painter employed at the court of the duke of Ferrara who is thought to have painted arms. As to its provenance, the shield was said to come from the collections of the dukes of Ferrara and of Archduke Franz Ferdinand d'Este, but documentary evidence was not offered to support these claims.

Further research has shed considerable new light on the Kienbusch shield regarding its iconography, authorship, and provenance. The painted scenes, inhabited by warriors wearing armor *all'antica*, can be shown to represent episodes from the Second Punic War. The style of the painting bears no obvious relation to the work of Pordenone but rather is much closer to the style of Giulio Romano (1492/99–1546) and his circle. Indeed, the Kienbusch shield is one of at least ten examples, all with classical themes painted in grisaille on gold, that can be attributed to Girolamo di Tommaso da Treviso (c. 1497–1544), who is known to have worked with Giulio in Mantua in 1527. This attribution will be discussed by Everett Fahy in the second part of this article. Finally, the provenance, too, must be reassessed, as the Kienbusch shield is now known to have entered into Este possession only in the nineteenth century. Before that it appears to have belonged to the famous armory of the Medici, dukes of Florence and later grand dukes of Tuscany, in their galleries in the Uffizi.

The shield is circular, convex in section, and measures 24 inches (61 cm) in diameter. X-radiograph photographs indicate that it is constructed of three layers of thin wooden boards overlaid at right angles to one another, the layers originally held together by metal staples and, presumably, glue. The wooden surfaces inside and out are covered with coarse-woven linen, then layers of gesso and bole, on which is laid a ground of gold leaf. The gold ground is painted over with figures whose flesh is rendered in grisaille (white with shadings in gray). The elaborate costumes and other details in gold are achieved either by leaving the gold ground in reserve, with highlights in black, or by painting over the gold with black and then scratching through the upper paint layer to reveal the gold ground below, a technique known as *sgraffito*. Much of the exposed gold leaf is impressed with comma-shaped marks that enhance its light-catching quality. A technical note on the construction and decoration of the shield is provided by Melissa Meighan below.

The convex outer side, or front, of the shield (fig. 71) is painted with an elaborate multifigured scene of soldiers in pseudoclassical armor storming a fortress. The black and gold border decoration, rendered in sgraffito, consists of a wide center band of strapwork and foliage framed by narrow bands of scrolls within two parallel lines (see frontispiece). The border and the center of the shield at its highest point on the exterior have suffered considerable damage and paint loss.

At its center, the concave inner side, or back (fig. 72), has an unpainted oblong area where the red bole ground is exposed. This area was originally covered by an upholstered arm-pad, obviating the need for gold leaf and paint. A series of holes around the edges, now filled in, formerly held the nails that secured the arm-pad and the two straps (*brases*) by which the shield was carried on the forearm. Above and below the arm-pad are two flattened semicircular fields painted with narrative scenes. The upper one contains a battle between horsemen in classical costume within a wooded landscape (fig. 76); the lower one depicts horsemen departing from a camp set within a forest (fig. 77). The two scenes are visually (and presumably also thematically) linked by the presence of trees on each side of the arm-pad. The scenes on the inside are much smaller in scale and are more finely painted than that on the exterior. This change in scale presumably reflects the desire to have the outer scene more easily recognizable from a distance, whereas the inner scenes were intended for appreciation at close range by the wearer. The sgraffito border along the edge of the outer area consists of contiguous circles overlaid with a pattern of strapwork and foliated scrolls, with a row of white dots framed on each side by pairs of gold lines. The same border frames the arm-pad areas (fig. 75). The marks made by the compass points in the drawing of the circles in these borders are still visible. At the extreme outer edge is a series of scallops, or scales, painted in white, each with a white dot in the center.

The fragile medium of painted wood and the painstakingly detailed decoration indicate that the Kienbusch shield was undoubtedly created as a parade piece and was most likely never intended for use in the field or in the tournament, where its surfaces would have suffered irreparable damage. Painted shields of this type belong to a distinctive category of sixteenth-century armor in the antique style, reflecting the Renaissance interest in all aspects

Fig. 71. Exterior of pageant shield, Italian, c. 1535.
Kienbusch Collection of Armor and Arms; 1977-167-751.

STUART W. PYHRR AND EVERETT FAHY

Fig. 72. Interior of the Kienbusch shield (fig. 71).

of classical culture, including costume and armament.[2] Inspired by their customers' humanistic interests, Italian armorers looked to Roman sculpture, painting, and coinage for models. The "muscled" cuirass, the open-faced helmet with its tall crest, the circular shield, and the short sword suspended from a baldric were essential elements of the revived style of antique military dress that became commonplace in triumphal entries and feast-day parades. Dressed in armor *all'antica,* the prince or *condottiere* saw himself in the guise of heroes of classical history and literature, such as Julius Caesar, Scipio, and Ulysses, with the suggestion of legitimate power, military prowess, and the prestige associated with an earlier golden age.

Armor *all'antica* was undoubtedly worn in the fifteenth century, but is usually thought of as a sixteenth-century phenomenon because of the survival of so many elements of classically inspired armor of embossed steel fashioned by Milanese armorers, notably Filippo Negroli (recorded 1532–51) and his workshop. Painted shields are not usually thought of in the same category, although they are indeed part of the same phenomenon. The Kienbusch shield's round shape, classical subject matter, and even the rendering of its decoration in grisaille, which was considered an antique mode of painting by Renaissance theorists, leave no doubt as to its humanist inspiration.

Painted shields of the sixteenth century seem to have been an Italian specialty. Invariably circular in shape and convex in section, they are usually painted with antique subject matter in polychrome or grisaille, sometimes on the exterior only. At least fifty painted shields are known, with attributions to a variety of centers: Venice, Mantua, Bologna, Florence, Rome, and Naples.[3] Although essentially decorative costume adjuncts, painted shields provided an unusual medium for narrative subjects and, presumably, maximum public exposure in pageants. Shield painting could be considered a serious undertaking even by major artists: Leonardo da Vinci (1452–1519) is reputed to have painted one, and two shields survive by the hands of Giovanni Stradano (the Flemish artist Jan van der Straet, 1523–1605) and Caravaggio (1571–1610).[4]

Little documentation exists concerning this category of sixteenth-century circular pageant shields with painted decoration. The earliest record I know of such a shield is one depicted in the painting *Warrior* (fig. 73), dating to the decade 1510–20, by a follower of Giorgione, Lorenzo Luzzo (Morto) da Feltre (c.1470–1526/27).[5] The warrior holds forth a shield painted with two equestrian figures, one carrying a lance or spear, surrounded by a wide decorative border. As the painting is at present known only from a black and white illustration, it is not possible to comment on the colors used on the shield.

Inventories indicate that a number of these painted shields were in existence by the mid-sixteenth century and that they were widely distributed throughout Europe. The shields were invariably referred to in terms implying a round shape: *rondache, rotella, rodela, Rundell.* In English, the term *target* was used, a word that today still suggests a circular form. The earliest record I have found that lists circular painted shields is the 1543 inventory of the Gonzaga armory in Mantua. Fifteen examples are mentioned, although unfortunately without

Fig. 73. The Warrior, c. 1510–20, by Lorenzo Luzzo (Morto) da Feltre (Italian, c. 1470–1526/27). Present location unknown.

Fig. 74. Detail of a fallen soldier from the battle scene above the arm-pad on the interior of the Kienbusch shield.

Fig. 75. Detail of the sgraffito border around the arm-pad of the Kienbusch shield.

Fig. 76. Detail of the battle scene above the arm-pad on the interior of the Kienbusch shield.

Fig. 77. Detail of the scene below the arm-pad on the interior of the Kienbusch shield.

reference to the subject of their decoration.[6] The armories of the Medici, grand dukes of Tuscany, and of the della Rovere family, dukes of Urbino, also contained numerous painted shields. Inventories dating from 1631, the year the two collections were united in Florence,[7] and 1639 list fourteen painted shields in the Medici section and seven in that coming from Urbino.[8] Again, the brief descriptions give no indication as to the decoration, although in later inventories several of the shields are described in sufficient detail to allow them to be identified among the surviving examples.[9]

Circular painted shields are also recorded in collections north of the Alps. No inventories of the French royal armory appear to survive for the sixteenth century, but painted shields are recorded in other French collections. The 1556 inventory of the Paris hôtel of Anne de Montmorency, Constable of France, lists "une rondelle paincte de coulleur d'or et de vert, avec une histoire de bataille."[10] Twenty-three painted *rondaches*, presumably also of sixteenth-century date, are recorded in the 1642 inventory of the armory of the dukes of Bouillon at Sedan.[11]

In Spain, the inventory of the armory of Emperor Charles V, the so-called *Relacíon de Valladolid*, probably compiled soon after the emperor's death in 1558, records several painted shields (*rodelas*). One of these was said to depict the battle of Pavia,[12] where, in 1524, the imperial forces defeated the French and took their king, Francis I, prisoner. Another of the emperor's shields, painted with a boar hunt, presumably illustrating the story of Meleager and the Hunt of the Calydonian Boar from Ovid's *Metamorphoses*, is represented in the *Inventario Iluminado*, the famous illustrated inventory of the armory of Charles V, a manuscript dating between 1544 and 1558 preserved in the Real Armería, Madrid (fig. 88).[13] The inventory of goods belonging to the 3rd Duke of Albuquerque, drawn up in 1560, lists four circular painted shields, three painted in gold on a black ground with battles and classical subjects, said to be of Neapolitan origin ("de Nápoles").[14]

A surprisingly large number of painted shields are mentioned in the inventories of the English royal armories and arsenals made in 1547–48, following the death of Henry VIII. The Tower of London contained over two hundred painted shields of diverse types, including twenty-three "rounde targettes painted blacke gilt rounde aboute by the edge and in the myddest a round circle w^t sondry antiques paynted gilte w^{t}in them," and another thirty-three "rounde targettes alle over gilte and paynted w^t sondry antiques and sondry collours."[15] The armory at Westminster contained eight "targettes of woode painted w^t divers histories and trimmed w^t vellet and girdells of them of crymsen satten."[16]

While a comprehensive and critical study of sixteenth-century painted shields has yet to be made, a cursory survey of surviving examples indicates that, on the basis of the different styles of decoration, the shields were painted in a number of different workshops. The largest and artistically most distinguished of these is a series of about ten shields painted in grisaille on gold that depict scenes from Roman history and classical legend on both their outer and inner surfaces. The Kienbusch shield is one of the finest of these, and a study of its origins and iconography provides a point of departure for exploring the entire series.

The scene on the exterior of the Kienbusch shield can be identified as the *Storming of New Carthage*. It is based on a design of the same subject by Giulio Romano, Raphael's principal assistant and collaborator in Rome, and from 1524 court artist to Federigo Gonzaga, Marquis of Mantua. Giulio's drawing belongs to a series of twenty-two designs that he executed in collaboration with Francesco Penne (another of Raphael's assistants in Rome) for a tapestry cycle *The History of Scipio*, which was commissioned by Francis I of France.[17] The cycle consisted of ten scenes illustrating the military feats of the Roman general Scipio Africanus (Publius Cornelius Scipio, 237–183 B.C.), and another twelve illustrating the triumphs. Three of the tapestries were finished by July 1532, when they were shown to Francis I, who then commissioned the remaining nineteen. The completed series, woven in gold and silk thread in the Brussels atelier of Marc Cretif, was delivered and paid for by April 1535. The cycle, one of the largest, costliest, and most important of the sixteenth century, was preserved in the French royal collections until the Revolution, when in 1797 the tapestries were burned to extract the gold content.

Giulio's original design for the *Storming of New Carthage* is preserved in the Musée du Louvre (fig. 78), where there is also a contemporary and more legible copy (fig. 79).[18] It was presumably through such workshop copies that Giulio's composition achieved wide circulation in Italy and thereby served as a model for similar scenes in sixteenth-century painting and decorative arts.[19] The subject was also engraved (in reverse) by the Nuremberg painter and printmaker Georg Pencz (c.1500–1550), who was working in Rome in the years from 1535 to 1540. The Pencz engraving (fig. 80), his largest, is dated 1539 and in the second and later states gives credit to the design's author, IVLIVS ROMANS INVENTOR.[20]

Giulio's conception of the assault on New Carthage follows closely an episode related by Livy in his account of the Second Punic War.[21] The text recounts the career of the Roman general Scipio (after whose later African campaigns he acquired the appellation ''Africanus'') who, in 209 B.C., laid siege to the fortified town of New Carthage (Carthago Nova, modern Cartagena), the headquarters of the Carthaginian army in Spain. The city was situated along the coast, on a peninsula with a bay to the south and a channel to the west leading to a large lagoon at the north. New Carthage was a city of many towers and high walls that had never yielded to attack. The Roman assault came from two directions: from the south, by sea, with Gaius Laelius in charge of naval forces; and from the east, over land, with Scipio commanding the attack. Repeated attempts to scale the walls proved futile, so densely packed were its parapets with Carthaginian defenders. In an attempt to break the spirit of their enemy, the Carthaginian commander Mago ordered an attachment of his troops to counterattack the Romans outside the walls, but they were met and matched by an equally strong Roman force that forced the Carthaginians back through the city gate. Then, as if by a miracle, the lagoon protecting the northern ramparts of the town ran low with the tide. Scipio exhorted his troops to take advantage of this ''act of the gods'' and the Romans attacked the unprotected flank of the city while continuing to assail from the south and east. The walls were scaled and the Romans gained entrance to the city. New Carthage capitulated, surrendering to the Romans

Fig. 78. The Storming of New Carthage, *by Giulio Romano (Italian, 1492/99–1546). Pen and wash with white highlights on paper. Musée du Louvre, Paris; inv. no. 3535.*

her great store of war matériel, rich booty, valuable hostages, and an important harbor on the coast of Spain. With this victory young Scipio won praise from his countrymen and fame in the annals of history.

Giulio's interpretation of Livy's text is quite literal, although he conflates several episodes into a single narrative scene. In his drawing, the storming of New Carthage occupies most of the sheet, and the earlier episode of the Carthaginians meeting the Romans in battle outside the walls is depicted in the background at the left. The naval attack is omitted altogether. The composition is clear in its organization, unified by a sinuous arabesque of figures leading back from the foreground, around the foremost tower and winding deep into the background. In the left foreground a group of gesticulating Roman soldiers, among whom Scipio may be represented, watch as their comrades scale the walls.[22] These foreground figures and the hillock they occupy have the character of a repoussoir, magnifying the illusion of depth and heightening the sense of immediacy. Many of the figures, especially those scaling the walls, display a plasticity of form and an energy that look back to the animated figures in Raphael's frescoes in the Stanza dell'Incendio and those completed by Giulio in the Sala di Constantino in the Vatican.[23] The drama of the composition is echoed by the forceful wind that whips the hair and draperies of the soldiers and the billowing standard occupying the center of the design. The *Storming of New Carthage* has an almost proto-Baroque quality in its bravura of action, violence, and excitement.

Giulio's drawing (or a copy of it), rather than Pencz's engraving, seems to have served as the model for the Kienbusch shield, as the scene on the shield's exterior follows the direction of the former rather than that of the latter. In light of the fact that the design may have been in existence by 1532, and certainly well before 1535, it seems quite possible that the Kienbusch

Fig. 79. The Storming of New Carthage, *after Giulio Romano. Pen and wash on paper. Musée du Louvre, Paris; inv. no. 3720.*

Fig. 80. The Storming of New Carthage, *dated 1539, by Georg Pencz (German, c. 1500–1550) after Giulio Romano. 1st state, engraving. The Metropolitan Museum of Art, New York, Rogers Fund; acc. no. 62.602.110.*

shield could have been painted as early as the mid-1530s. A date around 1535 is, in fact, most likely, and consistent with the activities of the shield's painter, Girolamo da Treviso.

A comparison of the Kienbusch shield to Giulio's design demonstrates that the shield's painter followed Giulio's composition closely, but not slavishly. A great many differences between the two works may be observed. At the outset, the painter was required to adapt Giulio's rectangular composition to a circular shape, which necessitated cropping the image and relocating certain figures. But rather than eliminate details to simplify his labor, he multiplied the figures and added elaborate costumes and architectural ornament of his own invention. For example, a second figure of a soldier carrying a scaling ladder has been inserted in the foreground, and another ladder, mounted with attackers, has been raised against the turret at the right. The soldiers, who in Giulio's design were dressed in robes or armor of comparatively simple design, now wear elaborately detailed costumes, suggesting armor of embossed leather or metal, with plumes on their helmets, decorative motifs on their shields, and elaborate jewelry-like mounts on their cloaks and baldrics. The banners bear emblems where they were originally plain, and their number has increased. The towers of New Carthage, which Giulio seems to have modeled on the Castel Sant'Angelo in Rome, have been multiplied and embellished with garlands and lion masks. The Roman banner, emblazoned SPQR (*Senatus Populus Que Romanus*—the People and Senate of Rome) already flies over one of the towers, leaving no doubt as to the outcome of the siege. A fleet of ships presses close to the towers at the right: this is the naval attack cited in Livy's text that was missing from Giulio's drawing and the tapestries that followed from it. The scene on the exterior of the Kienbusch shield is thus not as derivative as it might first appear, but reveals a highly personal interpretation of Giulio's original design, and, indeed, a more faithful rendering of the historical account.

The sources and subjects of the two scenes on the inside of the shield are more difficult to identify. The two equestrian scenes are not part of the original Scipio tapestry series, nor can they be identified with certainty as deriving from Livy's account of the Second Punic War. They do, however, appear to represent two moments of a single episode and were intended to be viewed sequentially. In the lower scene, soldiers ride out from camp into the forest. The principal figure is the bearded warrior who rides in front of his four comrades-in-arms. This figure wears an elaborate classical armor, with a plumed helmet surmounted by a harpie, a "muscled" cuirass with lion heads at the shoulders, and a fluttering cape. He carries a shield on his left arm and holds a spear in his right hand. His richly caparisoned horse has elaborate chest and rump girdles and tassels hanging from the headstall. This same figure can be identified by his distinctive costume and the details of his horse's trappings as the warrior who is killed by the thrust of a spear in the battle raging in the center of the upper scene.

Like the painting on the front of the shield, that on the inside, both in spirit and in detail, reflects the influence of Raphael and his school, particularly Giulio Romano. The figure on horseback in the center of the upper scene (fig. 76), with his lance poised overhead to strike a

Fig. 81. Detail of the Battle of Constantine *by Giulio Romano. Fresco, Sala di Constantino, Vatican, Rome.*

deadly blow to his opponent, appears to have been inspired by the figure of Constantine in the depiction of the *Battle of Constantine* (fig. 81), in the Sala di Constantino. Many of the poses from this fresco—the quintessential High Renaissance battle scene—were repeated by later artists, including Giulio, for reuse in other contexts. Details such as the wild-eyed horses with rippling manes, the figures of warriors collapsing to the ground with their steeds underneath, and many of the individual figural poses are found in Giulio's work. The pose of the fallen warrior at the left, just above the border of the arm-pad, with his leg bent and his arm stretched overhead, is found, for example, in Giulio's fresco showing gladiatorial combat in the Sala dei Venti in the Palazzo del Te, Mantua, painted about 1528–29.[24] The frequent repetition of figures such as these indicates not only the high esteem with which Raphael and Giulio were held, but also the authority of antiquity, the source from which many of these motifs ultimately derive. Thus, figures such as these can be found on Roman sarcophagi and in battle scenes such as those found on the column of Trajan.[25] This reflects the Renaissance practice of transposing into painting motifs borrowed from antique statues, sarcophagi, coins, and gems.[26] The painter of the Kienbusch shield took ancient history as his subject and adopted, through the intermediary works of Raphael and Giulio Romano, a number of motifs from classical art. It is likely, too, that in his use of grisaille, he was attempting to emulate the ancient mode of painting. Grisaille, monochrome painting only in shades of gray, was a method highly praised in antiquity—by Pliny, for example—and in the Renaissance by Leon-Baptista Alberti.[27] In the sixteenth century, large-scale grisaille frescoes in imitation of antique reliefs adorned the facades of palaces. Polidoro da Caravaggio (1492–1543) is perhaps the best-known High Renaissance artist working in this technique, and it is to him that several of the grisaille-painted shields related to the Kienbusch example have in the past been attributed. Grisaille was also used in temporary decorations such as triumphal arches created for festivals and ceremonial entries into cities, where the technique served to suggest fictive architecture and sculpture in the classical style.

The lavish use of gold in the rendering of these antique scenes does, however, belie the qualities of austerity and gravity that were imputed to grisaille painting in the Renaissance. Clearly the artist was interested in more decorative effects, achieving as a result a palette not unlike that found on Limoges enamel. It would be logical to suppose that the shield painter was attempting to imitate the elaborate embossed iron shields damascened in gold and silver that were the specialty of Milanese armorers. The Kienbusch Collection possesses a fine example of this type as a point of comparison.[28] The format of these iron shields is similar, with the center of the shield's exterior occupied by a narrative scene from ancient history surrounded by a border of ornamental strapwork and trophies. It must be noted, however, that this type of shield of embossed and damascened iron with elaborate multifigured narrative subjects appears to be unknown, or at least undocumented, before about 1550. Indeed, it may be that, on the contrary, the Kienbusch shield and others like it preceded the familiar embossed iron shield and conceivably may have served as inspiration for the armorer to expand decoration to include narrative scenes.

In the 1963 Kienbusch catalogue, the provenance of the shield was given as the dukes of Ferrara, Archduke Franz Ferdinand d'Este, and an anonymous sale in Paris in 1954. Additional information on this subject is found in the Kienbusch files in the Philadelphia Museum of Art and in the Department of Arms and Armor at the Metropolitan Museum of Art, New York. The shield was last recorded in the armory at Konopiště Castle, near Prague, in 1944, the contents of which were inventoried by Hans Schedelmann that year.[29] After World War II the shield appears to have been traded out of Konopiště in an exchange with a private collector, Theodore Wollner,[30] who sold it at a sale conducted by Galerie Charpentier in Paris on April 1–2, 1954, lot 23.[31] The shield was bought in and was subsequently acquired privately by Mr. Kienbusch directly from the owner.

The armory at Konopiště Castle is known to contain portions of the former armory of the Este family, dukes of Ferrara from 1208 to 1597, and this no doubt suggested to the cataloguers of the Kienbusch shield that it, too, had once belonged to the Este family. A closer look at the formation of the Konopiště armory does not, however, support these conclusions. Konopiště Castle contains a large and important collection of arms and armor, much of it of Italian origin.[32] The nucleus of the collection does indeed come from the Este family. With the death of Alfonso II in 1597, the Ferrara line became extinct, and the ducal title, together with the Este collection, was transferred to the Este branch at Modena. The last of the line, Ercole III, Duke of Modena and Reggio, died in 1803, and with that the Este inheritance passed by marriage into the hands of the Austrian archdukes, founding a new Hapsburg-Este line. In 1875 this branch, too, died out and the title and inheritance passed to Archduke Franz Ferdinand (1863–1914), who later became heir to the imperial throne. Following the union of Modena with the new Italian state in 1860, the Hapsburgs were allowed to remove portions of the Este Collection to Vienna, where much of it remains today in the Kunsthistorisches Museum. The armory, on the other hand, was moved in 1904 from Vienna to the neo-Gothic castle of Konopiště, which Franz Ferdinand had purchased at the end of the previous century. Following the assassination of its owner at Sarajevo in 1914 and the collapse of the Austro-Hungarian monarchy following World War I, the Konopiště collections were nationalized by the Czechoslovakian state, and the castle was eventually opened as a public museum.

In spite of the presumed Este provenance of many of the pieces in the Konopiště armory, the majority seems to have come from other sources. A large portion of the armory is made up of pieces coming from Catajo Castle, near Padua, where a large collection of arms and armor had been assembled by several generations of the counts Obizzi.[33] Some of the arms were those actually used by the Obizzi, who were *condottiere* in Venetian service from the fifteenth through the seventeenth century. The last of the line, Tommaso degli Obizzi, seems to have been a collector in the modern sense, and he is thought to have acquired many pieces from the Medici armory following its dispersal around 1775. Catajo Castle and its contents were bequeathed by Tommaso in 1803 to Ercole III, the last Este duke of Modena, who died in the same year. The Catajo armory, merged with that of the Este, thus passed into Hapsburg possession and ultimately to Konopiště. In addition to the Este and Obizzi sources, the Konopiště armory seems to have included pieces from Archduke Franz Ferdinand's collection, some of which may have been of old Hapsburg provenance, while others must have been acquired on the art market in the late nineteenth century.[34] Given the eclectic nature of the collection, a Konopiště provenance cannot be taken as *prima facie* evidence for the Kienbusch shield having once belonged to the dukes of Ferrara.

The Kienbusch shield has not been identified in any of the Este inventories preserved today in the Archivio di Stato, Modena, nor in the contents of Catajo Castle that were inventoried following the death of its owner in 1803. Dating from the seventeenth and eighteenth centuries, and therefore before the inclusion of the Catajo armory, the Este inventories contain no reference to painted shields of any kind.[35] The Catajo inventory lists a number of wooden shields, but none is described as having painted decoration.[36]

By sheer good fortune a shield exactly matching the description of that now in the Kienbusch Collection has been discovered in the inventories of the Medici armory in Florence. Perhaps the largest and most important collection of its kind in Italy, the Medici armory was housed from about 1588 to 1775 in four galleries of the Uffizi.[37] The collection was augmented in 1631 with the armory of the dukes of Urbino, which was transferred to Florence on the occasion of the betrothal of Vittoria della Rovere, the last of the Urbino line, to Ferdinando II de'Medici. An inventory begun on October 14, 1631, records the contents of both armories, though the descriptions tend to be very summary. Subsequent inventories contain progressively more detailed descriptions and are therefore more helpful in identifying surviving pieces. The Kienbusch shield is identifiable in several of these.

It is first recognizable in the Medici inventory of 1695, where it is listed as "a wooden shield painted with a battle in chiaroscuro, with gilded costumes, showing the assault on a fortress, with a border around it with tiny gold arabesques, and painted similarly underneath with another battle, with an arm sling of green velvet."[38] In 1730 it caught the attention of the German tourist Johann Georg Keyssler (1693–1743), who observed in the Medici armory "some shields painted by Raphael, another which represents the storming of a city by Julius Romanus."[39] It is interesting to note that the perceptive attribution of the painting to Giulio Romano may be that of Keyssler himself, or perhaps his guide, but it is not repeated in the Medici inventories. The shield is found again in the last complete inventory of the armory, that made in 1747.[40]

In 1773 the Medici armory was deemed an unnecessary relic of the feudal past, and its dispersal was ordered by the director of the galleries. While some objects were retained for their historic associations or technical interest, many others were sold or destroyed to extract the value of their precious metal or stones. In October 1775, several hundred pieces were sent to the director of artillery at the Fortezza da Basso, possibly for decorative display. The list of these items includes the final mention in Florentine documents of the Kienbusch shield: "No. 221. A shield of fig wood varnished black, with touches of gold, representing an assault on a fortress."[41] While some of the arms sent to the Fortezza remained in Florence and are now housed with the remnants of the Medici armory in the Museo Nazionale del Bargello, the Kienbusch shield seems to have passed out of Florence, perhaps by means of the antiquarian trade.

The presence of the Kienbusch shield in the Medici armory suggests that, depending on its dating, it could have belonged either to Alessandro de'Medici (1511–1537), Duke of Florence from 1530, or Cosimo I de'Medici (1519–1574), his successor in 1537 and Grand Duke of Tuscany from 1569. On the other hand, if the shield entered the Florentine collections with the transfer of the Urbino armory in 1631, then it presumably belonged either to Francesco Maria della Rovere (1490–1538), Duke of Urbino from 1508, or to his son, Guidobaldo II (1514–1574). Unfortunately, because the two armories had already been combined by 1695, the date of the first inventory in which the Kienbusch shield is identifiable, it is impossible now to identify from which of the two sources it comes.

Related Shields

As noted above, painted shields formerly existed in considerable numbers, though many have presumably perished as a result of their fragile construction and decoration. Among the known examples, however, six can be identified as sufficiently close to the Kienbusch shield in medium, style, and subject matter as to have been painted in the same atelier. Three additional shields can be associated with that workshop, although there are certain differences in style that suggest a different hand. Another example, known only from a drawing, can also be included in this group. The corpus thus comprises eleven shields, including the Kienbusch example.

These shields are of the same circular, convex shape, the same construction, and approximately the same size. Each is painted on both sides in grisaille on a gold ground, with many details rendered by means of sgraffito. The principal surfaces are covered with densely packed figural scenes after ancient history or classical legend, with the costumes and accouterments rendered in painstaking detail. The faces of the men and women are expressive, especially the eyes, and the thick hair and beards of the men are rendered in elaborate curls. The horses, particularly those engaged in battle, are intensely animated, their bulging eyes and bared teeth suggesting the height of fury. The exterior of each shield is painted with a single scene with large figures, and the interior, with its two scenes above and below the arm-pad, is invariably more delicately painted. The interiors are generally better preserved than the exteriors, the concave shape having protected the inner surfaces from abrasion. These shields also have the same style of border, usually with bands of circles, strapwork, and arabesques incised through the paint to the gold ground, the bands framed by gold lines and dots of white paint. The rims are further embellished with scales painted in white, usually with a dot in the center of each.

Four of the shields are painted on their exteriors with scenes from Roman history, although—unlike the Kienbusch shield—the subjects of their narrative episodes have yet to be satisfactorily identified. One of these is in the Metropolitan Museum of Art, New York (fig. 82).[42] The condition of the shield, particularly the exterior, is better preserved than that in the Kienbusch Collection, having suffered comparatively minor paint loss. On its exterior is a crowded scene of Roman soldiers gathered in a wooded encampment. The commander is seated on a dais at the center, before whom a kneeling figure offers a wide bowl. Two other soldiers, one to each side of the seated figure, hold similar bowls, which appear to be filled with coins. Figures in the foreground examine pieces of armor, presumably trophies of war. The scene may represent the presentation to Scipio of the rich booty captured at New Carthage, an account Livy gives in considerable detail.[43] The interior of the shield is painted with two battle scenes, the upper one taking place outside the encampment, the lower one around the camp's tents. Neither scene has been specifically identified, although they are presumably related to the subject of the narrative on the shield's exterior.

The provenance of the Metropolitan's shield can be traced to the early nineteenth century, when it was part of the small but choice collection of arms and armor assembled by the English painter James Philippe Loutherbourg (1740–1812). Following the artist's death his collection was purchased and exhibited in London by the entrepreneur and dealer Thomas Gwennap. In the earliest of Gwennap's catalogues the shield is said to have belonged to Loutherbourg "who supposed it to be painted by Julio Romano," an attribution of particular interest in light of the Giulio influence seen in the Kienbusch shield. Gwennap, on the other hand, added an opinion of his own that "it was probably more of the manner of the equally eminent disciple of Raphael's Polidoro Da Caravaggio."[44] Polidoro's name has in subsequent years become attached to several of these shields because of their grisaille decoration, a

*Fig. 82. Exterior and interior (p. 115) of pageant shield. The Metropolitan Museum of Art,
New York, Gift of Stephen V. Grancsay, 1942; acc. no. 42.50.16.*

specialty of that artist. The Gwennap Collection was sold in 1833, and the shield subsequently passed into the collections of Sir Adam Hay, Clarence H. Mackay, and Stephen V. Grancsay.[45]

Two other shields from this series are in the Louvre (figs. 83, 84).[46] Both were formerly part of the collection of drawings and paintings assembled by Everard Jabach, which was purchased in its entirety by Louis XIV in 1671. Catalogued by the painter Charles LeBrun in 1681, the shields were attributed to Giulio Romano. It has recently been suggested that both may have come from the Earl of Arundel's collection, from which Jabach is known to have acquired many items, and before that possibly the Gonzaga armory in Mantua. The validity of this suggestion will be considered in connection with one shield still at Arundel. Like the Kienbusch shield and that in the Metropolitan Museum, the Louvre shields illustrate events in

A RENAISSANCE PAINTED SHIELD

115

Fig. 83. Exterior and details of the exterior (p. 117) of pageant shield. Musée du Louvre, Paris; inv. no. OA1138.

Roman history. On one (no. OA1138), the exterior is painted with a naval battle between two distinct groups of warriors (fig. 83). One group, readily identifiable as Romans, wears classical armor, carries banners bearing the letters SPQR, and fights with straight swords. Their opponents, a fierce-looking band dressed in exotic hats and turbans, and armed with curved swords, are probably intended to be understood as one of the Asian, Middle Eastern, or North African (Carthaginian?) nations with which Rome was periodically at war. The interior is painted with two battle scenes between warriors dressed similarly in classical armor. Roman banners with the SPQR emblem are visible, but the identity of the opposing forces is not distinguishable.

The second Louvre shield (no. OA 1139) depicts on its exterior the abduction of a queen, distinguished by her crown, who is pulled into an awaiting boat (fig. 84). Around her soldiers fight a pitched battle while other females are seized and carried off toward the shore. In the rear, at the top of the shield, is a high-walled city. The interior is painted with two closely related scenes that presumably refer to the same tale. Above the arm-pad is a scene of soldiers bearing spoils and crossing a narrow bridge while a coastal city burns behind them. The soldiers are met midway by a group of females, guarded by soldiers, who seem to stop them. Below the arm-pad, the story appears to continue, with the females and booty-carrying soldiers continuing across the bridge.

Fig. 84. Exterior (top), interior (bottom), and detail of the upper exterior (p. 119) of pageant shield. Musée du Louvre, Paris; inv. no. OA1139.

STUART W. PYHRR AND EVERETT FAHY

118

The shield belonging to the Duke of Norfolk at Arundel Castle (fig. 85) can also be attributed to the same hand.[47] The exterior represents a pitched battle between two forces dressed in classical armor. In the background, soldiers carrying sacks of booty emerge from the swirling smoke of a burning city and hurry across a bridge; anchored ships are seen in the distance. The equestrian figure in the center has his spear poised above a warrior on the ground below. The pose of the horseman clearly derives from that of the figure of Constantine in Giulio Romano's *Battle of Constantine* (fig. 81), echoes of which were also noted in the figures on the interior of the Kienbusch shield and that in the Metropolitan Museum. The elaborate caparisons of the horses are also very similar to those depicted on the Kienbusch and the Metropolitan Museum shields.

The scenes on the interior of the Arundel shield are more readily identifiable. They illustrate two legendary deeds of Roman valor and self-sacrifice recorded by Livy (Book VII)— Mucius Scaevola plunging his hand into the flames, and Marcus Curtius jumping into the abyss. Both heroes were popular examples of virtue during the Renaissance, as they were in antiquity, and are frequently encountered in the decoration of sixteenth-century armor.[48]

The borders on the interior and exterior of the Arundel shield are notably different in design from one another. The band on the exterior has delicate foliate scrollwork reminiscent

Fig. 85. Exterior and interior
(p. 121) of pageant shield.
Arundel Castle.

of that encircling the exterior of the Kienbusch shield and, to a lesser extent, on the
Metropolitan Museum's example, and is very close to that on the Louvre shield number OA
1138. The interior of the Arundel shield has wide borders painted with a continuous,
undulating scroll of vines with broad leaves and encircling tendrils. This pattern is not repeated
on any of the shields previously discussed, although its large scale and bold design recall the
borders on the interior of the Metropolitan Museum's shield. The rim of the Arundel shield is
also painted with white scales and dots.

   With the two examples in the Louvre, the Arundel shield is one of the few whose history
can be traced prior to the nineteenth century. The shield belonged to Thomas Howard (1585–
1646), Earl of Arundel, one of the greatest English art patrons of the seventeenth century. The
shield seems to have been highly valued by its owner, as it appeared in several versions (one
dated 1643) of the Howard family portrait (fig. 86) by the Antwerp-born painter Philip
Fruytiers (1610–1665).[49] In this portrait the earl and his wife receive their grandchildren, who
approach the seated couple carrying what is clearly this shield, as well as a gilt rapier of early
seventeenth-century type, a burgonet with embossed decoration, probably Italian about
1560–70, and a gauntlet of sixteenth-century type.[50] The portrait would appear to have

dynastic implications, as the earl and his wife are seated in front of Holbein's portraits of Arundel's ancestors Thomas Howard (1473–1554), 3rd Duke of Norfolk, and his son Henry Howard (1517–1547), the Earl of Surrey. In this context, it is possible that the shield and other arms, seemingly out of date and out of place for the non-militant earl, may be those of Thomas Howard, who served as Earl Marshal of England. Whatever their iconographic significance in connection with the portrait, the pieces may have had no direct family associations but could have been acquired by Arundel, a noted antiquarian, for their artistic and historic interest. This is almost certainly true for the shield.

The Arundel shield is probably one of the ten wooden painted and gilded shields recorded in the countess of Arundel's inventory of 1654 ("10 scudi de legno depinto et lavorato con oro").[51] It has been suggested that these shields may have been acquired by Arundel from the Gonzaga Collection in Mantua, from which the earl is known to have acquired important works of art.[52] However, the fifteen painted shields recorded in the Gonzaga inventory of 1542 are not encountered in the later inventories of the Mantuan armory and may have been lost in the fire that badly damaged the armory in 1609, four years before Arundel visited Mantua.[53] Whatever the source of the shields, it is likely that the earl,

Fig. 86. The Earl of Arundel and His Family, *by Philip Fruytiers (Flemish, 1610–1665). Oil on canvas. Arundel Castle.*

like Jabach later in the seventeenth century, acquired them as works of art, as examples of Italian design and painting of which he was a recognized connoisseur.

The shield eventually passed into the hands of the Earl of Stafford, but was reacquired for Arundel in the mid-eighteenth century by Stafford's cousin, the 9th Duke of Norfolk. By that time a legend had developed that it had been given to the Earl of Surrey by the Grand Duke of Tuscany at a tournament. This legend, first recorded by the antiquary George Vertue (1684–1756), who also made a careful drawing of the shield, is entirely without basis, however, as the poet earl never went to Florence.[54] This apocryphal story has also been repeated several times in arms and armor literature and has contributed to the otherwise unfounded belief that this and other shields like it were created as tournament prizes.[55]

A second group of shields attributable to the same workshop as those discussed above are painted with scenes from Ovid's *Metamorphoses* (Book VIII). Three of these depict the Hunt of the Calydonian Boar, in which Ovid recounts the tale of the hero Meleager who, with the assistance of the huntress Atalanta, slayed the fierce boar that had been sent by Diana to terrify the land of Calydon.[56] The finest of the shields, indeed the only complete one, is in the Historisches Museum in Dresden (fig. 87).[57] The hunt is painted on the exterior with the boar in the center of a knot of hunters on horseback whose spears are aimed, ready for the kill. The equestrian figure at the center and the boar beneath his leaping horse appear to have been inspired by a Roman sarcophagus relief, presumably transmitted by means of sixteenth-century sketches.[58] On the interior are two scenes, presumably episodes of Roman history, that are apparently unrelated to the Meleager theme. The upper scene is set in a richly furnished interior, with tapestries depicting battles lining the walls, spiral columns decorated with garlands, a tiled floor, and a multibranched chandelier overhead. Around two sides of the room are seated fifteen gesticulating figures wearing heavy robes and turbans and other elaborate headdresses. Their attention is focused on a fully armed soldier standing before them, his right hand holding a sword aloft, the left extended forward. Behind him a group of similarly dressed soldiers, apparently his comrades, motion toward him. This scene has previously been identified as Rome's declaration of war on Carthage,[59] but, on the other hand, it might also be interpreted as Scipio's exhorting his fearful comrades not to flee Italy after Rome's disastrous defeat by Hannibal at Cannae.[60] The scene below the arm-pad and the narrow spaces at its sides are filled with a violent battle of soldiers on horseback engaged in hand-to-hand combat. This shield retains what appears to be an original arm-pad and portions of the matching arm-straps covered in green velvet, the same color fabric as was originally on the Kienbusch shield.[61] The borders along the exterior and interior, forming a pattern of overlapping circles and arabesques, are related to the borders found on the inside of the Kienbusch shield and the outside of the Louvre shield number OA 1139.

The Dresden shield comes from the armory of the prince electors of Saxony and is probably the one described in the inventory of 1606 as "a round shield on which a hunt is painted in colors."[62] The source from which the shield entered the Saxon collections is not known.

The Hunt of the Calydonian Boar is also the subject of two other shields from this group. One, now apparently lost, belonged to Emperor Charles V and is represented in the *Inventario Iluminado*, the illustrated inventory of his personal armory, made between 1544 and 1558 (fig. 88).[63] The shield is illustrated in pen and ink, washed with white, black, and yellow, colors suggesting that it was painted in grisaille on gold. Though only summarily sketched, the scene on the exterior clearly shows a boar hunt with figures on horseback placed approximately in the same positions as those on the Dresden shield, with the exception of the boar, whose pose is reversed. Each depiction has at its center a bearded male figure (Meleager) on a rearing horse, his arm raised overhead to thrust his spear; to each side are hunters, one of them, Atalanta, drawing her bow, another hurling a spear. A leaping stag pursued by dogs is seen in the wooded background of each composition. Were it not for the reversal of the boar, one would almost assume that the shield of Charles V, which can no longer be traced, is that found today in Dresden. It is not likely, however, that the artist recording the shield in the *Inventario Iluminado* would have reversed the boar by mistake, and there is no evidence to indicate that the Dresden shield came from Madrid before it was recorded in the prince elector's armory in 1606. The likely explanation is that the Dresden shield is a replica of that in Charles V's collection. It is logical to assume that both were painted in the same atelier.

The same subject is found on a third example that was formerly in the private collection

*Fig. 87. Exterior (top), interior (bottom; p. 124), and detail of exterior (above) of pageant shield.
Historisches Museum, Dresden; inv. no. N. 71.*

Fig. 88. Illustration of a painted shield in the Inventario Iluminado, *album of pen and wash drawings illustrating the contents of the armory of Emperor Charles V, c. 1544–58, Real Amería, Madrid; inv. no. N18.*

Fig. 89. Portions from the interior of pageant shield formerly in the collection of Bashford Dean.

of Dr. Bashford Dean, Curator of Arms and Armor at the Metropolitan Museum (fig. 89). All that survives of the shield are the painted cloth portions that were originally located above and below the arm-pad on the shield's inner side. The shield's exterior and wooden core were probably so badly damaged that only the painted areas on the inside could be salvaged. These were cut out and glued to a flat board. Not surprisingly, the surfaces are heavily abraded, with major losses of paint. Nothing is known of this shield before 1919, at which time the shield was in its present altered state.[64]

The boar hunt on the upper half of the Dean shield corresponds closely to that on the Dresden shield, with the boar in the center encircled by dogs, and male and female hunters on horseback riding in for the kill. The gold costumes and horse trappings are generally similar to those on the Dresden example, although they are not direct copies. The pose of the male figure at the center of the hunters, presumably Meleager, and that of his horse, his costume, and such details as his plumed helmet and forked beard, are similar to the corresponding figure on the Dresden shield. A second boar hunt on the lower half of the shield appears to be a variant of the upper one, although in the lower scene Atalanta is the only female, and the majority of the hunters are on foot. Atalanta, with her elaborate coiffure, prominent breasts, and fluttering cape, is especially close to her Dresden counterpart. The border decoration, which consists of bands filled with overlapping circles, with scrollwork in the background, is almost identical to that on the inner side of the Dresden shield. The outer edge of the Dean shield is painted with the same pattern of scales, with a dot inside each scale, as on the other shields in this group.

Another painted shield with scenes inspired by Ovid's tales of the Olympian gods is in the Victoria and Albert Museum, London (fig. 90).[65] Its exterior is painted with the Battle of the Lapiths and Centaurs at the wedding of Hippodamia (*Metamorphoses*, Book XII). In the center is the centaur Eurytus, who, driven by wine and lust, attempts to abduct the bride while fighting off Hercules (distinguished by his golden lion skin cloak), one of the invited guests. A melée ensues around this group, with women shrieking in terror as swords are flashed among the guests. A clutter of plates and food and overturned tables are scattered beneath the feet of the protagonists. The scene is set in a columned loggia of four bays, with a classical cityscape in the distance.

The interior of the shield is painted at the top with a scene of Mucius Scaevola plunging his hand into the fire, a variant of the image found in the same place on the Arundel shield. The organization of the scene is generally similar to that on the Arundel shield, but many details have been changed, including the positions of the figures and the details of the costumes. The overall quality of the drawing and the rendering of the faces are much cruder, suggesting that it may have been painted by another craftsman within the same workshop. The coloring, too, is different, with less area of white and gold, and a greater emphasis on scratched or hatched areas.

The impression that a different hand is at work is further reinforced by the battle scene at the bottom of the interior, now almost obliterated by paint loss. The figures are dressed in sixteenth-century armor and wear the puffed and slashed costumes associated with the

German mercenaries (*Landsknechte*) of the first half of the sixteenth century. The elaborate horse trappings relate the figures to the other shields of this group, but only on this example is contemporary costume mixed with the antique.

The borders of this shield on the front and the back are different. The border of overlapping concentric circles on the exterior matches those found on the Dresden shield and on the fragmentary Dean example. The border on the interior, formed of interlaced scrolling foliage, is comparable to those on the exteriors of the Metropolitan Museum shield, the Louvre shield OA1138, and the Arundel shield. The rim is painted with scales in white as on the other shields, but within each scale is a fleur-de-lis rather than a dot. This feature also distinguishes the Victoria and Albert Museum shield from the rest.

Two more shields can be added to this group in so far as they relate by size, technique, and iconography. They differ, however, from the Kienbusch shield and the related examples already discussed, in the absence of the distinctive detail of costumes and accessories. The compositions are more simplified and the painting is more broadly rendered. Despite these differences, they are sufficiently close to the Kienbusch group as to have been painted in the same atelier but perhaps by a different hand.

The first of these shields, in the Museo Civico, Turin, is, like the Kienbusch shield, painted on its exterior with the *Storming of New Carthage* (fig. 91).[66] The Turin example, however, follows Giulio's drawing quite literally and does not elaborate on the composition or costumes as does the Kienbusch shield. The Turin shield parts from Giulio's model by the addition of the della Rovere arms (a golden oak tree on a red field) on the shield of one of the soldiers scaling the walls. It must also be noted that some of the simplification and occasionally rather crude details on the outer surface of the Turin shield appear to be the result of the restoration and overpainting to which it has been subjected.

The style and quality of the painting on the Turin shield can be appreciated better on the interior, which is still well preserved. Here, in contrast to the battle scenes on the inside of the Kienbusch shield, we find two mythological scenes set within a forest clearing. In the upper scene, the mischievous Cupid, accompanied by a young hunter, fires an arrow at a nymph while her companions flee in alarm; in the scene below, the young man and Cupid emerge from the trees into the clearing, around which sit the nymphs. The lack of alarm among the females suggests that Cupid's arrow has hit its intended mark. The bows and arrows carried by the nymphs relate these episodes to the legend of Diana, but neither scene corresponds exactly to the Olympian tales recounted by Ovid.

Comparing the interiors of the Turin and Philadelphia shields, one finds in the former a more open and calm rendering of the scene, with fewer fussy details than on the Kienbusch shield. The faces on the Turin shield are cruder and more homely. There are, however, a number of similarities that indicate a close connection between the two shields, notably the use of a forest backdrop for the interior scenes, and the similar manner in which the narrow areas between the sides of the arm-pad and the edge of the shield are filled with trees. The

Fig. 90. Exterior (top) and interior (bottom)
of pageant shield. Victoria and Albert Museum, London; inv. no. 174-1869.

Fig. 91. Exterior and interior
(p. 131) of pageant shield. Museo
Civico D'Arte Antica, Turin; inv.
no. 5.

border of the arm-pad on the Turin shield is painted with intertwining branches entirely
appropriate to the forest scenes above and below. This border, and the framing bands of
double gilt lines and white dots, are features very similar to those of the Kienbusch shield.

The shield in Turin was donated to the Museo Civico in 1890 by Marchese Emanuele
d'Azelio, without reference to its earlier provenance. However, the incorporation of the della
Rovere arms in the decoration on the exterior suggests that it belonged to one of the dukes of
Urbino, presumably either Francesco Maria della Rovere, duke from 1508 to 1537, or his son
Guidobaldo II, who ruled from 1537 to 1574. One of these men may also have owned the
Kienbusch shield. The scene on the shield's exterior has been identified as the siege of Pesaro,
which was conducted by Francesco Maria in 1512. In light of the discovery of the source of
this scene as the *Storming of New Carthage,* this identification must be corrected. The painting
has been ascribed to Polidoro de Caravaggio, who, as noted earlier, was famous in the 1520s
for his building facades and interiors decorated with Roman histories painted in grisaille;
however, this attribution has generally not met with critical acceptance.[67]

At the time of the Medici exhibition in Florence in 1980, the Turin shield was published
as fitting the description in the Medici armory inventories beginning in 1695; the Kienbusch

shield was cited as a comparable example.[68] Looking at the inventory descriptions more carefully, with their references to the underside painted with "another battle," there can be no doubt that it is indeed the Kienbusch shield, not the Turin example, that is referred to. It seems unlikely that the Ovidian scenes on the interior of the Turin shield, in which the majority of figures are female, would have been mistaken for a battle scene. The presence of the della Rovere arms on the Turin shield points to it as having once been in the Urbino armory, but it would seem that the shield either passed out of the collection before it was transferred to Florence, or it is unidentifiable among the surviving inventories. The Medici inventories mention in great detail a number of painted shields, but only one is described as depicting a siege on the outside and battle scenes on the inside.[69] The Kienbusch shield matches this description exactly.

The last shield of this group is more closely related to the Turin example than to that in Philadelphia. It is presently in the possession of Wildenstein and Company, New York, where it is currently attributed to Baldassare Peruzzi (Italian, 1481–1536; fig. 92).[70] The exterior is painted in grisaille on a gold and black ground with what appears to be a version of the Diana legend. In the center stands a robed female holding a spear, her left arm raised in a gesture to

Fig. 92. Exterior and interior
(p. 133) of pageant shield.
Wildenstein and Company,
New York.

the females around her, one of whom holds a bow. To the viewer's left, Cupid ushers into this
sylvan setting a male hunter, presumably Actaeon. Behind the figures is a deep wooded
landscape, including mountains and rustic buildings.

The interior is painted with two scenes from Ovid's story of Diana and Actaeon
(*Metamorphoses*, Book III). In the upper scene the hunter Actaeon accidentally encounters
Diana and her nymphs at their bath. The hunter stands in the center, his hands outstretched in
surprise. Facing him, Diana cups her hands with water in preparation to splash him, which
will result in his transformation into a stag. In the lower scene the stag/Actaeon is attacked by
six hunters and their dogs and is killed.

The style of painting of the Wildenstein shield is more closely related to the example in
Turin than to any of the other previously discussed shields. While it is painted in the same
grisaille and sgraffito technique as the Kienbusch shield, one notes a greater simplification in
the figures, their costumes, and even the borders. The faces on the Wildenstein shield are
coarser, like those on the Turin example, the movements more awkward and less animated.
The overall effect is calmer and more classical, and decidedly less decorative. One notices, too,

that the border decoration is less inventive and the framework for the arm-pad is more rigidly rectangular in shape. The heavy "roping," suggested by parallel slashes of white paint, that frames the arabesque border is unlike that found on any of the other shields. As the outer edges are now hidden from view by a heavy wooden frame, it is difficult to know if the rim is painted with scales, as on the other shields of this group. The border around the exterior scene, with its band of gold arabesques and strapwork framed by double gold lines and white dots, is very similar to the decorative framework on the aforementioned shields and thus, despite the differences, firmly connects this shield to the main group.

The existence of so many shields of similar form, technique, and theme, not to mention stylistic unity, suggests that at least some of them may have been created for a specific event such as a court pageant or a triumph. The quality of the painting, full of Renaissance invention and painstakingly rendered detail, implies considerable expense as well as artistic talent and bespeaks the importance of the event. Retracing the early history of the surviving shields has not revealed a common source, as none has been identified with certainty before the early seventeenth century. However, the presence of at least one of these shields in the collection of

Charles V, with others imputed to the ownership of the Medici or della Rovere families, as well as the Gonzaga of Mantua, suggests the possibility that they might have been created for use in the ceremonies surrounding the triumphal progress of Charles V through Italy in 1535–36.[71] In August 1535 Charles V landed in Sicily, as his first stop in an eighteen-month-long stay in Italy. The emperor had just concluded a successful military campaign against Barbarossa's pirates in North Africa, with the taking of their stronghold at La Goletta and the subjugation of Tunis. Charles entered Messina in triumph, with *all'antica* decorations that evoked humanistic and historical parallels of Scipio and Hannibal, as well as references to Alexander the Great and Julius Caesar. Polidoro da Caravaggio, a master of antique-style painting in grisaille to whom several painted shields have been attributed, was in charge of the decoration. The emperor repeated his triumphal entries *all'antica* on the peninsula in Naples and then Rome, where Battista Franco (1510–1580) executed great canvases of the triumphs of the two Scipios, father and son, hailing Charles as the "Third Scipio," and where Francesco Salviati (1510–1563) painted *storie di chiaroscuro* (histories in grisaille). Similar celebrations were offered in Siena and Florence before the emperor returned to Spain in December 1536.

The siege of New Carthage by Scipio, the subject of the exterior of the Kienbusch shield, is particularly relevant in connection with Charles V's African campaign. The Muslim pirates had often plundered Spanish coastal towns, as well as those in Charles's domain in Sicily and Naples. Barbarossa commanded a large Turkish fleet, which was harbored beneath the walls of La Goletta. Personally leading his troops, Charles V besieged the fortress for three weeks, finally storming the walls on July 14, 1535. Like the combined land and sea forces commanded by Scipio against New Carthage, imperial artillery on land and at sea commenced the attack; under this bombardment sappers mined the walls. Following a bloody assault, the walls were breached and the imperial banner was raised overhead. The victory yielded considerable booty and the capture of Barbarossa's fleet of eighty-two ships.

As the descriptions of the imagery employed in the emperor's triumphs attest, the historic parallel between Charles V's victories in Africa and those of Scipio were certainly not lost on his contemporaries. With the reference to Scipio on the Kienbusch shield, and possibly also on those in New York, Paris, Dresden, and Arundel Castle, it is tempting to speculate that they may have served as an illustrated account of this celebrated chapter of Roman history that had such timely relevance in 1535–36. A date in the mid-1530s would also correspond to the activity of the painter Girolamo da Treviso, to whom these shields have been convincingly attributed.

Fig. 93. The Adoration of the Shepherds *(and detail), by Girolamo da Treviso (Italian, c. 1497–1544). Panel, Fogg Art Museum, Cambridge, Massachusetts.*

PART II · BY EVERETT FAHY

An Attribution to Girolamo da Treviso

Over ten years ago Stuart Pyhrr drew my attention to several early sixteenth-century parade shields that I recognized as the work of Girolamo di Tommaso da Treviso (c. 1497–1544), a versatile North Italian artist who worked as a painter, sculptor, printmaker, and engineer. The style of the shields' decoration is identical to that of two pictures by Girolamo in the Fogg Art Museum, Cambridge, Massachusetts (figs. 93, 94).[72] Moreover all are executed in the same curious technique. In making the pictures in the Fogg Art Museum and in decorating the processional shields, Girolamo employed an unconventional and highly demanding procedure. Their designs were achieved by a complex process incorporating painting in grisaille with sgraffito (here, the scraping away of paint applied over gold leaf) and impressing the exposed gold with a blunt stylus. Girolamo's intention may have been to imitate the effect of damascened metalwork, which is inlaid with gold or silver.

94

94

 95

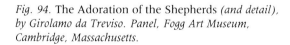

Fig. 94. The Adoration of the Shepherds *(and detail),* by Girolamo da Treviso. *Panel, Fogg Art Museum, Cambridge, Massachusetts.*

Fig. 95. The Adoration of the Magi, *by Girolamo da Treviso. Panel, National Gallery, London.*

Sometimes called Girolamo the Younger—to distinguish him from another painter from Treviso, Girolamo Pennacchi (c. 1450–1496)—Girolamo di Tommaso was born about 1497. The date of his birth is based upon Vasari's statement that he died in 1544 at the age of forty-six.[73] The first secure date concerning Girolamo is November 1523, when the artist was commissioned to paint an altarpiece for the hospital of San Biagio, Bologna, which unfortunately was destroyed in Dresden during World War II. Girolamo presumably moved from Treviso to Bologna when Bernardo de' Rossi, the bishop of Treviso (of whom Lorenzo Lotto made an unforgettable portrait in 1505, now in the Galleria Nazionale di Capodimonte, Naples), was elected papal legate to Bologna in 1519.[74] In 1524 the artist enrolled in the Bolognese guild of the Matricola delle Quattro Arti, and in the same year he carved several of the reliefs surrounding a portal on the facade of San Petronio. On November 24, 1525, Giovanni Antonio Saraceni, a wealthy Bolognese, commissioned Girolamo to decorate his family chapel in San Petronio with grisaille murals ("in chiaro e scuro") depicting the miracles of Saint Anthony of Padua. In the document for these surviving frescoes, Girolamo is called "viro magistro Hieronimo quondam Thome de Trivisio pictori ac sculptori" (master Girolamo, son of Tommaso of Treviso, painter and sculptor).[75] This citation provides evidence for the artist's standing as an independent master and also supplies his patronymic (proving that he could not have been the son of Girolamo Pennacchi, as many writers claim). From September to December 1527, Girolamo received payments for the frescoes he executed on Giulio Romano's designs in the Sala dei Venti of the Palazzo del Te, Mantua.[76] Shortly before 1529, Andrea Doria employed him to help decorate the facade of Palazzo del Principe, Genoa. In 1531 he completed an altarpiece for the church of San Salvatore, Venice, in which city he befriended the notorious Pietro Aretino. For Sabba da Castiglione, a knight of the Order of Saint John of Jerusalem, he painted in 1533 the exceptionally beautiful frescoes in the church of the Commenda at Faenza. (In his memoirs, published in Venice in 1584, Sabba da Castiglione remembered "Tarvisio" as a man "of quickness and resolution, and of excellent practice in all the secrets of his craft."[77]) In 1534 Girolamo worked in the Oratory of Santa Croce at Castelbolognese, on the road between Bologna and Faenza. From a letter of December 1537, we learn that the artist, still in Bologna, was willing to complete the carving of a funeral monument for Francesco Gonzaga of Mantua.[78] The last work Girolamo painted in Italy may have been the *Presentation of the Virgin in the Temple with Saint Thomas of Canterbury*, in San Salvatore, Bologna. As this picture originally stood over the altar of the English university students in Bologna, it may have led to the invitation Girolamo received to work for Henry VIII.[79] By August 1538, Pietro Aretino had heard from Girolamo in England.

Vasari, no doubt informed by Aretino, recorded that Girolamo "was thought a wonder by the king, who richly rewarded him with a pension of 400 crowns a year and the means to build a stately house." But this good fortune was not to last. England sided with Charles V of Spain in his fourth war against Francis I of France, and "Girolamo supervised the making of bastions and forts for the artillery. One day while riding a horse during the siege of Boulogne

[September 10, 1544] he was cut in two by a cannon ball, thereby losing his life and all his newly won honors."[80]

Girolamo da Treviso's career thus may be divided into three chronological phases, corresponding to the places of his principal activity: Treviso, Bologna, and England. From the first no documented work survives, but a handful of paintings and a woodcut of *Susanna and the Elders*, variously monogrammed *HIRTV*, *H.R.T.V.*, and *HIER.T.* (which may be deciphered as Hieronymous Tarvisii or Hieronymous Tarvisius), are now generally accepted as Girolamo's juvenilia. They are the work of an artist influenced on one hand by contemporary Venetian paintings and on the other by the prints of such diverse artists as Dürer and Marcantonio Raimondi. In one recently identified work of this period, a painting of the *Descent into Limbo*, in the Alte Pinakothek, Munich, the pose of Christ is a quotation from Dürer's woodcut of the same subject in the *Large Passion*.[81]

While resident in Bologna during the 1520s and 1530s, Girolamo must have studied Raphael's Saint Cecilia altarpiece (Pinacoteca Nazionale, Bologna), then in the church of San Giovanni in Monte, Bologna, and his *Vision of Ezekiel* (Galleria Palatina, Florence), then in the possession of Count Vincenzo Ercolani in Bologna. Girolamo also was exposed to Raphael's style through Raphael's pupils Giulio Romano, who settled at nearby Mantua in 1524, and Perino del Vaga, with whom Girolamo worked at Genoa in 1528. Girolamo's mature work also manifests an awareness of Parmigianino, who had settled in Bologna after the Sack of Rome in 1527.

Although Girolamo is said to have worked for Henry VIII "not as a painter but as an engineer,"[82] at least one painting by him survives from the last six years of his life. It is the *Anti-Papal Allegory* at Hampton Court Palace, which is feebly executed in grisaille with some touches of gold.[83]

The style of Girolamo's pictures in the Fogg Art Museum corresponds with that of his Bolognese work. The symmetrical compositions, teeming with figures in classical poses, depend more on Central Italian sources than on Girolamo's North Italian experience. In fact, their designs owe not a little to a celebrated drawing of which Girolamo painted a full-size copy (fig. 95). According to Vasari, Count Giambattista Bentivoglio commissioned the drawing from Baldassare Peruzzi (1481–1536), the great Sienese painter and architect, who, in 1522–23, worked at Bologna on plans to remodel the facade of San Petronio. Peruzzi's drawing was a "Nativity with the Magi, rendered in chiaroscuro [in this context, meaning with strong contrast between the ink and the lavish highlighting] . . . most gracefully executed. . . . The count subsequently had this work colored by Girolamo da Treviso, who did it most successfully."[84]

Centuries later both Peruzzi's drawing and Girolamo's copy of it followed the artist to England. They entered the collection of the National Gallery, London, in 1839 and 1849, respectively. The unusually large drawing (44¼ by 42⅛ inches) is signed by Peruzzi and corresponds to Vasari's description; the pedigree of the somewhat larger painting has some gaps but the facial types and the palette match those of Girolamo's documented work.[85]

Fig. 96. The Raising of the Cross, *by Girolamo da Treviso. Panel, London, art market, c. 1965.*

Fig. 97. Madonna of Saint George, *by Girolamo Comi (Italian, c. 1507–1581) after Correggio. Panel, City Art Gallery, York.*

In the much smaller pictures in the Fogg Art Museum, Girolamo, like the true eclectic artist he was, combined elements of Peruzzi's design with the heavy physical types of Giulio Romano. He also borrowed specific inventions, such as the figures cut off by the lower edge of one of the pictures (fig. 93), from Giulio's design for the fresco of the *Discovery of the Sacred Blood* in the basilica of Sant' Andrea, Mantua.[86]

The wooden supports of the pictures, as well as the shields, were prepared in the traditional method described in medieval treatises such as Cennino Cennini's *Il libro dell'arte*.[87] Fabric was then glued to the wood and several layers of white gesso were applied. When dry, the gesso was polished smooth, and the surface was covered with gold leaf. The artist then applied gray and black paint over the gold, modeling the pigment to achieve a grisaille effect. Some gold was left exposed for particulars such as the soldiers' sandals, indicating that the entire composition must have been worked out to the finest detail before the application of any paint. The artist then delicately scratched into the grisaille to expose bits of the underlying gold. The scratches are usually parallel and follow the fall of shadows. Girolamo's last refinement was also his most subtle. Taking a blunt stylus in hand, he scored selected areas of the gold ground, making tight *C* strokes, giving the surface a rough texture. The gold thus shimmers with varying intensity of reflected light.

Girolamo used the same technique in a small panel of the *Raising of the Cross* (fig. 96). As Andrea Bayer kindly pointed out to me, its design derives quite faithfully from Albrecht Altdorfer's woodcut of the same subject.[88]

Sgraffito is quite common in medieval paintings, particularly in the depiction of cloth-of-gold textiles. In the early fifteenth century, Gentile da Fabriano exploited its illusionistic potential. By the end of the century, however, only provincial artists employed the technique, and it was ignored by progressive painters such as Giovanni Bellini and Leonardo. From the sixteenth century I know of only one example outside Girolamo's oeuvre, a small grisaille copy of Correggio's *Madonna of Saint George*, at York (fig. 97).[89] Inscribed by Girolamo Comi (c. 1507–1581), a little-known painter from Modena, and dated 1530, it is executed in light gray paint over a stippled gold ground.

While the technique is thus almost unparalleled in sixteenth-century religious paintings and may even have struck some eyes as being rather odd for the rendering of biblical subjects, it certainly suited the decoration of parade shields. The style of the sgraffito decoration of the shields corresponds with that of Girolamo's Bolognese work of the 1530s. Given their uniform dimensions and the consistent format of the sgraffito decorations, the shields presumably are part of one commission. The varying level of quality of the decoration suggests that Girolamo entrusted some of the work to assistants. The variations may also be due to the state of preservation of the individual shields. Being fragile objects, they have not come down to us in pristine condition.

APPENDIX

Technical Note by Melissa S. Meighan

The sixteenth-century Italian parade shield from the Kienbusch collection was examined in the conservation laboratory of the Philadelphia Museum of Art in order to better understand the materials and methods of its manufacture.[90] For comparison, related shields in Philadelphia, at the Metropolitan Museum of Art in New York, and in several European and other American collections underwent more limited study.[91]

The Philadelphia shield is a well-crafted, complex object: circular and convex with some minor distortion of its form probably due to the warping of the wood core.[92] X-radiography has shown the core to be constructed of three thin strata, each stratum consisting of from eight to eleven wooden strips (*Populus*).[93] The strips, which taper in both width and thickness (coopering), are laid tightly against one another, presumably with adhesive between, and are clamped at a number of points with iron devices resembling staples. The middle stratum is horizontal and turned 90 degrees with respect to the strata above and below, and the strips in the outer layers are staggered with respect to each other.[94]

Bending the wood for this shield would have been relatively simple. Although steam is commonly used to soften and bend wood, strips this thin (maximum of 0.38 cm) can be shaped without any specialized technology. It is possible that these strips were bent when still green and therefore especially flexible.[95] In addition, moisture introduced by a water-soluble adhesive such as hide glue would have facilitated the shaping process. The shaping was probably assisted by the use of a simple convex form or a two-piece mold (a caul).

The Philadelphia and the Metropolitan shields have similar, notable features related to their manufacture that are visible in their x-radiographs (fig. 98), and non-existent on the x-radiographs of other shields examined. Approximately forty-six iron staples were counted in the Philadelphia shield, and over one hundred locations where staples have been removed (fig. 99). These locations are random except for a rather orderly progression around the rim, approximately 3 to 7.5 cm apart.[96]

Out of the forty-six extant staples more than 60 percent can be located on the obverse, and two or three staples can be associated with the middle layer. Taken with the numerous indications of areas where staples were pulled out, this tentatively suggests the following technique of manufacture.[97] Thin strips of wood were laid out on a solid convex form, held with staples to keep the strips pressed tightly one against the other and attached to the form while the layer was being assembled and adhesive applied. When proceeding to the next layer the majority of the staples would have been pulled out, probably reused, and the holes filled with a material such as gesso, which happens to be more radiographically opaque than wood. Some staples have been left in the final layer, with their "heads" countersunk and filled around to smooth the surface. The re-

maining staples would hold all three layers together, impart additional strength to the front, and yet still allow the completed shield to be removed from the underlying form.

Over the wooden core of the shield is a tabby-weave linen,[98] covered by a white ground, which has been identified as gypsum, the major component of common Italian gesso.[99] On top of the ground is an orange-red bole and a layer of gilding, which appears to cover the entire shield surface,[100] with the exception of a rectangle on the reverse which would have been covered by the arm-pad. Applied onto the gold are the pigment layers. A substantial number of the images (armor, tents, trees) are reserved in gold, that is, either left unpainted or scraped clean, with details added in black. For the remainder, there appears to be an overall, very medium-rich, black layer laid down directly on the gold with white, gray, and additional black paint building up the grisaille images. The pigments have been identified as carbon black and lead white. The medium appears to be egg tempera with additional protein glue in the black.[101] See figure 100 for a cross-section of the paint, gilding, and ground layers.

The final step, save the possible application of a varnish layer,[102] would have been the scratching of a rich variety of decorative patterns through the paint, exposing and impressing the gold. This technique, called sgraffito, is extensively and very effectively used on both the Philadelphia and the Metropolitan shields. Sgraffito (fig. 101) was used to make the elaborately decorated borders, to delineate details, and to enliven the background and introduce an overall glitter of gold, for example, in the towers of Carthage and on the ground beneath the warriors and the horses on the reverse.

Structurally the shield is relatively sound. Although its composite nature makes it vulnerable to variations in temperature and relative humidity, stability is imparted to the structure by the use of techniques that were probably developed for functional shields, primarily the cross-lamellar wood strips bound in cloth. The virtually complete layer of gold, albeit very thin, may additionally act as a moisture barrier. Nonetheless, vertical cracks on both the obverse and reverse reveal the joins between the wood strips. Along the edges there are numerous small areas where all layers down to the wood have been lost or seriously damaged. In several areas the iron staples have either expanded due to corrosion or moved and have raised the surface into low bulges. Many of these areas have been restored, making it difficult to understand exactly how serious such lifting was in the past. In general, the most obvious damage is the loss of original surface, which is more severe on the obverse than the reverse. There is a substantial amount of inpainting in the areas of loss.

The Metropolitan's shield is very similar in structure and in painting style to the Philadelphia example.[103] The x-radiographs of three other round, sixteenth-

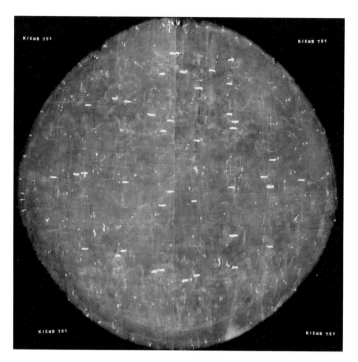

Fig. 98. X-radiograph
of the Kienbusch shield.

*Fig. 100. Cross-section of paint sample of
the Kienbusch shield under ultraviolet
illumination (taken at 400x
magnification).*

*Fig. 101. Photomicrograph of sgraffito on
the Kienbusch shield: detail of sword tip
touching horse's hoof in interior scene
above the arm-pad (see lower-right corner
of fig. 76).*

*Fig. 99. Detail of x-radiograph of the
Kienbusch shield showing several remaining
staples on the left and the locations of removed
staples on the right.*

century Italian shields in the Kienbusch Collection all show similar lamellar wood cores, with the lamellae ranging in number from two to four.[104] One of these (1977-167-753) is among examples of the known "Venetian-Salzburg" type, where the lamellar structure is covered with leather, metal foil, and glazed in several colors. Two examples of this type in the Museo Stibbert in Florence have been published as lamellar in structure.[105] At least five other round shields at the Museo Stibbert were observed to have lamellar structures: one attributed to the seventeenth century, two to the sixteenth century, and two to the fifteenth century.[106] The "Medusa" shield of Caravaggio, dated to c. 1596, presently in the Uffizi, Florence, is described as having a structure of layered poplar, seven horizontal pieces glued to eight vertical ones and covered with cloth then gesso.[107]

One of the most interesting group of shields examined during this investigation is that identified in the 1547 post-mortem inventory of the Tudor Royal Ar-

moury of Henry VIII. This group of round, convex shields have wood forms covered with iron plates, in several cases colored (blued or russeted) with gold decoration, and each is fitted with a matchlock gun, either placed in the middle of a central boss with a small window just above, or placed just above center. The group has long been associated with Giovanbattista de Ravenna because of a recorded letter dated 1544 documenting his offer to serve the court of Henry VIII and supply "several round shields and arm pieces with guns inside them that fire upon the enemy and pierce any armour."[108] Examination of fifteen of this group in London and one in the Walters Art Gallery in Baltimore, indicates that the wood substrate was cross-lamellar, apparently two layers thick.[109] This group is significant because it represents the use of lamellar wood structure for an apparently nonceremonial, albeit highly elaborate, shield type.[110] The common use of this structure for round shields is demonstrated by a comment in an Italian manuscript on ceramics technol-

modern varnish
warm white
gray-white with black
cool white (stray black)
black in fluorescent medium

red bole

traces of gesso

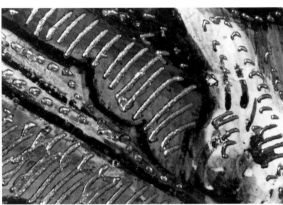

ogy, dated 1557, which recommends a similar method for making a potter's wheel, adding ''after the same fashion of overlay as round shields, or targes.''[111]

In addition to the structure of these shields, technical aspects of the surface decoration are of interest. As noted above, the surface of the Philadelphia shield consists virtually entirely of paint on top of gilding in order to allow for the large amount of sgraffito that makes up the decoration. This method presents problems due to the difficulty of the paint adhering to such a smooth, relatively non-porous surface. It is suggested by the unusual amount of medium added to the black paint directly on top of the gold layer, that the artist was aware of this problem and adjusted his formula to make the paint adhere better. The additional medium may also have facilitated the sgraffito process itself.[112]

Technically and stylistically, the large amount of gilding and sgraffito on these shields is not typical of sixteenth-century Italian panel painting or wooden objects. The gold, white, or silver and black scheme of these painted shields is more similar to that seen on the most elaborate metal ceremonial shields and armor of the period. Such metal pieces were sometimes highly worked with colored base metal and etched or engraved with patterns filled with gold, silver, or niello.[113] Whether these grisaille and sgraffito shields offered a less time-consuming and less expensive method of producing a shield for a special event, or were in and of themselves a prestigious commission for a painter has not been determined. However, given the metal objects known to be in production and given the tradition of monochromatic painting often being used to represent other materials, it seems clear that these wooden shields with grisaille painting and elaborate patterning in gold were created to imitate, even emulate, the metalwork of the armorers of the period.

NOTES / PART I

1 C. Otto von Kienbusch, *The Kretzschmar von Kienbusch Collection of Armor and Arms* (Princeton, N.J., 1963), p. 146, no. 299, pl. XCI.

2 See John F. Hayward, "The Revival of Roman Armour in the Renaissance," in *Art, Arms and Armour: An International Anthology*, edited by Robert Held (Chiasso, 1979), pp. 144–63.

3 On the subject of Renaissance painted shields, see Lionello G. Boccia, "Un inedito dello Stradano: la 'rotella Odescalchi,'" *L'Arte*, vol. 5 (1969), p. 113, n. 3, who lists about thirty examples dating from the late fifteenth century to the late sixteenth century. This list is by no means complete. Unfortunately, no serious attempt has been made by paintings specialists to identify the various groups by technique or style.

4 For Vasari's anecdote relating Leonardo's painting a shield, see Giorgio Vasari, *Le vite dé più eccellenti pittori, scultori, ed architettori* [1568], edited by Giovanni Milanesi, 9 vols. (Florence, 1878–85), vol. 4, p. 24. The shield signed by Stradano and dated 1574 was formerly part of the Odescalchi Collection (inv. no. 114), and is now in the Museo di Palazzo Venezia, Rome; see Boccia 1969, cited above. Not previously noted, this important shield corresponds to the description of one sold as part of the collection of Prince Pierre Soltykoff at the Hôtel Drouot, Paris, on April 18–22, 1854, lot 244. The famous "Medusa" shield by Caravaggio, painted c. 1596 for Cardinal Del Monte, is now in the Uffizi, Florence; see Detlef Heikamp, "La Medusa del Caravaggio e l'armatura dello Scià 'Abbâs di Persia,'" *Paragone*, n.s., vol. 17, no. 199 (September 1966), pp. 62–76.

5 See Adolfo Venturi, "Di un quadro inedito del Morto da Feltre," *L'Arte*, vol. 33 (1930), pp. 473–74, fig. 1. The painting was then in the hands of the London dealer A. L. Nicholson, who, twenty years later, lent it for exhibition in the Arcade Gallery, London, 1950, cat. no. 1 (according to a note on a photograph of the painting in the Witt Library, University of London), but its present whereabouts are unknown. I am grateful to A.V.B. Norman for bringing this painting to my attention.

6 James G. Mann, "The Lost Armoury of the Gonzagas, Part II: The Libro Aquila," *The Archaeological Journal*, vol. 100 (1943), pp. 72–73, item 220: "*Quindici rudelle depente adorate co le sue imbrazzade et fate a diverse foze* (Fifteen bucklers painted and gilt, with their enarmes, of various patterns)."

7 For the history of the Medici and Urbino armories, see the introduction by Lionello G. Boccia in Bruno Thomas and Lionello G. Boccia, *Mostra delle armi storiche restaurate dall'aiuto austriaco dopo l'alluvione* (Florence, 1971), pp. 13–22.

8 Archivio di Stato, Florence, Guardaroba Medicea, vol. 513 [inventory of 1631], c. 54 (Urbino section): "Sette scudi di legno di fico o altro legno dipinti e dorati di diverse sorte che parte picholo, e sei grande usati bene" (Seven shields of fig wood or other wood painted and gilt, of diverse types, of which one is small

and six large, well used); and vol. 539 [inventory of 1539], c. 4v (Medici section): "Quattordici scudi di legno neri miniati d'oro, in diverse storie" (Fourteen shields, black, painted in gold with different subjects). The fourteen shields noted in the Medici inventory of 1639 were probably also included in the inventory of 1631, but are not described in sufficient detail so as to be identifiable. They are most likely included in the reference on c. 6 (Medici section): "Sedici rotelle di legno che tre coperti di quoio e neri e dorati" (Sixteen circular shields of wood, of which three are covered with leather, black and gilt). In this and other citations from the Medici inventories, I have spelled out the abbreviations and modernized the punctuation.

9 For my identification of other painted shields in the Medici armory, see Lionello G. Boccia, "Le armi medicee negli inventari del Cinquecento," *Le arti del principato mediceo* (Florence, 1980), pp. 399–400, n. 27.

10 See Léon Mirot, "L'Hôtel et les collections du Connétable de Montmorency," *Bibliothèque de l'Ecole des Chartres*, vol. 80 (1919), p. 107, no. 378. The shield is listed again in the inventory made in 1568, following the constable's death on the battlefield of Dreux (ibid., p. 145, no. 1020).

11 See Francis H. Cripps-Day, "Ein Harnish aus Sedan," *Zeitschrift für Historische Waffen- und Kostümkunde*, n.s., vol. 4 (1933), p. 122, citing a volume in the Archives Nationales, Paris, vol. R^2 177.

12 "Una rodela de madera labrada, en ella pintada la batalla de Pavía, desguarnecida," quoted in Conde de Valencia de Don Juan, "Bildinventar der Waffen, Rüstungen, Gewänder und Standarten Karl V. in der Armeria Real zu Madrid," *Jahrbuch der Kunsthistorisches Sammlungen des Alterhöchsten Kaiserhauses*, vol. 11 (1890), pt. 2, p. CCLIV. Another transcription of this inventory, with an English translation, is provided by Francis H. Cripps-Day, "An Inventory of the Armour of Charles V," *Fragmenta Armamentaria*, vol. 2, part V (n.p., 1951), with the description of the Pavia shield found on pp. 66–67.

13 The two-volume manuscript, inv. no. N18 in the Real Armería, Madrid, is described and reproduced, in part, by Conde Valencia de Don Juan, "Bildinventar . . . ," *Jahrbuch der Kunsthistorisches Sammlungen des Alterhöchsten Kaiserhauses*, vol. 10 (1889), pp. CCCLIII–CCCLIV, pls. 1–23; and ibid., vol. 11 (1890), pp. CCXLII–CCLVIII, pls. 24–55. The shield painted with the boar hunt is reproduced on plate 45.

14 *Inventario del moviliario, alhajas, ropas, armería y otros efectos del excmo. sr. D. Beltrán de la Cueva, tercer Duque de Albuquerque, hecho en el año 1560* (Madrid, 1883), pp. 75–76. The inventory of the Spanish royal armory of 1594 (p. 89 verso) lists "Diez Rodelas de las de Napp^s pintadas de diferentes ystorias y colores" (Ten round shields of those of Naples painted with different histories and colors; personal communication from José Godoy, May 17, 1991). I am also grateful to Mr. Godoy for information that, at least in Spanish sources, painted shields, saddles, and other such

equipment were said to be "of Naples," although the reason behind this attribution is unclear.

The unique, and often overlooked, group of painted wooden saddles in the Real Armería, Madrid, inv. nos. F 52–70, provide an important contemporary parallel to the painted shields under discussion. Some of the saddles are painted in polychrome, others in grisaille, and several depict antique battle scenes. None of those examined by me in May 1988, however, appear to have been painted by the author of the Kienbusch shield. For the Madrid saddles, see Valencia de Don Juan 1898, pp. 177–178; and especially Maria Teresa Ruiz Alcon, "Real Armería: Sillas de Montar de Diego de Arroyo," *Reales Sitios*, vol. 10, no. 37 (1973), pp. 49–54, where the attribution of several of these saddles to the Spanish painter Diego de Arroyo (active 1498–1551) is discussed.

15 See H. A. Dillon, "Arms and Armour at Westminster, the Tower, and Greenwich, 1547," *Archaeologia*, vol. 51 (1888), pp. 267–68; see also J. R. Kenyon, "Ordnance and the King's Fortifications in 1547–48: Society of Antiquaries, MS. 129, folio 250–374ʳ," *Archaeologia*, vol. 107 (1982), p. 171.

16 See Dillon 1888, p. 299.

17 See Bertrand Jestaz and Roseline Bacou, *L'Historie de Scipion: tapisseries et dessins* (Paris, 1978). Unless otherwise noted, my discussion of these tapestries and the related designs by Giulio Romano is based on this source.

18 Musée du Louvre, Département des Arts Graphiques, inv. nos. 3535 and 3720, respectively. The Giulio drawing is damaged and was retouched by Peter Paul Rubens, according to Michael Jaffé, "Rubens as a Collector of Drawings, Part One," *Master Drawings*, vol. 2, no. 4 (1964), p. 396, n. 28; and "Part Two," ibid., vol. 3, no. 1 (1965), pp. 29 and 35, n. 41; see also Jestaz and Bacou 1978, pp. 33–36.

19 Giulio's design seems to have been the source for a number of similar scenes, including Vasari's fresco *The Taking of Milan*, in the Stanza di Leone in the Palazzo Vecchio, Florence, begun in 1561 (see Paolo Barocchi, *Vasari Pittore* [Milan, 1964], pp. 47–48 and pl. 65); a fresco in the Palazzo dei Conservatori, Rome (see Catherine Dumont, *Francesco Salviati au Palais Sacchetti di Rome et la décoration murale italienne [1520–1560]* [Geneva, 1973], pp. 62–64, pl. 22, fig. 50); and *The Storming of [New] Carthage*, from a series of tapestry designs for *The History of Rome* executed by Giovanni Stradano (Jan van der Straet), c. 1563 (Windsor Castle, inv. no. 6864; L. van Puyvelde, *The Flemish Drawings in the Collection of His Majesty the King at Windsor Castle* [London, 1942], cat. no. 185).

20 Adam Bartsch, *Le Peinture-Graveur*, 22 vols. (Leipzig, 1843–76), vol. 8 (1866), p. 344, no. 86; see also *The Illustrated Bartsch*, vol. 16, *Early German Masters: Jacob Bink, George Pencz, Heinrich Aldegrever*, edited by Robert A. Koch (New York, 1980), p. 115, fig. 86.

21 Livy, *History of Rome*, translated by F. G. Moore (Loeb Classical Library), vol. 7 (Cambridge, Mass., and London, 1943), Book XXVI, 42–46; see also H. H. Scullard, *Scipio Africanus: Soldier and Politician* (Ithaca, 1970), pp. 39–67.

22 This figure is identified as Scipio by Bertrand Jestaz in Jestaz and Bacou 1978, p. 320.

23 For the history of these frescoes, and their importance in the emergence of Giulio's vigorous painting style, see especially S. J. Freedberg, *Painting in Italy 1500 to 1600* (Harmondsworth, 1971), pp. 132–35.

24 Frederick Hartt, *Guilio Romano*, 2 vols. (New Haven, 1958), vol. 2, pl. 197.

25 Phyllis P. Bober and Ruth Rubenstein, *Renaissance Artists and Antique Sculpture: A Handbook of Sources* (London, 1986), p. 175.

26 A useful introduction to this subject is found in Bober and Rubenstein 1986, pp. 31–40.

27 On the palette of antique painting, see Ernst Gombrich, "Dark Varnishes: Variations on a Theme from Pliny," *The Burlington Magazine*, vol. 104 (1962), pp. 51–55; and Ruth Wedgewood Kennedy, "Apelles Redivivus," *Essays in Memory of Karl Lehmann*, edited by L. F. Sandler (New York, 1964), pp. 167–70. I am grateful to Lois R. Granato for these references.

28 Kienbusch 1963, p. 143, no. 293, pl. XC; acc. no. 1977-167-766.

29 Hans Schedelmann, "Inventar der Waffensammlung des Erzherzogs Franz Ferdinand (Schloss Konopischt) aufgenommen in Heeres Museum zu Prag, 1944," not paginated, inv. no. K669 (LH.298) (typed manuscript; a copy annotated by Schedelmann is in the Department of Arms and Armor, The Metropolitan Museum of Art, New York).

30 Hans Schedelmann to Kienbusch, December 2, 1952, archives of the Kienbusch Collection of Armor and Arms, Philadelphia Museum of Art.

31 The shield, which was not illustrated and for which no provenance was given, was described as follows: "Ecole italiene (style de Pordenone). Modèle de rondache à décor de sujets guerriers avec rehauts de dorure. Suivant une tradition, il aurait été executé à Ferrare dans la premiére motié du XVIᵉ siècle, pour les Princes de la famille d'Este, et peint par Pordenone à la fin de sa vie (?)." The sale catalogue obviously served as the primary source of information for the subsequent description of the shield in the 1963 Kienbusch catalogue.

32 See Ludiše Letošníková, *The Armoury at Konopiště Castle* (Prague, 1970), pp. 7–17; Konstantina Blechová, "Storia dell'Armeria Estense," in *Le Armi degli Estensi: La collezione di Konopiště* (Bologna, 1986), p. xi (exhibition catalogue, Castello di Ferrara). For the Este armor, see especially Lionello G. Boccia, *Le Armerie Estensi nel Settecento* (Florence, privately printed, 1988); and, by the same author, "Armature 'estensi,'" *Schifanoia: Notizie dell'Instituto di Studi Rinascimentali di Ferrara*, vol. 5 (1988), pp. 9–22.

33 For the history of the Obizzi Collection, including a transcription of the inventory of Catajo Castle made in 1803, see Paola and Pier Luigi Fantelli, "L'inventario della collezione Obizzi al Catajo," *Bolletino del Museo Civico di Padova*, vol. 71 (1982), pp. 101–238.

34 The Konopiště armory contains many pieces that appear to have been heavily restored in the nineteenth century, or are outright fakes. For example, armor no. 1044, ostensibly complete, in fact consists only of a genuine close-helmet with falling buffe and an infantry breastplate; the remaining plates (including the waist lames and tassets attached to the breastplate) are

modern. This armor is illustrated by Letošníková 1970, fig. 7; Blechová et al. 1986, fig. 12; and is discussed by Boccia 1988, p. 19, who also noted the restored parts.

35 Boccia 1988, p. 20.

36 See Fantelli 1982, pp. 217–20, where various *scudi di legno* are mentioned.

37 See Thomas and Boccia 1971, pp. 14–15.

38 Archivio di Stato, Florence, Guardaroba Medicea, vol. 710, quaderno 4 [an inventory begun April 12, 1695], c. 37, no. 272: "Uno scudo di legno dipintovi una battaglia a chiaroscuro con i vestimenti dorati, in atto d'assaltare una fortezza, con fregio attorno di rabeschi d'oro minuti; e per di sotto dipintovi simile altra battaglia, con imbracciatura di velluto verde." The same shield is also described, with little variation, in successive inventories: Guardaroba Medicea, vol. 1091, begun November 5, 1696, c. 87v, no. 1729; vol. 1231 *bis*, begun August 6, 1715, c. 127r-v; and vol. 1275, dated 1719, c. 156v.

39 Johann Georg Keyssler, *Travels Through Germany, Bohemia, Hungary, Switzerland, Italy, and Lorraine*, 4 vols. (London, 1756–57), vol. 1, p. 442; quoted by Heikamp 1966, p. 75, n. 22.

40 Archivio di Stato, Florence, Guardaroba Medicea, vol. appendice 60 [begun on January 7, 1746 (1747)], c. 170. "Due scudi di chiaroscuro che in uno in vestimenti dorato gente che assaliscono una fortezza . . . " (Two shields in grisaille, in one men in gilt costumes who attack a fortress . . .).

41 "Uno scudo di fico verniciato di nero, tocco d'oro, figurato un assalto di una fortezza." Offices of the Soprintendenza alle Galerie, Florence, Regie Gallerie, vol. IX [1776], quaderno 55, inventory entitled "Nota di Capi dell' Armeria consegnati alla Direzione dell' Artiglieria . . . 17 ottobre 1775," c. 5, item no. 14.

42 Acc. no. 42.50.16. For the history of this shield, see note 45 below.

43 Livy, *History of Rome*, translated by F. G. Moore (Loeb Classical Library), vol. 7 (Cambridge, Mass., and London, 1943), Book XXVI, 47: "Of gold also and silver a large quantity was brought to the general. There were two hundred and seventy-six *paterae* [deep saucers used as drinking cups], nearly all of them weighing a pound; of silver, the unwrought and coined, there were eighteen thousand three hundred pounds, of silver vessels a large number."

44 *Catalogue of a Most Splendid and Instructive Collection of Ancient Armour Exhibiting at the Oplotheca, No. 20, Lower Brook Street, Bond Street* (London, 1816), p. 15, no. 108.

45 The early history of this shield has been discussed in detail by Claude Blair, *The Waddesdon Manor Collection: Arms, Armour and Base Metalwork* (Fribourg, 1974), pp. 46–52. The shield was first illustrated when it was in the hands of the London dealer George Durlacher, in Sir Guy Francis Laking, *A Record of European Armour and Arms through Seven Centuries*, 5 vols. (London, 1920–22), vol. 4, pp. 237–38, fig. 1309. It was acquired in 1921 by the New York collector Clarence H. Mackay and was subsequently lent by him to *The Metropolitan Museum of Art: Loan Exhibition of European Arms and Armor* (New York, 1931), no. 101, catalogue by Stephen V. Grancsay. Following Mackay's death in

1938, Grancsay acquired the shield and in 1942 presented it, together with many other Mackay pieces, to the Metropolitan Museum.

46 Inv. nos. OA1138, 1139. The history and attribution of these shields are discussed in detail for the first time by Sylvie Béguin in Roseline Bacou, *Autour de Raphaël: Dessins et peintures du Musée du Louvre* (Paris, 1983), pp. 127–29, nos. P5, P6.

47 See A.R.E. North, "Arms and Armour from Arundel Castle," *The Connoiseur*, vol. 197, no. 793 (March 1978), pp. 188–90, where the exterior of the shield is illustrated in color. North correctly identified the Arundel shield as being by the same artist who painted the shield in the Kienbusch Collection, and noted its close relation to another in the Victoria and Albert Museum, London (see note 65 below). For the Arundel shield, see also the Ashmolean Museum, Oxford, *Patronage and Collecting in the Seventeenth Century: Thomas Howard, Earl of Arundel* (Oxford, 1985), p. 25, no. 16, where the base material of the shield is mistakenly implied to be papier-mâché.

48 As, for example, on the morions worn by the bodyguard of the prince electors of Saxony, of which the Kienbusch Collection possesses an example (Kienbusch 1963, p. 76, no. 102, pl. LII; acc. no. 1977-167-130).

49 For the two versions of this painting, see the discussion by Nicholas Penny in Ashmolean Museum 1985, p. 20, no. 11.

50 The sword, gauntlet, and helmet are by tradition those taken from James IV of Scotland after the battle of Flodden Field in 1513, but the style of the arms indicates their manufacture well after this date. See North 1978, p. 190.

51 Mary L. Cox, "Notes on the Collections formed by Thomas Howard. Inventory of Pictures, Etc., in the Possession of Alethea, Countess of Arundel, at the Time of Her Death at Amsterdam in 1654," *The Burlington Magazine*, vol. 19 (1911), p. 285.

52 Sylvie Béguin, in Bacou 1983, pp. 127–29.

53 James G. Mann, "The Lost Armoury of the Gonzagas, Part I," *The Archaeological Journal*, vol. 95 (1939), p. 256.

54 Ashmolean Museum 1985, p. 25; J. M. Robinson, "Antiquarian Taste at Arundel Castle," *Country Life*, vol. 173 (February 10, 1983), pp. 333–34.

55 See John F. Hayward, *Victoria and Albert Museum: European Armour* (London, 1965), text accompanying cat. no. 22; North 1978, p. 190.

56 Ovid, *Metamorphoses*, translated by F. J. Miller (Loeb Classical Library; Cambridge, Mass., and London, 1916), Book VIII, 270–545.

57 Inv. no. 71. See Erich Haenel, *Kostbare Waffen aus der Dresdner Rüstkammer* (Leipzig, 1923), p. 74, pl. 37; Johannes Schöbel, *Helme und Schilde* (Dresden, n.d.), p.5, pl. 5.

58 Bober and Rubenstein 1986, pp. 143–45, fig. 113.

59 Schöbel n.d., p. 5.

60 Livy, *History of Rome*, translated by B. O. Foster (Loeb Classical Library), vol. 5 (London and New York, 1929), Book XXII, 53. An important element in identifying this episode is Scipio's drawn sword, by which he threatens his followers: "some of the young nobles . . . were looking to the sea and ships, proposing to

abandon Italy and flee for refuge to some king. . . . But when they would have called a council to talk the matter over, young Scipio, the predestined leader in this war, declared that it was no matter for taking counsel: they must be bold and act, not deliberate, in the face of this great evil; let them take arms and go with him at once, as many as wished to save the state; no camp was so truly the camp of the enemy as one where such thoughts were rife. He proceeded, with only a few followers, to the quarters of Metellus, where he found a gathering of young men of whom he had been informed. Raising his sword over their heads, as they sat in consultation, 'I solemnly swear,' he said, 'that even as I myself shall not desert the republic of the Roman people, so likewise shall I suffer no other Roman citizen to do so. . . .' "

The same scene, painted in grisaille, appears on the interior of a shield by a different hand in the collection at Maxstoke Castle near Birmingham. The painter of the Maxstoke shield may, however, also be responsible for the painted shield in the Royal Armouries, Tower of London, V. 16; see A.V.B. Norman and G. Wilson, *Treasures from the Tower* (London, 1982), p. 44, no. 13. I am grateful to Claude Blair for bringing the Maxstoke Castle shield to my attention.

61 A green velvet-covered arm-pad and arm-straps were originally on the Kienbusch shield, as described in the Medici inventory (see note 38), and are also found on two other painted shields now at Konopiště, nos. K659 and K664, which are also identifiable in the same Medici inventories. It is quite possible that the green upholstery was specific to the Medici (or della Rovere) collection. The Konopiště shield painted with the triumph of Scipio (K664), illustrated in Blechová et al. 1986, p. 36, is described in the Medici inventory of 1695, already cited, c. 274; the shield painted with a scene of Orpheus and the Muses on Parnassus (K659), a scene adapted from a Giorgio Ghisi print of the same subject after a drawing by Luca Penni, is described on c. 280. These inventory references have been published, following my notes, by Lionello G. Boccia, "Le armi medicee negli inventari del Cinquecento," *Le Arti del Principato Mediceo* (Florence, 1980), pp. 390–400, n. 27. The Konopiště shields are especially close in style to the Turin shield and further study may prove them to be from a closely related workshop.

62 "Ein Rundel, darauff eine jagt mit farben gemalt ist in des alten Rüstkammer gewest." I am grateful to Dr. Dieter Schaal, Director of the Historisches Museum, Dresden, for this reference (letter of February 2, 1979, archives, Department of Arms and Armor, The Metropolitan Museum of Art, New York). Haenel 1923, p. 74, quotes a description of the shield in the inventory of 1674. As to the provenance of the Dresden shield, it should be noted that Christian I, Prince Elector of Saxony, received a gift of arms and armor from Francesco I de'Medici, Grand Duke of Tuscany, in 1587. It is quite possible that the Dresden shield, with its green upholstery matching that of other shields from the Medici armory, may have been included in this gift. Unfortunately, no documentary evidence from the Dresden archives is yet known that would support this hypothesis.

63 For this manuscript, see note 13. On the dating of the

Inventario Iluminado, see José A. Godoy in *Resplendence of the Spanish Monarchy: Renaissance Tapestries and Armor* (New York, 1991) p. 101, n. 1.

64 The shield was purchased at the sale of the George Hellman Collection at the Anderson Galleries, New York, November 21, 1919, lot 8. I am grateful to the late Anita Reinhard for this reference. The shield remained in Dean's collection until his death in 1928, and belonged to his widow until her death in 1950; it was sold as part of Mrs. Dean's estate at Parke-Bernet Galleries, New York, October 26, 1950, lot 120A. The shield reappeared at Parke-Bernet, October 7, 1971, lot 316 (bought in). In the early 1980s, it passed into the European art trade.

Several other painted shields, possibly belonging to the group under discussion, had earlier appeared on the American art market. In an anonymous sale conducted by the auction firm of Leavitt in New York City on May 15–17, 1873, there were three painted shields in this manner: "1026. Shield: measures two feet in diameter on the outside; made of wood, covered with thick cloth, painted or enameled on both sides; bears a spirited drawing in gold, representing a conflict of cavalry. May be referred to the time of Elizabeth, or perhaps earlier, when tournaments and other pageants were common. Rare. 1027. Shield. Another for use in pageants. Similar to the above. 1028. Shield. Another; wants the covering on the hollow side. Similar to the above."

65 Inv. no. 174–1869; 23½ inches (60 cm) in diameter. See Hayward 1965, cat. no. 22. I am grateful to Gillian Walking, formerly of the Department of Furniture and Woodwork of the Victoria and Albert Museum, London, who provided me with photographs and the technical report made on the shield in 1971. This report, which was made in conjunction with another on a painted shield by a different workshop, inv. no. 1–1865, suggests that the shield is composed of three layers of boards (poplar), exactly as the x-radiographs of the Kienbusch shield and that in the Metropolitan Museum have indicated. The upholstery of the fragmentary arm-straps is said to be green velvet.

66 Inv. no. 5; 23½ inches (60 cm) in diameter. See Luigi Mallè, *Museo Civico di Torino, I Dipinti del Museo D'Arte Antica, Catalogo* (Turin, 1963), pp. 160–61, pl. XII and fig. 100, where the shield is attributed to Polidoro da Caravaggio and, because of the presence of the della Rovere arms, the scene on the exterior is identified as that of the siege of Pesaro in 1512.

67 In a review of Luigi Mallè's catalogue, Andreina Griseri disputed the attribution to Polidoro and suggested instead that it was the work of the Peruzzi circle. She noted that "the outside is flawed by a touching-up of the battle-scene which derives from designs by Perino but achieves only an *intarsio* effect, like that of majolica" (*The Burlington Magazine*, vol. 107 [November 1965], p. 582).

68 See note 38. Although exhibited in Florence in the exhibition *Firenze e la Toscana dei Medici nell'Europa del Cinquecento. Palazzo Vecchio: committenza e collezionismo medicei*, 1980, the shield was not published in the accompanying catalogue. It was, however, published after the exhibition in Boccia 1980, pp. 403–4. In his discussion of the shield, Boccia mentions my discov-

ery of the related inventory references to a similar shield in the Medici armory and, following my error at the time, also identifies it with the Turin example rather than the Kienbusch shield. The correct identification of the subject represented on the exterior of the Turin shield was recognized independently by Sylvie Béguin, in Bacou 1983, pp. 127–29.

69 See note 40. The Konopiště armory possesses another shield depicting the storming of a fortress, no. K669, although it is less directly inspired by the design of Giulio Romano. This shield is smaller (19¼ inches, 49 cm in diameter) than the others discussed and is painted in a different technique (gold paint on a black ground, without grisaille or sgraffito). Perhaps these are the painted shields "de Nápoles" referred to in the inventory of the Duke of Albuquerque (see note 14). These differences, together with the general crudeness of the painting, indicate that this shield and others related to it in Konopiště (no. K626) and the Victoria and Albert Museum (no. 1–1865) are from a different workshop. For the two Konopiště shields, see Blechová 1986, figs. 6 and 108.

70 Diameter 21¼ inches (54 cm); ex-collection F. Engel-Gros, sale, Galerie Georges Petit, Paris, May 30–31,

June 1, 1921, lot 225; and Madame P., sale, Galerie Charpentier, Paris, December 6, 1952, lot 3. The attribution to Peruzzi appears to follow the suggestion made by Griseri in her review of Mallè's catalogue (see note 67). I am grateful to Dr. Roy Fisher and Alan E. Salz, both formerly of Wildenstein and Company, for having provided information on the provenance and attribution of this shield.

71 For the political importance of Charles V's African campaigns and the Italian sojourn that followed, see Karl Brandi, *The Emperor Charles V* (London, 1970), pp. 365–83. For the triumphs, see André Chastel, "Les entrées de Charles Quint en Italie," in *Fêtes et cérémonies au temps de Charles Quint*, edited by Jean Jacquot (Paris, 1960), pp. 197–206; Roy Strong, *Splendor at Court: Renaissance Spectacle and the Theater of Power* (Boston, 1973), pp. 93–97. A compendium of contemporary printed accounts of these triumphs is found in Andre Sala, "Ordine, pompe, apparati, et ceremonie, delle solenne intrate, di Carlo V Imp. sempre aug. nella città di Roma, Sienna, et Fiorenza" (n.p., n.d.), a copy of which is found in the Biblioteca Riccardiana, Florence (Moreniana B5 64).

NOTES / PART II

72 Acc. nos. 1927.60 (gift of the Ehrich Galleries, New York) and 1946.42 (gift of the Dumbarton Oaks Research Library and Collection). Both are executed on wood and measure 20½ by 20 inches (52.1 x 50.8 cm) and 10⁵⁄₁₆ by 7 inches (26.2 x 17.8 cm), respectively. Bernard Berenson, quoted by Luisa Vertova in a letter of April 2, 1955, to the Fogg Art Museum, first suggested that 1927.60 might be by Girolamo da Treviso the Younger or a copy after him by a Flemish hand. Berenson listed it as a late autograph work in *Italian Pictures of the Renaissance: Venetian School* (London, 1957), vol. 1, p. 90. In 1963 I found the second *Adoration* in a closet in the Fogg Art Museum and recognized that it was by the same artist. These attributions are accepted by Burton B. Fredericksen and Federico Zeri, *Census of Pre-Nineteenth-Century Italian Paintings in North American Public Collections* (Cambridge, Mass., 1972), p. 93; and by Alessandra Speziali, "Girolamo da Treviso," in *Pittura bolognese del '500,* edited by Vera Fortunati Pietrantonio (Bologna, 1986), vol. 1, p. 151.

73 Giorgio Vasari, *Le vite dé più eccellenti pittori, scultori, ed architettori nelle redazioni 1550 e 1568,* edited by Rosanna Bettarini and Paola Barocchi (Florence, 1976), vol. 4, p. 452. In the 1568 edition, Vasari says Girolamo died at the age of thirty-six in 1544.

74 Luigi Coletti, "Intorno ad un nuovo ritratto del vescovo Bernardo de' Rossi," *Rassegna d'arte antica e moderna,* no. 8 (December 1921), pp. 407–20.

75 I. B. Supino, *Le sculture delle Porte di S. Petronio in Bologna illustrate con documenti inediti* (Florence, 1914), p. 104, no. 78.

76 Vincenzo Mancini, "Un insospettato collaboratore di

Giulio Romano a Palazzo del Te: Gerolamo da Treviso," *Paragone,* vol. 38, no. 453 (November 1987), pp. 3–21. See also Manfredo Tafuri, "Giulio Romano: linguaggio, mentalità, committenti," in Manfredo Tafuri et al., *Giulio Romano* (Milan, 1989), pp. 57, 63 n. 114 (exhibition catalogue, Palazzo del Te and Palazzo Ducale, Mantua, September 1–November 12, 1989).

77 Quoted by J. A. Crowe and G. B. Cavalcaselle, *A History of Painting in North Italy,* edited by Tancred Borenius (London, 1912), vol. 3, p. 126. On Castiglione's interest in painting, see Marco Collareta, "La miniatura di Simone Martini per il Petrarca descritta da Sabba da Castiglione," *Prospettiva,* nos. 53–56 (April 1988–January 1989), pp. 334–37.

78 Letter of Francesco dell'Arme to Giangiacomo Calandra, published by Willelmo Braghirolli, in *Alfonso Cittadella: scultore del secolo XVI* (Mantua, 1878), p. 51, no. VI (originally published in *Atti e Memorie della R. Accademia Virgiliana* [Mantua, 1874–78], p. 127, no. VI). Cited by Mancini 1987, p. 7; and by Speziali 1986, vol. 1, p. 149. The monument was begun by the sculptor Alfonzo Cittadella, who died during the early stages of its execution.

79 Philip Pouncey, "Girolamo da Treviso in the Service of Henry VIII," *The Burlington Magazine,* vol. 95 (June 1953), p. 211; Speziali 1986, vol. 1, p. 148, dates the *Presentation* a decade earlier.

80 Vasari, *Le vite,* ed. Bettarini and Barocchi 1976, vol. 4, pp. 451–52 (author's translation).

81 See Anchise Tempestini, "Un 'Cristo al Limbo' di Girolamo da Treviso il Giovane (1498–1544)," *Antichità Viva,* vol. 28, nos. 2–3 (1989), p. 17.

82 Vasari, *Le vite*, ed. Bettarini and Barocchi 1976, vol. 4, p. 451 (author's translation).

83 As John Shearman has observed, "Girolamo's standards, especially of drawing, were relaxed in the less critical English atmosphere" in *The Early Italian Pictures in the Collection of Her Majesty the Queen* (Cambridge, 1983), p. 118.

84 Vasari, *Le vite*, ed. Bettarini and Barocchi 1976, vol. 4, pp. 321, 450 (author's translation).

85 For arguments in favor of the painting being by Girolamo, see Cecil Gould, *National Gallery Catalogues: The Sixteenth-Century Italian Schools* (London, 1975), pp. 115–16.

86 For a reproduction of this fresco, which was executed in the 1530s by Rinaldo Mantovano, see Konrad Oberhuber, "I disegni e i dipinti mantovani," in Tafuri et al. 1989, p. 431.

87 An edition of Cennino Cennini's text was edited by Fernando Tempesti and published in 1975. For more recent information, see David Bomford, Jill Dunkerton, Dillian Gordon, and Ashok Roy, *Art in the Making: Italian Painting before 1400* (London, 1989). For help with the technical examination of the shield in the Metropolitan Museum of Art (acc. no. 42.50.16), I am indebted to Gisela Helmkampf and Matthew Heath Kennedy.

88 Panel, 14³⁄₈ by 12¹⁄₂ inches (36.5 x 32 cm). See *The Illustrated Bartsch*, vol. 14, *Early German Masters: Albrecht Altdorfer, Monogrammists*, edited by Robert A. Koch (New York, 1980), p. 135.

89 Acc. no. 12, panel, 20 by 12³⁄₄ inches (50.8 x 32.3 cm); *City of York Art Gallery: Catalogue of Paintings, I. Foreign Schools, 1350–1800* (York, 1961), pp. 14–15.

NOTES / APPENDIX

90 The shield was examined macroscopically under visible and ultraviolet illumination, and by means of infrared reflectography (Hamamatsu C1000 with Conrac Monitor) and x-radiography (Picker x-ray equipment). Microscopic examination of the shield itself was made on a Wild M8 stereomicroscope at from 6 to 50 times magnification. Samples and cross-sections were examined at up to 400 times magnification in normal and polarized light on a Zeiss Universal Research Microscope, and in some cases with ultraviolet light on a Leitz Laborlux S Microscope with an LEP Ltd. 50W Hg vapor source or a Nicolet 510P FT-IR Spectrometer, using Nic-Plan IR microscope. In the case of ultraviolet microscopy, fluorescent stains were used on cross-sections, as well as observing auto-fluorescence. X-ray diffraction was carried out on Philips equipment, PW 1729 and 1840 using Gondolfi cameras.

91 Examined x-radiographically were: Philadelphia Museum of Art acc. nos. 1977-167-752, 1977-167-753 (Kienbusch 1963, p. 147, no. 302, pl. LXXXIX), 1977-167-757 (Kienbusch 1963, p. 147, no. 300, pl. LXXXIX), and 29-147-1; and the Metropolitan Museum of Art acc. no. 42.50.16. Examined visually only were shields in the following museums: in New York, The Metropolitan Museum of Art; in Baltimore, The Walters Art Gallery; in Florence, the Museo Stibbert, the Museo Baldini, and the Uffizi; in Paris, the Musée de l'Armée at the Invalides and the Louvre; and in London, the Victoria and Albert Museum, the British Museum, the Wallace Collection, and the Tower of London.

92 The maximum diameter of the shield is 61 cm, with a variation of approximately 1 cm between the narrower (left and right sides, which are dropped) and wider (top and bottom, lifted) dimensions. The maximum overall depth is 12.5 cm. The thickness of the shell is about 1.15 cm at the center, tapering to about 0.75 cm at the rim.

93 The wood species *Populus* includes aspen, cottonwood, and European poplar, which can be *P. fastigiata* (Lombardy), *P. nigra* (black), *P. canescens*, or *P. alba* (both white poplar). The latter was commonly used in Italian panel painting (David Bomford, *Art in the Making: Italian Painting Before 1400* [London, 1989], p. 11). It has been identified as being used in a late sixteenth-century round, lamellar shield by Caravaggio (see note 95 below). The sample, from a damaged area at the top center edge of the shield, was analyzed by Melvin Wachowiak, Jr., at the Winterthur Museum conservation laboratories, Delaware.

94 The x-radiographs were taken by Joe Mikuliak, Philadelphia Museum of Art. The exposures were 21 kV, 2.8 ma for 145 seconds, or 19.5 kV, 3 ma for 180 seconds. The vertical joins between the wood strips of the two outermost strata do not fall in precisely the same location, as is observable in the surface crack patterns.

95 In his article on Caravaggio's "Medusa" shield, Detlef Heikamp stated that "pioppa (*populus alba*)" was specifically used for that lamellar shield because this "tender wood easily lends itself to being pressed into a convex form" (author's translation). See Heikamp, "La Medusa del Caravaggio e l'armatura dello Scià 'Abbâs di Persia,'" *Paragone*, n.s., vol. 17, no. 199 (September 1966), p. 62.

96 The removed staples are characterized by small rectangular areas (0.5 to 1.5 cm long by 0.3 to 0.5 cm wide), which are relatively dark on the x-radiograph, and which contain one or commonly two smaller spots (0.3 to 0.5 cm square), which are white. The larger, darker marks are areas of thinner wood where the cross-bar of the staple previously occupied the space; and the small, square white marks are dense fills in the cavities left by staple legs (see fig. 99).

97 The extant staples were located by means of a magnetic "stud finder," which allowed the author to quantify the strength of the magnetic pull and to make some assumptions about increased distance.

The staples associated with the middle stratum were identified as such because they are perpendicular to the majority of staples and presumably span the horizontal joins of that layer.

98 The weave was identified under the binocular microscope. Samples were taken from two exposed areas along the obverse right and left edges. Polarized-light microscopy at 400 times magnification identified the fibers as a bast fiber, most probably linen: individual fibers have a diameter of 9 to 15 microns, with narrow lumens; and single fibers have parallel extinction, which is incomplete at the nodules (Walter C. McCrone and John Gustav Delly, *The Particle Atlas*, 2nd ed., 4 vols. [Ann Arbor, 1973], vol. 2, p. 354, no. 63).

99 X-ray diffraction, at 40 kV, 5 ma for a minimum of 3 hours, was carried out in a Gondolfi camera. The sample matched 15 d-spacings of the JCPDS reference 21-816 for $CaSO_4 \cdot 2H_2O$, calcium sulfate hydrate, or gypsum. See Bomford 1989, p. 17; and Rutherford J. Gettens and George L. Stout, *Painting Materials: A Short Encyclopedia* (New York, 1966), p. 233, for comments on Italian gesso.

100 The bole was not successfully analyzed but traditionally is a soft, greasy-textured clay, colored red by iron oxides and mixed with either a dilute animal-skin glue or egg white. The gold, most probably burnished water gilding, which is necessary to sustain the sgraffito without tearing, was only occasionally visible in the cross-sections. However, the omnipresent bole, and the very sharp line between the bole and the black-paint layer confirms its presence. See Bomford 1989, pp. 21–24, 130.

101 The black pigment was identified as a carbon black using polarized light microscopy. It is isotropic with dense, large, irregular particles; its brownish tone suggests bone black; and its refractive index is close to the mounting material, respectively, 1.65–1.70/1.66 (Gettens and Stout 1966, p. 99). The white pigment, apparently in two slightly different shades, is a lead white, basic lead carbonate, $2PbCO_3 \cdot Pb(OH)_2$, identified by microchemical testing (potassium iodide added to an acidic solution of the pigment, producing a yellow lead-iodide precipitate), its opacity in the x-radiograph, and by means of polarized light microscopy. The particles are very fine, highly birefringent, and have a refractive index higher than the medium, which is 1.66 (Gettens and Stout 1966, pp. 174–75). The medium is more difficult to identify. Ultraviolet fluorescent microscopy has indicated the presence in the paint layers of both lipids (positive staining with Rhodamine B using filter block D, BP 355–425) and protein (positive staining with fluorecein isothiocyanate [FITC], filter block H_3, BP 420–490), suggesting egg tempera, which is consistent with the very thin, discrete paint layers (thickness from varnish through gesso varies from 55 to 110 microns), and with the historic literature about sgraffito on gold. The medium-rich black layer that is directly on the gold autofluoresces very strongly, indicating the addition of either protein glue or resin, although the historical literature suggests oil (see note 112). Fourier-transform infrared spectroscopy confirms the presence of protein, suggesting additional glue. The modern varnish appears to be an oil-resin (strong autofluorescence, positive Rhodamine B, negative FITC).

102 The cross-sections have shown only one varnish layer, which is "modern" in that it covers damage and restoration.

103 Shields very similar in form and decorative style were seen by the author at the Musée du Louvre, Paris, OA1138 and OA1139, and at the Tower of London, NO. V-16. The structure of the former two could not be seen. However, the latter, dated 1550, with a lantern set into its upper edge, c. 1600, and an elaborate grisaille painting of Camillus Attacking the Gauls on the reverse, clearly has a lamellar structure, which can be seen by the crack pattern and in damage on the upper proper left. A photograph of the unpainted obverse is reproduced in A.V.B. Norman and G. M. Wilson, *Treasures from the Tower of London* (Norwich, 1982), pp. 43–44, cat. no. 12.

104 Acc. no. 1977-167-753 (Kienbusch 1963, p. 147, no. 302, pl. LXXXIX) is covered with leather, metallic foils and painted or glazed with orientalizing ornamental patterns and has at least two layers; acc. no. 1977-167-752 (not in Kienbusch 1963) has four layers of wood, covered with elaborately embossed leather, with the Judgment of Paris in the central panel and putti in the borders, of a type considered to be Florentine (see Helmut Nickel, Stuart W. Pyhrr, and Leonid Tarassuk, *The Art of Chivalry* [New York, 1982], pp. 48–49, cat. no. 16); acc. no. 1977-167-757 (Kienbusch 1963, p. 147, no. 300, pl. LXXXIX) has two layers of wood, covered with cloth and gesso and painted with a narrative image.

105 Lionello G. Boccia, *Il Museo Stibbert*, vol. 3, *L'armería Europea* (Milan, 1975), cat. nos. 176 and 177, book 1, pp. 49, 87–88, book 2, pls. 169, 170 (Stibbert nos. 2180 and 2190).

106 Assigned to the seventeenth century is no. 1412: two layers of wood, black and gold with loose sgraffito of Turkish motifs. Assigned to the sixteenth century are nos. 3806 and 4900, both with lamellar structures, black and gold with loose, open sgraffito drawings, the former depicting the Siege of Carthage as on the Philadelphia shield. Stibbert nos. 2386 and 2387 are attributed to the battle of Giornico in 1478 (Boccia 1975, vol. 3, cat. nos. 169 and 170).

107 Heikamp 1966, p. 62.

108 Quoted by John F. Hayward, *European Armour: Victoria and Albert Museum* (London, 1965), cat. no. 10.

109 The examples on display at the Tower of London were not identified numerically. Examples can be seen in Norman and Wilson 1982, cat. no. 11, pp. 42–43, described as russeted steel, etched and fire gilt, with a classical scene; and Peter Hammond, *Royal Armouries* (London, 1986), p. 35. Walters Art Gallery, acc. no. 51.1414.

110 The attribution of these metal-covered shields to Italian craftsmanship is not confirmed. It is known, however, that due to the inferiority of the local product, Henry VIII brought Italian armorers to England in 1511 to establish workshops at his palace in Greenwich (see Hayward 1965, p. 1). Although the practical nature of these shields can be questioned, the suggestion passed on to me by Thom Richardson

of the Tower of London that they might have been useful on-board ship has been supported by the finding of examples aboard the *Mary Rose*, Henry VIII's flagship, which sank in 1545.

111 Cipriano Piccolpasso, *The Three Books of the Potter's Art*, translated by Ronald Lightbown and Alan Caiger-Smith (London, 1980), vol. 2, p. 18.

112 The tendency for tempera painting to flake from gold has been commented on (see Bomford 1989, p. 70). There are various remarks in the early technical literature regarding the medium used to paint on metal or gilded surfaces. When egg tempera was the common medium, various oils were sometimes recommended. See Theophilus, *On Diverse Arts*, translated by J. G. Hawthorne and C. S. Smith (Chicago, 1963), pp. 32–33, n. 1; and Cennino Cennini, *Il libro dell'arte* (*The Craftsman's Handbook*), translated by C. V. Thompson, Jr. (New York, 1960), pp. 88–89.

113 See Lionello G. Boccia and E. T. Coelho, *L'Arte dell'armatura in Italia* (Milan, 1967), figs. 237–60 for examples of the elaborate Italian armor of similar date.

ACKNOWLEDGMENTS

During the preparation of the study I have relied on the valuable advice and information provided by a number of friends and colleagues, notably Everett Fahy, Gisela Helmkampf, Helmut Nickel, Donald LaRocca, José Godoy, Tony North, Dieter Schaal, Bertrand Jestaz, Ian Eaves, Nolfo di Carpegna, Mario Scalini, Claude Blair, A.V.B. Norman, and Lois Granato. I also wish to acknowledge the friendship, encouragement, and assistance given by Mr. C. O. von Kienbusch, who allowed me frequent access to his collection during my years as a graduate student in New York (1971–75), and who provided a fellowship in the Department of Arms and Armor at the Metropolitan Museum, of which I was the first recipient.

—S.W.P.

Many people have generously discussed these issues with me, as well as having contributed in a variety of ways to the paper. I would like to thank them all for their kindness and support, most particularly, Andrew Lins, Sally Malenka, and Jane Watkins at the Philadelphia Museum of Art, and Donald LaRocca, Assistant Curator of Arms and Armor at the Metropolitan Museum of Art, New York, as well as the following: at the Philadelphia Museum of Art, Marigene Butler, David DeMuzio, Gina Erdreich, Joe Mikuliak, and Mark Tucker; at the Metropolitan Museum of Art, Stuart W. Pyhrr and Gisela Helmkampf; in Florence, Mario Scalini and Carl Strehlke; and in London, A.V.B. Norman and Thom Richardson.

—M.S.M.

Crediton: The Story of Two Helmets

CLAUDE BLAIR

Early in 1933 an important "Loan Exhibition Depicting the Reign of Queen Elizabeth" was held in London in aid of the Young Women's Christian Association. Item 59 in the catalogue was a helmet described as follows: "*CLOSE HELMET*, embossed with conventional foliage with an acorn at the apex, very similar to one in the Whawell collection, 1927. Bever [*sic*] and visor pivoted at the sides. Russet./*Lent by the Governors of Crediton Church.*"[1]

The Whawell referred to was Samuel James Whawell (1857–1926) of London, a leading dealer in arms and armor, whose "collection" had been sold by Sotheby's during May 3–6, 1927 (see figs. 105, 106).[2] The other helmet mentioned in the entry as being "very similar" to the Crediton one appeared as lot 243 in the sale catalogue (fig. 104), where it was illustrated, and described as follows:

A FINE CLOSE HELMET, with embossed decoration, the skull formed of one piece drawn out at the apex to an acorn terminal. The visor with two apertures for sight projects well forward, the so-called ventail entirely without the usual breathing apertures falls low over the chin-piece. The decoration, which is of a most restrained character, consists of radiating acanthus leaves in strong relief. This fine helmet, which now has a brown patine surface with traces of gilding, is undoubtedly the production of a member of the celebrated Negroli family, and the presence of a hole piercing the crown (together with its general aspect) suggests that it has been used for funerary purposes and hung in a church. *Italian, Mid. 16th Cent.*

The helmet was sold for £200 to Raymond Bartel, acting for William Randolph Hearst, whose armorer he was. Hearst kept it until 1941, when he included it among the many pieces from his collection that he put on public sale at Gimbel's department store in New York.[3] It was bought there by Carl Otto von Kienbusch and passed in due course with the rest of the Kienbusch Collection to the Philadelphia Museum of Art (figs. 102, 103).[4]

The story of the two helmets told here is an interesting one, as much for the light it throws on the activities of a number of distinguished personalities in the field of antique arms and armor in the first quarter of this century as for its contribution to the study of Renaissance armor. It has never previously been fully told, and I welcome the opportunity to place it on permanent record, the more so because part of it came to me in oral form.

The members of the organizing committee for the 1933 Elizabethan exhibition included C. J. ffoulkes, then Curator (later Master) of the Tower of London Armouries, and his successor, James G. Mann, the most respected British armor scholar of the interwar period.

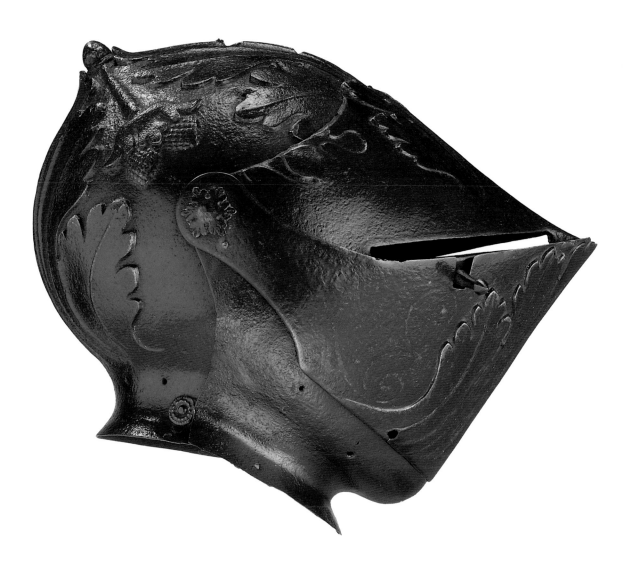

Fig. 102. Kienbusch close-helmet, c.1550, photographed in 1990. Embossed steel; 1977-167-105.

Despite this formidable support for the authenticity of the helmet at Crediton, there were those who had doubts about it. Among them was Francis Henry Cripps-Day, the distinguished writer on early armor who was, respectively, author and coauthor (in 1922 and 1939) of the two standard published lists of armor then remaining in English churches.[5] Cripps-Day noted that the helmet at Crediton was "a dud" in his interleaved copy of these lists, which he eventually deposited in the library of the Victoria and Albert Museum, London.[6]

On January 3, 1940, it was suggested, apparently for the first time in print, that the helmet was a fake, in the *Western Morning News*, a newspaper published in Plymouth, Devonshire, the county in which Crediton is also situated. It is worth quoting in full:

HELMET RELIC CONTROVERSY
Crediton Forgery Suggestion

REPLICA CLAIM DISCREDITED
Crediton Parish Church authorities are inclined to discredit the possibility that an ancient and valuable helmet, which had been in the possession of the church for centuries, has been replaced by a comparatively valueless replica.

According to an armour expert, the original helmet has disappeared from the church, and is now possibly in a private collection. He considers the loss should be made known, in the hope that the helmet will be restored.

To a "Western Morning News" reporter he recalled that he last saw the helmet in the church as long ago as 1920. "It was a beautiful helmet," he said, "and was certainly not a forgery." In about 1925 I received a letter from a gentleman interested in armour, stating that there was then in a private collection in London a helmet exactly similar to the one at Crediton.

"A little later I saw another such helmet in the rooms of an armour dealer. It was offered to me for £80. I did not buy it. At the sale of the dealer's effects a year or two later the helmet realized at auction a very considerable sum. I do not know in whose hands the helmet now is."

INQUIRY SUGGESTED
"The other day I received a letter from a correspondent interested in church armour, telling me that the helmet now in Crediton Church is undoubtedly a forgery.

"The fact that a helmet of this unique form finds its way to London, within a few years of the discovery that the real Crediton helmet has been replaced by a forgery, makes it very desirable that the authorities of the diocese should investigate the matter, and that the public should receive any information which the diocese is able to furnish. It is possible that the present possessor, when he learns of the loss by Crediton Church, would restore the helmet to the church, for happily in our Empire and in the United States of America most collectors would not care to retain a piece with such a doubtful pedigree."

Although the helmet cannot be associated with any particular individual, experts are agreed that it is of the Cromwellian period. It has been described by Col. L.A.D. Montague, of Crediton, as "a beautiful helmet, richly decorated with oak leaf ornamentation and with a movable visor, which may have possibly belonged to some knight buried in the church."

CONSIDERED GENUINE
Surprise was expressed by church officials yesterday when asked if they could throw any light on the alleged disappearance of the original helmet.

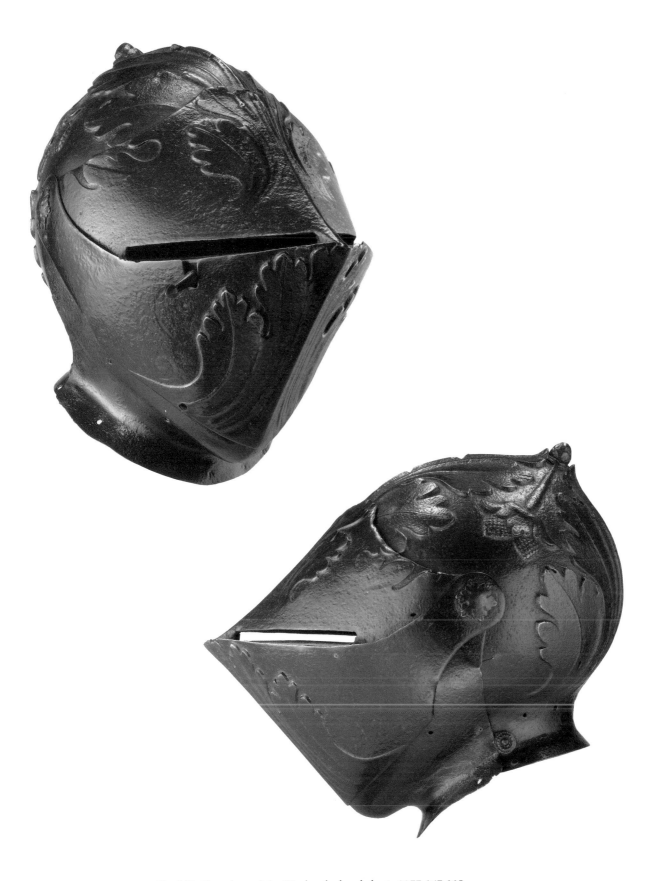

Fig. 103. Two views of the Kienbusch close-helmet; 1977-167-105.

Mr. J. Symes, clerk to the church governors, in whose care is the church armour, mentioned that the helmet was supposed to date from the Commonwealth period.

"A few years ago," he said, "we loaned it to an exhibition in London, and I have no doubt that the same helmet came back again. We have never suspected it as a forgery."

The Vicar of Crediton (Reverend J. A. Durling) had no reason to suppose that the original helmet had been replaced. "I do not think that there is any question about it," he said. "It has always been pointed out to visitors as a helmet of Cromwell's period."

Col. Montague regarded the helmet as a memorial helmet of the time of Charles I. He thought it was genuine when he wrote about it some years ago.

Five days later, on January 8, the *Western Morning News* published a letter from the previously mentioned Colonel Montague, a local antiquary, commenting on this report. The relevant portions are as follows:

I am no expert on English armour, but I think I know as much about the old helmet in the Governor's Room of Crediton Church as anybody else here.

I first came upon it about 1878, when (to quote from an article of mine in "Antiquarian Gossip," of May, 1898[7]—a bimonthly journal now long defunct) I had found:

"thrown pell mell in a damp cupboard, where they were rapidly rusting and rotting away, several highly-interesting antiquities deserving of a better fate. A beautiful helmet richly decorated with oak-leaf ornamentation and with a movable viser (illustrated) may have belonged to one of the knights buried in the church. Of armour there is a good breast-plate, three shoulder-pieces and an elbow-piece—also a leather coat worn under the armour. There is a saddle, bridle, bit, stirrup and holster, a good sword and a pair of the brown square-toed top boots as worn by Cromwell's dragoons."

. . . The helmet is of a pattern in use during the first half of the 17th century, and up to the Civil War, but helmets of the same type were often placed upon or hung over memorial monuments, so it is possible that it was one of these, overhung upon the church wall in memory of some departed knight . . . . As to the suggestion that it is a forgery, it was in a red and rusty state when I first saw it, and nothing about it in the least suggested that it was a fake, but when the Governors' room was rearranged some years ago, most of the former contents of the cupboard were hung up in full view, and I noticed that the helmet had been completely blackened over and "done up" in what struck me as an injudicious way. I did not examine it carefully and am unable to do so at present, but if the ornamentation shown on the drawing taken in 1898 is the same as that upon the helmet now exhibited, then this must be the original one. Who cleaned it I do not know, nor can anyone say how many years it had been in the church before 1878.

As a rider to this, it should be mentioned that the helmet must have been "completely blackened over and 'done up' " before 1918, since in that year Beatrix Cresswell wrote in *Devon and Cornwall Notes and Queries* that it had been "carefully painted with Brunswick black till it shone like a coal scuttle." Furthermore, the relics had already been "hung up in full view" at least seven years previously, as is made clear in a note by E. K. Prideaux on "Relics of Fairfax's Army in Crediton," in the 1911 issue of the same periodical.[8] Unfortunately, this note

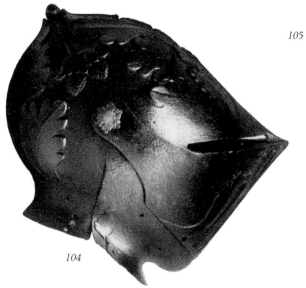

104

105

Fig. 104. Kienbusch close-helmet as it appeared in the
sale catalogue of the Samuel James Whawell Collection,
Sotheby's, London, May 3–6, 1927, plate 13.

Fig. 105. Samuel James Whawell (1857–1926) in front
of his London home in 1923 (photographed by C. Otto
von Kienbusch).

Fig. 106. Whawell Collection in 1923 (photographed by
C. Otto von Kienbusch).

106

neither mentioned nor illustrated the helmet, perhaps because—for reasons that will become clear—the helmet was not actually in the church when the article was written.

Colonel Montague's letter appears to have produced only one reply, published on January 20 in the *Western Morning News* and suggesting that "the Crediton Helmet be sent to the Tower [of London] with a request to the Master of the Armouries to give his opinion as to its date, and that the incumbent of the church at Crediton be asked if he, or his predecessor, ever parted with the possession of the helmet for a period." The letter was signed "H. de Povenasle," a misspelling of Cripps-Day's pseudonym, H. de Povenashe,[9] which leaves little doubt that he was the "armour expert" quoted at length in the original report in the *Morning News*. There is no reason to think that the suggestion made in his letter was ever acted upon.

When, in 1951 at the Tower of London Armouries, I first became professionally involved with early arms and armor, I knew nothing about the report and correspondence in the *Western Morning News* or Cripps-Day's note in his church-armor lists. I soon learned, however, that the helmet in Crediton Church—of which I had then only seen illustrations—was "supposed to be a fake" that had been substituted for the original, and that the latter was the helmet in the Whawell sale. I am not sure now who told me this, but it was probably the late Theodor Egli, who was then chief armorer at the Tower of London Armouries, but who before World War II had worked for H. Furmage, Whawell's successor in business.

In 1958, some time after I had transferred to the Department of Metalwork at the Victoria and Albert Museum, I was actively engaged in checking and expanding Cripps-Day's lists of church armor and decided to attempt to settle once and for all the question of the authenticity of the helmet at Crediton. I therefore obtained permission from the church authorities to examine and photograph it, which I did on May 30 of that year, together with A. R. Dufty (co-author of the second of Cripps-Day's church-armor lists,[10] who later became Master of the Tower of London Armouries). We found that its surface was completely covered with thick brown varnish, through which painted funerary scrollwork was visible, but which obscured the details of the metal and made proper assessment of the helmet very difficult. We nevertheless decided, after examining it carefully, that it was probably an authentic early piece. However, when I was subsequently able to compare the photographs I had taken of it (fig. 108) with photographs that C. Otto von Kienbusch had kindly sent me of the helmet in his possession, I discovered not only that the two were of identical form and decoration but that they also had rust holes and marks of damage and restoration in identical places! To accept that this could have occurred naturally would have been to stretch belief in coincidence beyond reason: further investigation was therefore clearly necessary. I accordingly wrote to the church authorities, offering to have the helmet cleaned and put in order without charge at the Victoria and Albert Museum, if they would arrange to send it to me in London, an offer that they accepted. As soon as the brown varnish had been removed, it was immediately revealed that the metal it concealed was modern (fig. 107).[11]

The discovery that the helmet was unquestionably a modern reproduction was

Fig. 107. Left, *Three views of the copy of the close-helmet photographed in 1958 shortly after cleaning in the Victoria and Albert Museum, London.*

Fig. 108. Above, *Copy of the close-helmet photographed in 1958 in Crediton Church, Plymouth, Devonshire, England (photographed by the author).*

immediately followed by the further discovery, by A. R. Dufty, in the English National Monument Record, of a photograph (fig. 111) of the armor in Crediton Church taken on June 9, 1908, by F. H. Crossley, the distinguished photographer of and writer on early churches and their contents.[12] The helmet shown in the photograph—viewed from the right-hand side—is slightly damaged, and its decoration differs in tiny details from that on the helmet now in the church. It is, however, identical to that on the one in the Kienbusch Collection. There can be no possible doubt, therefore, that this latter helmet was at Crediton in 1908.

Following these discoveries, I wrote to the Clerk of the Governors of Crediton Church,[13] to tell him about them and to ask if he had any record of the helmet having been removed from the church for any length of time after it was photographed by Crossley in 1908 and before May 1927, when it appeared in the Whawell sale. In a letter to me of December 8, 1958, he wrote:

With regard to your enquiries as to the loan of the helmet, the Governors' minute book states that on 11th January 1910 a Mr. Radford of Bovey House, Beer offered to put the old helmet into proper condition. The minute for 2nd April 1912 states "the thanks of the Governors be conveyed to Mr. A. L. Radford of Bovey House, Beer for repairing the old helmet in the Corporation Room." At some time between 11th January and 11th April 1933 the helmet was on loan to the Young Christian Women's Association [sic] for their loan exhibition of the reign of Queen Elizabeth. In 1940 a considerable amount of controversy appeared in the "Western Morning News" as to whether or not it was a fake and had been substituted for the original helmet. The Governors asked Lt. Col. L.A.D. Montague—a local antiquarian—for his views on the matter and he replied as follows on 22nd January 1940.

"I told him that I first came across this helmet about 1878, in a cupboard in the Governors' Room, together with a heap of Cromwellian relics including riding boots, sword, breastplate, holster, etc. etc., all rusty or needing restoration. In May 1898 I contributed an illustrated article about them to 'Antiquarian Gossip' (archaeological bimonthly of that period) in which a detailed drawing of the helmet appeared, being described as a type in use from the early 17th century up to the Civil War. It was then rusty and needed expert cleaning, but nothing about it suggested to me that it could possibly be a fake. I don't think I saw it again until these antiquities had been hung up in the room and was surprised to notice that it had been 'restored' by being blackened all over with grate polish or something of the kind instead of being de-rusted and oiled, though that it was the original helmet I never doubted."

The original helmet, then, was away from Crediton for an unknown period, which, for obvious reasons, must have been a fairly lengthy one, between January 11, 1910, and April 2, 1912. It can hardly be doubted that this was the occasion when the copy of it now in the church was made and covered with what Colonel Montague described as "grate polish or something of the kind," but which was presumably the varnish that was removed from it at the Victoria and Albert Museum in 1958.

It should be stated at the outset that not the slightest suspicion of complicity in the affair can be attached to A. L. Radford of Bovey House, Beer, Devonshire (fig. 110), to whom the

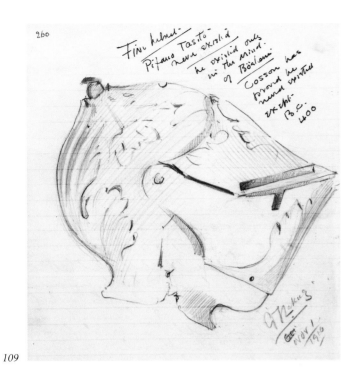

109

110

111

Fig.109. Drawing by Sir Guy Francis Laking (1875–1919) of the close-helmet in the minute book of the
Meyrick Society under the entry for November 1, 1910. The comment at the top is by Sir James G. Mann.
The Meyrick Society and the Royal Armouries, H.M. Tower of London.

Fig. 110. A. L. Radford (1862–1925), by J. Seymour Lucas, 1894. Chalk on paper. C. A. Ralegh Radford.

Fig. 111. The Kienbusch close-helmet and other relics as photographed in 1908
in Crediton Church. Courtauld Institute of Art, London (photographed by F. H. Crossley;
copyright by Canon M. H. Ridgway).

helmet was entrusted for restoration in 1910. He was a distinguished antiquary with an interest in, among other things, early arms and armor,[14] which no doubt accounts for his special concern for the helmet. He was a member of the exclusive London armor collectors' society, the Meyrick Society, and on November 1, 1910, exhibited the helmet at one of their meetings, at the home of the President, J. Seymour Lucas, in Hampstead, London. The minutes of the meeting,[15] which include an excellent drawing of the helmet by Guy Francis Laking (fig. 109), record the event:

> Mr. A. L. Radford exhibited a sword . . . but the gem of Mr. Radford's exhibition was of most remarkable interest in the shape of a very rare helmet from Crediton church (drawn on preceding page). This very fine & unique piece is of blued steel with remains of gilding & is embossed with an acanthus ornament expressed in a free and flowing manner. According to Mr. Laking it is the work of Pifane Tasito [*sic*] called il Principe & the date would be about 1540. It is probably the rarest & most interesting helmet ever exhibited to the Society & Mr. Radford was cordially thanked for its production.

The helmet is of the standard sixteenth- and seventeenth-century construction in which the visor and the upper- and lower-bevors are pivoted at the same points on either side of the skull. The 1908 Crossley photograph (fig. 111) shows it with the right-hand visor-pivot missing, and, as a result, with the lower-bevor pushed up inside the upper one, leaving only a small portion of what is, in fact, its rear edge visible just below the bottom edge of the upper-bevor. Enough of the edge can be seen to show that it had become jagged from rusting, as had also the corresponding lower right-hand corner of the skull. On the Kienbusch helmet both areas have been repaired with well-executed welded patches. They are almost certainly the work of Raymond Bartel, William Randolph Hearst's armorer, since the photograph of the helmet in the 1927 Whawell sale catalogue (fig. 104) shows riveted patches there, apparently exactly like those that remain on the reproduction helmet at Crediton. Both the Kienbusch helmet and the copy have visor-pivots with rosette-shaped heads with domed centers, of which the left-hand one on the Kienbusch helmet is possibly original,[16] the others, of course, being modern. Laking's drawing in the Meyrick Society's minute book (fig. 109)—a view similar to that in the Crossley photograph—shows the helmet as unrepaired but assembled correctly and with the missing visor-pivot replaced by a simple round-headed bolt. One can be certain, therefore, that it was the unrestored original helmet that was exhibited by Radford. In light of Colonel Montague's description of its condition in 1878, to say nothing of its present condition, the statement in the minutes that it was "of blued steel" must be regarded as an error: no doubt, the society's secretary was misled by the blue-black appearance of a heavily patinated surface that had been lightly cleaned and then oiled.

It is unlikely now that the story of how the fake helmet came to be made will ever be known for certain. I can, however, put forward a theory that seems to me to be convincing, based on knowledge of the personalities of the period derived from the reminiscences of some of the older generation of the antique arms and armor fraternity who were still alive when I joined the staff of the Tower of London Armouries. Notable among these were the following: Kienbusch himself; Francis Henry Cripps-Day, Laking's friend and literary executor, who died in 1961 at the age of ninety-eight; James G. Mann, Master of the Tower of London Armouries from 1939 until his death in 1962, and a protégé of the Baron C. A. de Cosson (1846–1929), a noted authority on armor who had also been Laking's mentor; Stephen V. Grancsay, Curator of Arms and Armor at the Metropolitan Museum of Art, New York, from 1929 to 1963; Richard Williams, the well-known armor collector; and, finally, Theodor Egli, chief armorer at the Tower of London Armouries when I knew him, but who had previously worked for H. Furmage (Whawell's business successor) and, before that, for another well-known and long-established armor dealer, S. G. Fenton.

As stated, there is no reason to suspect A. L. Radford of complicity in the substitution of the helmet. He was a man of the highest reputation, and there can be no doubt that he acted throughout from the best of motives and was as much an innocent victim of the deception as were the governors of Crediton Church. The same, however, cannot be said of Samuel James Whawell, the one person who we can be certain was deeply involved, since the original helmet finally surfaced at the sale of his "collection" in 1927 and was, in fact, seen at his home by Kienbusch in 1923. Kienbusch mentioned this in a letter to me of August 26, 1958, in which he also stated:

I bought a number of less important things from him at the time, but was not wealthy enough to buy this helmet. I think Whawell must have purchased it from someone connected with the church rather secretively on the basis of supplying a replica. Whawell wasn't particularly anxious to sell the helmet at the time. It remained with him until his death.

It will be recalled that "an armour expert"—undoubtedly Cripps-Day— was quoted in the *Western Morning News* of January 3, 1940, as saying that shortly after about 1925 the helmet had been offered to him for £80 by "an armour dealer," who can only have been Whawell.[17] The same expert also said that in about 1925 he had received a letter "from a gentleman interested in armour, stating that there was in a private collection in London a helmet exactly similar to the one at Crediton." This must refer to an undated letter from C. R. Beard—the antiquary and writer on arms and armor—to Cripps-Day, who marked it "c. 1924," now in the Crediton section of the latter's interleaved copy of his church-armor lists in the Victoria and Albert Museum library.[18] The relevant part reads:

On Thursday I looked up the Crediton (Greenwich) helmet, and compared it with a sketch I made some time ago of one then in the possession (permanent or temporary I don't know) of Dr. Jensen in Harley St. They are the same, there is no question. Jensen was very reticent, when he showed it to me about four years ago. I should very much like to know what he was doing with it, and if it has gone back to Devon. He wouldn't tell me whence it came or anything else regarding it. Kelly[19] saw it at the same time, and I think Furmage, but not Mann so far as I remember.

The Dr. Jensen referred to in this letter was E. T. Jensen, a well-known physician and armor collector.[20] As with Radford, there is no reason to suspect him of collaborating in the Crediton fraud: one may reasonably assume, therefore, that he had the helmet on approval from Whawell when Beard saw it in his possession, but eventually decided not to buy it. We may thus also surmise with some confidence that Whawell already owned it by about 1920, that is, eight years after the fake helmet had presumably been deposited in the church.

Whawell, as one of the leading dealers of his time, had an almost legendary reputation as a judge of armor among the collectors he served.[21] Laking acknowledged this in fulsome terms in the preface to his *Record of European Armour and Arms through Seven Centuries*:

Again, to Mr. S. J. Whawell, my old friend of very many years' standing, there is an obligation to be acknowledged; for, whenever a controversy has arisen over the authenticity of a specimen, he has always very generously come forward as consultant and given his opinion. In such predicaments, occasionally most difficult, I have always turned to him, and his decision has ever been final: for his knowledge of our subject is never at fault. It is not too much to say that a judgement of his, passed on any European weapon or armament, is one which cannot be disputed.[22]

Whawell, however, also had a reputation for both unpredictability and irascibility. He was for several years a sailor on deep-sea sailing ships and served through the Zulu War of 1879 in Baker's Horse before briefly joining the Cape Mounted Rifles. These experiences apparently had a lifelong effect on his temper and language, and I have been told by more than one person that, once his reputation was established, potential customers visiting his home, where he also kept his stock, might find themselves welcomed with open arms and lavish potions of whiskey or else told succinctly and impolitely to go away, however important they were. A once-celebrated story is told of Laking—in some versions Cripps-Day—going into the house and then emerging almost instantly, pursued by Whawell brandishing a sixteenth-century mace![23]

Born in London in 1857, Whawell came from a long line of armor repairers—allegedly going back to the seventeenth century—and while young had helped his widowed mother run the family business. Through his work he got to know many of the Victorian historical painters and, according to the memoir of him in the catalogue of his sale in 1927, was particularly encouraged by John Pettie, R.A. (1839–1893), who commissioned him to make a complete fluted armor in early-sixteenth-century German style. From 1883 onward, after his seafaring and other adventures, he devoted himself entirely to arms and armor. He was almost immediately employed by the wealthy publisher of boys' "penny-dreadful" magazines, Edwin J. Brett, to form a large collection of arms and armor,[24] and this was the foundation of his fortunes. Among his purchases for Brett was the Polish Gayeski Collection, which, according to another oft-told tale, he had to transport in sleighs across snow, pursued by hungry wolves kept at bay only by continuous gunfire. He became a central figure in the antique armor world, and this, coupled with his friendship with Laking, who, of course, had drawn the Crediton helmet at the Meyrick Society meeting, makes it inconceivable that he could have purchased the helmet innocently without knowing its origins.

The picture of Whawell that emerges from these anecdotes is of someone who was rumbustious, tough, probably also rather rough, and perhaps not overscrupulous in his business dealings when an opportunity for profit presented itself: Cripps-Day, in a note in his grangerized copy of the Whawell sale catalogue, now in the library of the Royal Armouries, says of him that "on the whole he was honest—but he was a 'wicked' man."[25] He was also, as we have seen, both a skilled armorer and someone whose opinion was sought about all matters to do with armor, which, according to Cripps-Day's note, "he really loved." A strong case could be made, therefore, for ascribing the whole of the Crediton fraud to him alone, including the actual making of the reproduction helmet.

Unfortunately, there appears to be no means of assessing whether Whawell's skill was up to the standard of the Crediton reproduction, which is very high indeed: from a purely technical viewpoint, it is in no way inferior to the original, and is only given away by the nature and appearance of the steel used to make it. It is also a remarkably accurate copy and, so far as one can judge by merely comparing photographs, it differs from the original only in such minute details as the configuration of the ends of the interstices of the embossed acanthus leaves and the form of the hatching on the pairs of strawberry-like fruit set in calyxes, one on each side of the skull. Cripps-Day certainly thought that Whawell was technically—and, by implication, morally—capable of having made the reproduction, since on August 30, 1958, he wrote to me: "Yes, Whawell could have made the copy. He could make anything & I have seen him at work making the missing pieces of armour for a suit. He worked only with the eye and two old tools."

I have no recollection of anyone else commenting on Whawell's skill as an armorer, so this testimonial is my only evidence on the subject. Unsupported, and in view of Cripps-Day's age when he wrote it—he was about ninety-five—it must be regarded with caution, especially since the production of a helmet decorated with high-quality embossing is quite different from "making the missing pieces of armour for a suit." There was, however, one extraordinary craftsman working in London in 1910 who would certainly have been capable of making the helmet and who is known to have produced fakes of all kinds. This was Felix Joubert (1872–1953; fig. 112), of The Pheasantry in the King's Road, Chelsea, the head of a large art and antique restoration business, who was referred to by the art dealer James Henry Duveen as the "Chelsea Wizard" and "the greatest artist in this kind of thing who has ever been known." Joubert's most celebrated fake was of the early fourteenth-century silver and enameled head reliquary of Saint Martin, from the church at Soudeilles (Corrèze), France, which was sold clandestinely and illegally by the parish priest to J. Pierpont Morgan via Duveen Brothers, a condition of the sale being that a substitute copy be provided for the church. James Henry Duveen tells how this copy was made so skillfully by Joubert that it could not be distinguished from the original, and that, as the result of a joke, the two became

CREDITON HELMET

1 6 5

confused, so that it was uncertain which was which. The story of the illegal sale eventually became public, and J. Pierpont Morgan presented what is believed to be the original reliquary—though incorporating some Joubert enamels—to the Musée du Louvre.[26]

Joubert was the subject of the acknowledgment immediately following that to Whawell in Laking's *Record*:

Among my other friends who collect armour, no one deserves greater credit for the good work that he has accomplished than Mr. Felix Joubert, from whose collection I have been privileged to take certain illustrations for this book. Mr. Joubert is an artist to his finger tips—modelling, painting, enamelling, and, indeed, interesting himself generally in all the arts of the past. He is a kind friend, ever ready with his staff of skilled workmen to assist in the repair of a weapon or harness of plate, with which time or the ignorant hand of a restorer has dealt hardly. A very skilled fencer, he has a most intimate knowledge of all types of arms, and, as an artist, appreciates what a weapon should be.[27]

A more recent writer has described Joubert as "an extraordinary craftsman, who could fake anything of any period . . . sculptor, jeweller, armourer, decorator."[28] He was also said to have included arms and armor among his fakes by some of the older generation of armor collectors mentioned here,[29] and their views are confirmed in a hitherto unpublished note by the late Earl of Crawford and Balcarres referring to comments made by his father, the 27th Earl (died 1940), in connection with an exhibition of fakes held by the Burlington Fine Arts Club in 1924, to which Joubert lent two helmets.[30]

I found the following in my father's diary:—

[16 April, 1924] To Joubert who has promised to lend for the B.F.A.C. [Burlington Fine Arts Club] show. He was quite frank about his own forgeries. He works to order and is often quite ignorant of the destination of the objects. When Miss Alice de Rothschild died a few years ago, Joubert discovered she was the owner of the little daggers with ivory handles and sheaths which he had made and sold to his agent. I doubt not that the old lady paid high prices for these sophistications. Joubert got one of them back, from the agent I think who had not "placed" it—I saw this sample, dainty and dextrous, but not at all convincing to my eye.

I remember Joubert and Pierre Cochette who worked for him. They were wonderful restorers as well as "honourable" forgers. "Honourable" because they never themselves sold their products as genuine—but only to people who would sell them as "genuine"!

Some twenty years ago I myself saw evidence of Joubert's abilities as a forger. An artist who had rented Joubert's former studio in Chelsea brought into the Victoria and Albert Museum for my opinion a few small pieces of armor and other metalwork that he had found there. Among them was a wheel-lock plate, of seventeenth-century form but obviously modern, which someone had started chiseling very skillfully with decoration in the style of the same period, but had not completed. In view of the source of the piece, it can hardly be doubted that the someone was Joubert or one of his assistants.

Fig. 112. Felix Joubert (1872–1952),
by Helen McKie. Ink on paper.
The Chelsea Library, London.

One other possible and relevant piece of evidence for Joubert's skill as a faker of armor can be mentioned. In the 1950s the collection of Claude Falkiner (the world-champion billiard player) contained a remarkable reproduction of an etched and gilt German helmet of about 1520, with a double visor and prominent S-shaped embossed roped ribs radiating across the skull from each side of the comb. The original helmet, of which this was an almost exact copy, is part of Joubert's own personal collection, now in the Musée Masséna, Nice,[31] and there is every probability, therefore, that the copy was made by him. It shows the same technical mastery as the copy of the Crediton helmet and could certainly have been made by the same hand.

In 1960 I wrote to Stephen V. Grancsay, who had a wide knowledge of armor faking, to ask his opinion about the possible authorship of the Crediton reproduction. He replied on May 5, 1960:

I wish I had some definite information about the armorer who made it. I do not think that Whawell made it, since he was active as a restorer in his younger days . . . . By 1910 Whawell was already sufficiently prosperous not to have to undertake the major operation of making a helmet. I would rather think that it was made under the supervision of Felix Joubert, who was very close to Laking and who I understand did some work on the armour in the Wallace Collection.

All in all, therefore, although certainty is not possible, there is a strong probability that the fake Crediton helmet was made either personally by Joubert or under his supervision, rather than by Whawell.

I come now to the more difficult question of the identity of the organizer of the fraud. Unfortunately, neither information about the way A. L. Radford set about arranging the helmet's repair in 1910, nor a record of whom he paid for the work, appears to have survived. As an armor-collector, he knew Whawell and he may well have gone directly to him. It is more likely, however, that he would first have approached Guy Francis Laking, the leading English armor expert of the period and a close friend, in addition to being a fellow member of the Meyrick Society. This opinion, which is held also by Radford's son, C. A. Ralegh Radford, appears to be supported by the fact that the helmet had apparently not yet been repaired when Laking sketched it at the meeting of the Meyrick Society on November 1, 1910. The missing visor-pivot had, it is true, been replaced with a plain bolt, but Radford very probably had had this done by one of his own employees, whom he is known to have entrusted with carrying out minor repairs and cleaning pieces in his own collection.

Laking (fig. 113) was an extraordinary character.[32] The son of the physician to the Prince of Wales (the future King Edward VII), he developed a passionate interest in antique arms and armor in early childhood. He always retained this love, and a touching story was told to me by Sir James G. Mann of how, in 1919, when Laking was dying, at the early age of forty-four, he asked for his latest armor acquisition to be brought to him so that he might have a last look at it. On leaving school, he first trained to become an artist, but soon became involved with Christie's, the London art auctioneers, an association that would last for the rest of his life. His expertise was remarkably extensive; the author of his obituary in *The Times* (London, November 24, 1919) wrote:

It was not only on armour that Laking was a recognised authority: he had a special knowledge, acquired by unremitting study, of every branch of the Fine Arts, both from an artistic as well as a commercial point of view. For this reason he enjoyed the confidence of many noted collectors.

His deep involvement in the art trade did not, however, prevent him from being appointed to a specially created royal office of Keeper of the King's Armoury at Windsor, and to the official museum posts of Inspector of the Armoury of the Wallace Collection and Keeper of the newly founded London Museum. At that time it would normally have been unthinkable for anyone to combine official and commercial involvement in art in this way, and one can only assume that Laking was able to do so because he enjoyed the personal friendships of both King Edward VII and his successor George V. Though the testimony of his contemporaries and the number of publications he produced in his short life leave no doubt about his dedication to his subject and his great industry, he was never a scholar in the academic sense, but rather what

Fig. 113. Sir Guy Francis Laking (1875–1919)
as "Esquire of the Knight Martial of the Lists"
in "The Triumph Presented at Shakespeare's England,"
Earls Court, London, July 1912.
The Meyrick Society, London.

his contemporaries would have called a connoisseur. Nevertheless, his magnum opus, the five-volume *Record of European Armour and Arms*, despite many imperfections, is a major work by any standard and still remains extremely useful because of its wealth of illustrations.

Laking's private life contrasted sharply with this exemplary public image. He was wildly extravagant—one friend said of him that he "spent his money like one who has a store of gold angels and gold nobles in an iron chest rather than one who draws cheques on a bank account"[33]—and when something that he wanted came into the market he would let nothing stand in his way until he acquired it.[34] In an article published in 1940, James Mann wrote of Laking and the Meyrick Society:

He inspired all around him with his intense enthusiasm for fine armour and arms, and his lavish entertainments are still spoken of with awe by older members. They tell how he had a peacock roasted in its feathers, and brought in with trumpets and preceded by Joan of Arc in armour.[35]

Mann omitted to mention that the woman who played this part, the governess of Laking's children, was reputed to be his mistress, and, if the stories once told about his amatory exploits are to be believed, she was only one of many.

Laking's life-style, then, was an expensive one, and, since he did not have great private wealth, he had to make money to maintain it. He naturally used his knowledge of art and his connections with the art trade for this purpose, but there is evidence to suggest that he was not always entirely scrupulous about his methods. A man of immense charm and, it should be mentioned, also of genuine kindness,[36] he was an extremely attractive personality, especially to women.[37] Because of these qualities, and probably also because of his royal connections, he had many wealthy friends, whom, according to Mann, he persuaded to collect arms and armor on the sale of which he would undoubtedly have received a commission from the dealers concerned. Two collections formed with Laking's assistance by wealthy people with no knowledge of arms and armor, Lord Astor of Hever and Alice de Rothschild of Waddesdon Manor, contained a high proportion of fakes of a kind that could not possibly have deceived him, and it is difficult to avoid the conclusion that he was party to the deceptions and financially rewarded for them.

In his *Secrets of an Art Dealer*, published in 1937, James Henry Duveen devoted a chapter to a story about a swindle practiced on an American collector, which he entitled "The Blackmailing of an Expert." It starts: "In 1905 there was in London a very brilliant and debonair young man who was an acknowledged authority on art and, in particular, on old armour," and goes on to say that the young man in question, who is given the pseudonym "Hugh Melmett," was a womanizer, an authority on vintage wine, had published works on armor, and had "died at an unexpectedly early age."[38] This description cannot refer to anyone other than Laking.

Duveen recounts how "Melmett" was threatened over the nonpayment of a debt of £800—a considerable sum in 1905—and turned for help to a leading London art dealer, who is given the name "Mr. George." This art dealer agreed to let him have the money, and more, but only on condition that he would help him to swindle a wealthy New York armor collector, to whom Duveen gives the pseudonym "Patrick P. Bordeaux." The swindle involved two plain "Gothic" armors that a "virtuoso-restorer" called "Halberd" (Joubert?), who had often been "the creator of 'works of art' which had fetched high prices," had offered to decorate with imitation gold inlay, thereby increasing their value from £800 to £20,000. The offer was accepted, and "Melmett" was required to certify that the armors were genuine, in return for the £800 and an additional commission, which he did, with the result that "Bordeaux" purchased them for £32,000.[39]

Duveen, who appears to have been profoundly ignorant about armor, undoubtedly embroidered this account to make it more readable. He stated that "Melmett" certified that the armors were "about 1480 and Verona," which is absurd, while nobody with any knowledge of the subject would decorate Gothic armor with gold inlay and hope to pass it off as genuine. His information, however, came from his friend "Frederick Alcker," who had worked for the "well-known Mr. George" and had been involved in the affair. The story is therefore likely to be accurate in outline, if not in detail.

One other piece of evidence pointing to Laking's lack of scruples can be mentioned. In 1913 the great Victorian art connoisseur Sir John Charles Robinson died,[40] leaving a collection, acquired in his dotage, consisting mostly of specimens of the splendid medieval fakes, including arms, associated with the faker Louis Marcy.[41] Laking discusses Marcy fakes in some detail in the chapter on fakes in the last volume of his *Record*, although without actually mentioning his name,[42] so he was undoubtedly familiar with them. However, according to a note in the issue of February 9, 1918, of the privately circulated and highly confidential *Mitteilungen* of the Berlin-based Federation of Museum Officials Against Fakes and Corrupt Trade Practices, the "dealer Fr. L." tried, after Robinson's death, to sell his collection in Berlin, then in America, and then in Berlin again.[43] The identity of "Fr. L." is not certain, but "Francis Laking" is an obvious, and probable, reading of the initials.

Finally, so far as this assessment of Laking's character is concerned, I can mention a comment made to me by Mann in the early days of our acquaintanceship. I remarked to him that it was sad that Laking had died so young. His reply, which I have always remembered because it astonished me, was that perhaps it was not so sad, because had Laking lived much longer, he would not have had any friends left!

In his commentary published as an appendix to this article, C. A. Ralegh Radford, the son of A. L. Radford, who had arranged for the Crediton helmet to be put in order in 1910, implies that, although Laking was almost certainly responsible for Whawell being entrusted with the work, it was the latter who, without his knowledge, took the opportunity to have the copy made: in short, Laking was as much an innocent victim as A. L. Radford and the church authorities. This possibility clearly cannot be ruled out, but it is difficult to accept in view of one crucial piece of negative evidence pointing strongly to Laking's complicity in the Crediton fraud: the helmet's omission from his *Record of European Armour and Arms*. The helmet is an important one, and, apart from a brass parade-shield in the Royal Armouries at the Tower of London (v.53), it is the only known example of embossed armor with English associations going back to the time when it might have been worn for use.[44] Laking discusses the shield,[45] but nowhere even mentions the helmet, although his coverage of the major pieces of English church-armor known at the time he was writing is otherwise virtually exhaustive. The obvious explanation for this quite extraordinary omission is that he knew the helmet at Crediton was a fake and, so devoted was he to his subject, could not bring himself to write about it in a work that he tried to make as honest as possible. This being so, he would equally obviously not have wanted to draw attention to the genuine helmet in Whawell's possession, and so did not mention it either.

In light of all the preceding information, I suggest that the inside story of the Crediton fraud is likely to have been as follows. When A. L. Radford first offered to have the helmet put in order he probably intended merely that his own man should carry out the work, which had already been done when it was exhibited to the Meyrick Society on November 1, 1910, since, judging by the Crossley photograph (fig. 111), its condition does not seem to have been very bad. It was natural enough, however, that Radford would have wanted to show the helmet to his fellow Meyrick Society members and to consult his friend Laking, the leading English authority on armor, about it. Laking no doubt persuaded him that such an outstandingly important piece required expert restoration and offered to have this done for him. He would then have made a deal with Whawell, and presumably also Joubert, with results as described here. We are unlikely ever to know whether the reproduction helmet was sent to Crediton via Radford as soon as it was ready or, as his son suggests in the appendix to this article, whether it was kept for a time and then taken surreptitiously to the church and substituted for the original, perhaps by Whawell. It appears to me, however, that the former course would have been by far the easier and safer, in view of the remarkably high quality of the fake: it will be recalled that it was good enough to deceive the distinguished armor experts who selected it for the 1933 Elizabethan exhibition, one of whom, James G. Mann, actually transported it personally to London for the purpose.

We can now turn to a brief discussion of the original helmet. Its form (figs. 102, 103) is that of a field helmet. The rounded, bluntly pointed skull is surmounted by a small strawberry-shaped finial, made separately on a short stem that passes through a hole and is riveted over on the inside. As already noted, the visor and upper- and lower-bevors are attached at the same points on each side on pivots with large, rosette-shaped heads with domed centers (the right-hand one certainly a replacement),[46] the rosettes being formed of acanthus-like leaves. The profile of the visor and upper-bevor together is that of a very wide isosceles triangle with slightly curved sides and its apex to the front. The top of the visor is cut to a shallow, concave curve on each side of the center point, and the long horizontal vision-slit—which is not stepped—has a single central division cut so close to the edge at the front that it only just clears the upper-bevor, and itself has a lower edge that barely projects beyond its upper one; on the right is a lifting peg (modern) with a conical knob of polygonal section. The upper-bevor is notched for this peg, and its lower edge on each side is cut to a dog's-leg shape, sloping down in a shallow concave curve to form an angle with a short straight section joining the front medial ridge. The lower-bevor has a strongly marked chin, and its lower edge, like that of the skull, curves out to form a flange pierced for rivets for the attachment of the missing gorget-plates. The edges of the face-opening are turned and file-roped—the turn across the brow being a hollow half turn—and bordered by lining-rivets, some of which are missing; a row of holes for similar rivets encircles the base of the skull. There are no signs of a locking device on the visor, but a hole near the right-hand lower edge of the upper-bevor and another adjacent to it on the lower-bevor presumably indicate the former presence of a pivot-hook and stud fastening of standard type. Two holes set one on each side of the skull near the lower front corners hold rivets attaching a modern strap and buckle that pass around the neck of the lower-bevor and hold it closed: this is presumably the original arrangement, since there are no signs of any other method of locking the lower-bevor to the skull. The whole surface is covered with varnish similar to that removed from the reproduction helmet in 1958.

The embossed decoration comprises single large acanthus leaves clasping, respectively, the back and top of the skull, the top of the visor, and the front of the upper-bevor; a pair of inverted acanthus-leaf calyxes, each containing a pair of strawberry-like berries, set one on each side of the top of the skull between the main acanthus leaves and linked to the finial by straight stems; and, finally, a shallow acanthus-leaf border to the upper edge of the visor. The last named was produced by recessing the background to the design along the edge of the visor, so that only the upper ends of the leaves are formed. All the other decoration is in relief, although the surfaces of the leaves are only modeled slightly and so have a flat appearance. If, as was frequently the case, the embossed decoration was supplemented with damascening, no traces now remain.

The evidence that the helmet—to quote the Whawell sale catalogue—"has been used for funerary purposes and hung in a church" needs to be emphasized. This, apart from the general appearance of its surface, is provided by the presence of a roughly punched hole in the skull, just forward of the finial, and of traces of gold-painted edging-lines and scrollwork (erroneously called "gilding" in the Whawell catalogue) on the visor and upper-bevor. Hundreds of helmets from English churches demonstrate that such a hole would originally have contained an iron spike for the attachment of a painted wooden crest of a kind that, like the painted scrollwork, is found only on helmets that have been used for funerary purposes.[47]

By the fourteenth century, if not before, it had become usual for a knight's crested helm, gauntlets, shield, coat-armor, sword, spurs, and banner to be carried at his funeral and then hung over his monument, forming what was known from the sixteenth century onward as an *achievement*. Many such achievements are still preserved, wholly or in part, in English churches[48]—the earliest known to survive being that of the Black Prince (died 1376) in Canterbury Cathedral—but the majority date from the middle of the sixteenth century onward. Initially, the achievement normally consisted mainly of pieces that had belonged to the person commemorated, and as late as 1556 the will of Sir Giles Capel of Rayne Hall, Essex, contained the instruction: "Also I will that my beste Helmett and my Armynge Sworde be sett over my funerall according to the demise of the harrauldes."[49] But the fashion for elaborate heraldic funerals, organized by the heralds, "had spread downwards by the middle of the sixteenth century from kings and noblemen to knights and citizens and their ladies,"[50] which explains why the vast majority of surviving achievements date from after this period. The increase in the numbers of heraldic funerals was a large one, and a high proportion of the people who produced it were not armor wearers, while the same period also saw the first faint signs of a decline in the use of armor, leading to its being generally discarded in the seventeenth century. These two factors must have produced a shortage of helmets and gauntlets for achievements, since, from at least the end of the sixteenth century onward, there are indications that the heralds were buying old armor—occasionally even medieval pieces— and doing it up for funerary use.[51] As the seventeenth century progressed, even this must have become more difficult to obtain, for the examples found in achievements of this time consist increasingly of degenerate and impractical pieces made specifically for funerary purposes, until, at the very end, they were often no more than carved wooden models.

There can be no doubt, therefore, that the helmet now in the Kienbusch Collection once formed part of the funeral achievement of a member of the aristocracy or gentry buried or commemorated in Crediton Church, and was originally displayed over or near his monument. Furthermore, the style of the funerary painting on it suggests that it was used for this purpose in either the late-sixteenth century or the first half of the seventeenth century. It must, therefore, have come from one or the other of the two major monuments of this period in Crediton Church, both of which are situated on the north side of the altar.[52] They commemorate, respectively, a member of a minor family of local gentry, John Tuckfield of Fulford (died 1630), and Sir William Peryam (1534–1604), also of Fulford, a distinguished judge who was of sufficient importance to merit an entry in the *Dictionary of National Biography*.[53] Unfortunately, there appears to be no way of establishing which monument is associated with the helmet,[54] but even if this were possible, it would be unlikely to throw any light on its origins, since neither Peryam nor Tuckfield seems to have had the personal experience or the family background to make ownership of armor of this kind and quality likely. There is a strong probability, therefore, that the helmet was an old piece supplied by the heralds who organized the funeral concerned.

We come finally to the questions of the date and provenance of the helmet. It would be well to start by clearing away the undergrowth of conflicting attributions already mentioned. These are that it is "of a pattern in use during the first half of the 17th century, and up to the Civil War," "of the Cromwellian period," "the time of Charles I," "about 1540," "undoubtedly the production of a member of the celebrated Negroli family [of Milan]," "Mid 16th Cent.," "the work of Pifane Tasito [*sic*] called il Principe," and was made in the English royal workshops at Greenwich. To these can be added the most recent attribution, in Kienbusch's own catalogue of 1963, "Probably ITALIAN, Third Quarter of XVI Century. . . . or it may be Flemish."[55]

Several of these attributions can be dismissed quickly. It requires only an elementary knowledge of armor to see that the helmet predates the seventeenth century; Pifanio Tacito, as Laking himself pointed out in his *Record*,[56] was the alleged maker of an armor for Hannibal the Carthaginian who was erroneously transported to the sixteenth century by Wendelin Boeheim of Vienna; and, not only is there no evidence to suggest that embossed armor of this kind was produced in the royal workshops at Greenwich, but the helmet does not have a single feature that would justify even a tentative attribution to them.[57] The remaining attributions deserve more serious consideration.

The best known of the artist armor-embossers belonged to the Negroli family of Milan. Their signed and attributed works cover the period from about 1532 to 1551, and the most famous of them was Filippo Negroli.[58] Their designs often include acanthus foliage, and some of Filippo's, in particular, superficially resemble that on the Crediton helmet, especially in the restrained way in which the ornament is used, interspersed with plain areas, instead of covering all surfaces in the manner usual on embossed armor of the latter part of the sixteenth century. The Whawell catalogue's attribution of the helmet to "a member of the celebrated Negroli family" was therefore reasonable enough. However, one need only compare the details of the decoration with that on signed Negroli pieces to see that it is quite different in style and, although the work of a skilled craftsman, not in the same class in terms of design or technical execution: Negroli work—and above all that of Filippo—is not only full of a strength and vitality that are completely lacking from the embossing on the Crediton helmet, but its details, instead of being raised in what are almost flat blocks, are fully modeled with great precision. A Negroli attribution for the helmet must, therefore, in my opinion, be rejected.[59]

The style of the embossing is closer to that of the work attributed to the next-best-known Italian artist-armorer of the first half of the sixteenth century, Caremolo Modrone, who was born in Milan but worked for the Gonzaga family in Mantua from before 1521 until his death in 1543.[60] This is characterized by the same widely spaced, rather broadly treated embossing on a completely uncluttered ground and the occasional use of leaves, including acanthus leaves, that, because of the minimal amount of modeling on their surfaces, also have an appearance of being raised in almost flat blocks. An attribution to Modrone's workshop is therefore a possibility, but no more than that. Current knowledge of Modrone's style is based on the decoration on the small handful of pieces that can be ascribed to him—with every probability, but no certainty—on historical grounds, and this is not particularly close in details of style or technique to that on the Crediton helmet.

The identification of embossed armor is notoriously difficult, and opinions on the subject have changed only marginally since the time, more than one hundred fifty years ago, when an auctioneer could describe a sixteenth-century shield as being "chased by the inimitable hand of Celini, from one of the finest designs of Raphael"![61] We have almost no detailed knowledge of workshop styles, and still less of variations within workshops, and tend to ascribe everything to the few important artists whose names we know, most of whom are Italian. A case in point is provided by an embossed burgonet in the Wallace Collection, London (fig. 114), the decoration on which has certain affinities with that on the Crediton helmet, in that it includes a large acanthus leaf clasping the back of the skull and also smaller ones raised in almost flat blocks. In 1958 this burgonet was attributed to Filippo Negroli by Bruno Thomas and Ortwin Gamber; in the 1962 edition of the Wallace Collection European arms and armor catalogue by James Mann, it was merely called "? Negroli"; it was subsequently attributed to Caremolo Modrone by both John F. Hayward and myself; and now, in A.V.B. Norman's supplement to the Wallace Collection catalogues, it has been returned once more to Filippo Negroli![62]

A further difficulty in attributing embossed decoration on armor is caused by the fact that it is almost invariably in the High Renaissance style that originated in Italy, so that, as we know next to nothing about the artist-embossers of other countries, we have a built-in bias toward

Fig. 114. Burgonet, North Italian, c.1540. Embossed steel, russeted and parcel gilt. Wallace Collection, London; A108.

ascribing all embossed armor automatically to Italy, unless there is strong evidence to the contrary. This being so, it is desirable to consider the Crediton helmet simply *as* a helmet, detached from its decoration, especially since no precise parallel to it can be found. This does not produce a definite answer to the problems of its origin, but it does, at least, clarify what these problems are.

The close-helmet construction, in which an upper- and lower-bevor and the visor are pivoted at the same points on either side, although apparently introduced in Germany in the 1520s, came to be used universally in Europe and survived well into the second half of the seventeenth century. It is not, therefore, in itself a guide to either date or provenance. The general form of the Crediton helmet, however, suggests that it dates from the middle years of the sixteenth century, that is, between the 1530s and 1560s, a period that is consistent with the restrained nature of the embossed decoration. The method of securing the lower-bevor and skull together by means of a neck strap is, on the whole, an Italian one, as are the absence of a locking device to hold the visor closed, and, although less exclusively, the use of a pivot-hook and stud to secure the upper- and lower-bevors together;[63] on German helmets of the same period, spring locking-catches are normally fitted for all these purposes. On the other

Fig. 115. Close-helmet, German, Augsburg?, c.1550. Steel, etched, and parcel gilt. The Metropolitan Museum of Art, Bashford Dean Memorial Collection; Gift of Mr. and Mrs. Alexander McMillan Welch, 1929, 29.153.3.

hand, the form of visor and upper-bevor that are together shaped like a broad-based isosceles triangle with its apex to the front, and having a single, unstepped, horizontal vision-slit set close to the front edge of the visor and with a central division, although not unknown in Italy, is distinctly German, as is any form of visor or lower-bevor with its lower edge cut to a dog's-leg shape: the normal Italian visor/upper-bevor is made with the bottom edge cut to a single slightly concave or convex curve, and has a vision-slit that is either stepped or has a lower edge that projects well beyond its upper one at the front, or both. Many German helmets with visors of a form generally similar to that of the Crediton helmet exist: one that is particularly close to it is on the splendid Augsburg(?) field helmet in the Metropolitan Museum of Art, New York (fig. 115), made for a member of the d'Avalos family.[64] It should also be mentioned that, whereas combless Italian helmets of the mid-sixteenth century with fruitlet or acorn finials are extremely rare, German ones are common, though the majority are burgonets and not close-helmets.[65]

The helmet, then, has features characteristic of both Italy and Germany. This may mean nothing more than that it was produced in one of those countries either for export to the other, or by an armorer who was a native of the other country or had been influenced by its styles.

Another possibility, however, is that it was made in an area outside Italy or Germany, but under the influence of both. The obvious places are France and the Low Countries or, possibly, although not very probably, England,[66] where there were other armorers besides those in the royal workshops at Greenwich, including some Italian craftsmen.[67] Unfortunately, we as yet know so little about armor produced in these areas during the period covered here, except that made in the Greenwich Armouries, which I have already discounted, that not even a tentative attribution to any of them is possible. It is worth noting, however, that the types of fastening and form of visor cited here are commonly represented, both singly and together, on a series of embossed armors associated with the French court, although none of the decoration on these relates to that on the Crediton helmet. One of them, an armor made for King Francis I about 1545 and formerly in the Hever Castle Collection, has been attributed to Giovanni Paolo Negroli;[68] the others date from the 1550s onward and are products of the French royal workshop, which is closely associated with the name of Eliseus Libaerts of Antwerp.[69] A French or Flemish origin for the Crediton helmet is therefore a distinct possibility. Until more definite evidence about its origins is available, however, the safest course is to call the helmet western European—perhaps French or Flemish, or Italian made for the western European market—and date it to the mid-sixteenth century.

APPENDIX

Comments on the Helmet in Crediton Church by C. A. Ralegh Radford

C. A. Ralegh Radford, the son of the late A. L. Radford, who arranged for the Crediton helmet to be repaired in 1910, has kindly written the following comments.

I preface these notes with a few dates, as the credibility of statements made from memory depends in part on the age of the person at the time of the events recorded. I was born in 1900. I matriculated at Exeter College, Oxford, in 1918, taking my degree in 1921. Between my father's death in 1925 and my appointment to the British School at Rome in 1936, I spent a certain amount of time putting his papers in order. They were voluminous. For example, every receipt over thirty years was filed—a case every two years; receipts for antiquities, armor, etc., were filed with those for mundane supplies, like car accessories. In 1940 our lease of Bradnich Manor allowed a break. I stored the furniture, not needed by my mother in her small flat in Exeter or by my sister. In 1942 the roof of the depository was destroyed by incendiary bombs. The greater part of my library and all the papers were dowsed with extinguishers and exposed to rain for some days. The papers, which were in the uppermost cases, were consolidated into an amorphous mass and had to be destroyed when I got access in 1950; the books were mostly saved, though damaged.

Lt. Col. L.A.D. Montague, to whom reference is made in the article, was a prominent member of the Devon Archaeological Exploration Society. He appears in published lists in 1938. In the next published list, in 1946, he is replaced on the committee by Mrs. Montague. I remember him well in the 1930s, a gentleman then in his seventies, with a memory beginning to fade in the later years of the decade. He was a numismatist—a Fellow of the Royal Numismatical Society—and outside coins his main interest was in Roman small antiquities.

As a schoolboy I saw the Crediton helmet several times while it was at Bovey House. I went with my father when he returned it to Crediton. It always appeared as bare metal—at first filthy and rusty, before its return clean. I accept the probability that it had been coated with transparent varnish, through which the gilding was visible; this is a point that I should not have noticed. Cripps-Day was a friend of my father and came more than once to our house between about 1916 and 1921. I still possess the presentation copy of *Church Armour* inscribed "A. L. Radford ex dono auctoris," together with a manuscript covering letter signed by Cripps-Day. His statement, cited in the *Western Morning News*, that the original helmet was in the church in 1920, should probably be interpreted as "in the period 1916–21."

I think the case against Whawell is irrefutable. He was the culprit, but I do not think my father would have entrusted the helmet to him. He would have sent it to Laking. That Laking employed Whawell to carry out the repairs and, incidentally, gave him the opportunity necessary to make the copy seems as near proof as we are ever likely to get. But I gravely doubt whether the copy was substituted at this date. My own view is that this was done after the war and after Cripps-Day's visit. It would not have been difficult for Whawell to gain access to the Governors' Room at any time between 1912 and 1923. He would have been granted access and allowed to handle the helmet. If he wished to take extensive notes he would probably have been left with it with a minimum of supervision. He was certainly in Devon at least twice in 1922–23. My father and I were lunching in the restaurant at St. David's Station, Exeter, in late autumn 1922 or early 1923. The restaurant was entered through the buffet, from which it was visible through a glass screen. I saw a man leave the buffet. He came into the restaurant and approached my father, who recognized him and introduced me. They spoke about armor for a few minutes and Whawell left to catch the London train. In the course of the conversation it emerged that he had come in on a local train to Exeter to catch the London express. He also said he had been in Devon a few weeks earlier and failed to make contact with my father by telephone. After he had left my father said "I have not seen him for years; he is a dealer and a great rogue."

I would suggest that on both these occasions Whawell went to Crediton. On the first visit he would note the then condition of the helmet, e.g., if the varnish had discolored, and its accessibility—I think it could have been removed by standing on a chair and that steps would not have been necessary. He would also probably have asked for permission to make a further visit and to take full notes. The substitution would have taken place on this second visit, which was also the occasion of his chance meeting with my father at St. David's Station, Exeter.

One small point. My father's notes on armor in Devon Churches, mostly made before 1914, were published in 1920 (*Devon and Cornwall Notes and Queries*, xi, 92). These were made available in manuscript to Cripps-Day at an earlier date. My father was in close touch with most of the local antiquaries, including at one remove those whose memory went back to 1850. The suggestion that the helmet came from the Peryam monument deserves credence. It was probably removed in the great restoration of the church about 1854, and people like Hamilton Rogers could well have seen it in position.

I make these points because I feel that the case against Laking is very thin. My father would never have believed that Laking was capable of such duplicity. He respected and admired him. There were hints about his private life and open criticism of his extravagance. I only met Laking once. I think it was at the Oriental Club, to which my father had taken me while I was an undergraduate. As a schoolboy the story of the "peacock feast" enthralled me. I had a photograph enlargement of the lady in plate armor with bare head and hands. She was a handsome girl in her twenties. I think it came from a relative who was a close friend of my father and died about 1916. It perished, alas, in 1942.

NOTES

1 Catalogue of *A Loan Exhibition Depicting the Reign of Queen Elizabeth. In Aid of the Young Women's Christian Association*, 22 and 23 Grosvenor Place, S.W.1, London, January 26–March 1933, p. 13, no. 59.

2 *Catalogue of the Magnificent Collection of Armour, Weapons, and Works of Art, The Property of the Late S. J. Whawell, Esq.*, Sotheby and Co., London, May 3–6, 1927.

3 *Art Objects and Furnishings from the William Randolph Hearst Collection*, Saks Fifth Avenue in cooperation with Gimbel Brothers, New York, 1941. The helmet can be identified from the Hearst inventory number on Kienbusch's receipt stub from Gimbel's as one described briefly on p. 275: "Embossed close helmet, Italian, XVI Century (1033-167)." It has usually been said that Hearst sold these pieces because he thought that he was in financial difficulties, but according to Marion Davies, it was merely because "he didn't have any more warehouse space to hold things." See Davies, *The Times We Had* (Indianapolis, 1975), p. 132, which also reproduces a photograph of the arms and armor on sale at Gimbel's.

4 Close-helmet, Philadelphia Museum of Art, acc. no. 1977-167-105 (C. Otto von Kienbusch, *The Kretzschmar von Kienbusch Collection of Armor and Arms* [Princeton, N.J., 1963], p. 68, no. 82, pl. XLVI).

5 Francis Henry Cripps-Day, "On Armour Preserved in English Churches," supplement to volume 5 of Sir Guy Francis Laking, *A Record of European Armour and Arms through Seven Centuries*, 5 vols. (London, 1920–22), also privately reprinted as a separate repaginated volume (London, 1922); Cripps-Day and A. R. Dufty, *Church Armour* (addendum to "On Armour Preserved"), in *Fragmenta Armamentaria*, vol. 4 (Frome, privately printed, 1939). The Crediton helmet is listed on page 172 (no. 22) of the former and pages 137–38 of the latter. James G. Mann's copy of the reprint of the earlier list, in my possession, bears the following note by him beside the Crediton entry: "Seen June 1926, & brought up for Elizabethan Exhibition 23 Grosvenor Place, 1933—a precisely similar embossed helmet was sold at the Whawell Sale (Lot 243) May 1927."

6 Victoria and Albert Museum, London, *M.S. L.* 1310-1312-1940.

7 Leopold A. D. Montague, "A Town with a Past," *Antiquarian Gossip* (London), vol. 1, no. 4 (May 1898), p. 43.

8 Beatrix Cresswell, "Armour, Etc., in Devon and Cornwall Churches," *Devon & Cornwall Notes and Queries*, vol. 10 (January 1918–October 1919), p. 85. E. K. Prideaux, "Relics of Fairfax's Army in Crediton," *Devon & Cornwall Notes and Queries*, vol. 6 (January 1910–October 1911), pp. 241–43.

9 See F. Gordon Roe, "Personal Reminiscences of Some Arms and Armour Collectors of the Past," *Journal of the Arms and Armour Society*, vol. 7 (1971–72), p. 164. The address appended to the *Western Morning News* letter was Cripps-Day's country one, Swanswood, Harvel, Meopham, Kent.

10 See note 5.

11 I am grateful to Kenneth Turner, formerly of the Art

Workroom (now the Conservation Department) at the Victoria and Albert Museum, London, for doing this work.

12 English National Monument Record negative number B47/3313. Reproduced in J. Charles Cox, *English Church Fittings, Furniture, and Accessories* (London, 1923), p. 171, fig. 163.

13 A. H. King Robinson, to whom I am extremely grateful for the information in his letters quoted later in these notes, and also for drawing my attention to the report and correspondence about the helmet in the *Western Morning News*.

14 I am very grateful to A. L. Radford's son, C. A. Ralegh Radford, for much personal information about his father, who died November 15, 1925. A short obituary was published in the *Antiquaries Journal* (Society of Antiquaries, London), vol. 6 (1926), p. 363. See also the appendix to this essay.

15 The minute books are still in the possession of the Meyrick Society. I am grateful to M. R. Holmes for locating the reference to the helmet for me in 1960 when he was Honorary Secretary. My attention was drawn to the fact that the helmet had been exhibited to the society by two sketches of it made by Major Victor H. Farquharson, who was a guest at the meeting concerned. These are now among the Crediton material in my own church-armor files and index in the Royal Armouries.

16 Unfortunately, all the known photographs and drawings of the helmet made before it was restored show the right-hand side only, so the form of the bolt then holding it together on the left is not recorded.

17 In his grangerized copy of the Whawell sale catalogue in the library of the Royal Armouries, Cripps-Day wrote beside the entry for the helmet, "This is Crediton church one," and beside an extra pasted-in illustration of the helmet, "J.S.W. [sic] offered it to me many times for £120. This is the real Crediton helmet sent to London to be done up—made a copy & sent copy back."

18 See note 6.

19 Francis M. Kelly, the distinguished authority on the history of costume.

20 His collection was sold by Sotheby and Co., London, February 27, 1951.

21 Much of the information following about Whawell's career derives from the biographical memoir published at the beginning of his 1927 sale catalogue (see note 2).

22 Laking 1920–22, vol. 1, p. ix.

23 A.V.B. Norman informs me that he was told the same story by James G. Mann, with the additional information that Whawell had started by going around smashing his own showcases with the mace.

24 One of the largest private collections of early arms and armor ever formed, it was sold by Christie's, London, on March 18–21 and 25–26, 1895. Drawings of pieces from it, said to be by Whawell, are the basis of Edwin J. Brett's own large book, *A Pictorial and Descriptive Record of the Origin and Development of Arms and Armour . . .* (London, 1894). Brett made his fortune from the "penny-dreadful" magazine *Boys of England*, and, according to Mann, who no doubt got the information from Baron De Cosson, formed the collection as what would now be called a status symbol, and sold it when it failed to help him socially. For an account of his publishing activities, see E. S. Turner, *Boys Will Be Boys* (London, 1940), *passim*.

25 Cripps-Day's note is worth quoting in full:

When Whawell died, Furmage installed himself in his home & took command. Some of the collection were [sic] never in this sale among them Cromwell's sword. It disappeared.

Whawell was buried in London. His coffin was the most magnificent I ever saw & the flowers were wonderful. No money was spared. It came out of the Whawell estate!

I called the day before he died. The Lady who lived with him took me upstairs to see him. I said "Have you sent for his relations, he is dying." She said "No." He died the next day. He had not a friend in the world, but he really loved armour. On the whole he was honest—but he was a "wicked" man.

26 See Nesta Macdonald, *The History of the Pheasantry, Chelsea, 1766–1977* (London, 1977), *passim*; James Henry Duveen, *Collections & Recollections: A Century and a Half of Art Deals* (London, 1934), pp. 134–36; Bevis Hillier, "Fowl Play in Chelsea," *The Times* (London), May 21, 1977; Grand Palais, Paris, *Les Fastes du Gothique*, October 9, 1981–February 1, 1982, no. 193. I am grateful to Barbara D. Boehm of the Department of Medieval Art at the Metropolitan Museum of Art, New York, for the information that the Duveen records confirm that it was Joubert who made the copy.

27 Laking 1920–22, vol. 1, p. ix.

28 Hillier 1977.

29 Joubert is mentioned in the scurrilous, but entertaining, papers of the imaginary Brayette Club, produced at intervals during 1924–31 by some unknown humorist who was extremely well informed about the antique arms and armor world. Each purports to give the club's program of activities for the coming year. That for 1929 includes the following:

Oct. A CURIOUS IMPLEMENT, BELIEVED TO BE A BRAYETTE OPENER, stamped ME FECIT CHELSEA, FABRICO DE FELIX. By Mr. R. L. Scott F.S.A., F.Z.S.

See Claude Blair and A. N. Kennard, "The Brayette Club Papers," *Journal of the Arms and Armour Society*, vol. 13, no. 4 (March 1991), pp. 233–55.

30 Burlington Fine Arts Club, London, *Catalogue of a Collection of Counterfeits, Imitations, and Copies of Works of Art* (London, 1924), nos. 44, 51. The former is catalogued as a genuine helmet and the latter as a reproduction, presumably by Joubert, although this is not actually stated.

31 Illustrated in Laking 1920–22, vol. 4, fig. 1187, p. 104. See also *The Joubert Collection of Arms and Armour* (London, privately printed, 1921); Musée Masséna, Nice, *Catalogue de la Collection Joubert* (Nice, 1926), no. 51.

32 For a short account of Laking's career, see John F. Hayward, "Profili Biografici. Sir Guy Francis Laking (1875–1919)," *Armi Antiche, Bollettino dell'Accademia di S. Marciano–Torino*, 1964, pp. 265–72.

33 Ibid.

34 C. J. ffoulkes, *Arms and the Tower* (London, 1939), p. 68.

35 James G. Mann, "The Meyrick Society and an Exhibition of Swords," *Connoisseur*, vol. 106 (August 1940),

p. 47. Mann also told me that Laking would sometimes decide in the morning to have a party the same evening and would go around by taxi issuing invitations to his friends; and that it was not uncommon for him still to be doing this when the first guests started to arrive!

36 I was once told that it was said of Laking that he would always find something kind to say about a fellow collector's object, however humble it or its owner was. See also ffoulkes's account (1939, p. 208) of how, when the British Government Stationery Office and Treasury were doubtful about publishing his large catalogue of the Tower of London Armouries (1916), "their doubts were set at rest by Sir Guy Laking ordering one hundred copies before the first words had been written, a generous act which is not easily surpassed." Compare also Roe 1971–72, p. 161.

37 In the early 1950s, Doreen Errol, the daughter of the collector Harry Plowman, founder of the Meyrick Society, told me that she had "never cried so much" as she did when she heard that Laking had died.

38 James Henry Duveen, *Secrets of an Art Dealer* (London, [1937]), pp. 102–117, 224–25.

39 Duveen referred elsewhere in this book, usually unfavorably, to "Mr. George," who was a major rival of his branch of the Duveen firm and therefore obviously one of the top dealers. A possible identification is Georges Wildenstein; another, suggested to me by R. T. Gwynn, is that it was Joseph, later Lord, Duveen, who was by no means popular with his family.

40 For an account of Robinson's life, see his entry in the British twentieth-century *Dictionary of National Biography*.

41 For a summary of the information available in print about the Marcy workshop, see the British Museum, London, *Fake? The Art of Deception* (London, 1990), pp. 185–87. Marcy was born in Reggio nell'Emilia, Italy, and his real name was Luigi Parmeggiani. His house and its contents, which include the largest single collection of his fakes in existence, are now part of the Museo Civico there, and a catalogue by the late John F. Hayward is to be published.

42 Laking 1920–22, vol. 5, pp. 142–47.

43 Verband von Museums-Beamten zur Abwehr von Fälschungen und unlauterem Geschäftsgebahren. An almost complete set of photocopies of their rare publications is in the Department of Metalwork, Victoria and Albert Museum, London.

44 All the other examples known to have been in England before the beginning of serious armor collecting in the late eighteenth century are first recorded either in cabinets of curiosities or artists' studios of the second half of the seventeenth century onward. See, for example, J. M. Levine, *Dr. Woodward's Shield* (Berkeley and Los Angeles, 1977), *passim*.

45 Laking 1920–22, vol. 4, p. 245.

46 See note 16.

47 See Cripps-Day, "Armour Preserved in English Churches," 1922, *passim*.

48 Ibid. See also Cripps-Day and Dufty 1939, *passim*.

49 See Claude Blair, "Sir Giles Capel's Funerary Instructions, 1556," *Church Monuments Society Newsletter*, vol. 2, no. 2 (winter 1986), pp. 14–15.

50 Sir Anthony Wagner, *Heralds of England* (London, 1967), p. 110.

51 See James G. Mann, "Two Fourteenth-Century Gauntlets from Ripon Cathedral," *Antiquaries' Journal* (Society of Antiquaries, London), vol. 22 (1942), pp. 113–22; Claude Blair, "The Blithfield Sallet," *Archaeological Journal*, vol. 111 (1955), pp. 160–67.

52 See David Cook, *The Church of the Holy Cross, Crediton* (1979), which includes a select bibliography; R. J. King, "The Church of St. Mary and of the Holy Cross, at Crediton," *Transactions of the Exeter Diocesan Architectural Society*, 2nd ser., vol. 4 (1878), p. 109; D. & S. Lysons, *Devonshire*, vol. 6 of *Magna Brittania* (London, 1822), p. 147.

53 *Dictionary of National Biography*, s.v. "Sir William Peryam." See also P. W. Hasler, *The House of Commons, 1558–1603* (London, 1981), p. 209; Rev. T. Moore, *The History of Devonshire*, vol. 2 [1829], pp. 352–53; W. H. Hamilton Rogers, *The Antient Sepulchral Effigies and Monumental Memorial Sculpture of Devon* (Exeter, 1877), pp. 154–55. Rather surprisingly, in view of the fact that Peryam was a lawyer, I have not been able to trace his will. John Tuckfield's will contains no information about his funeral or his monument (Public Record Office, London, Prob. 11/158, ff.403v.–404).

54 The only hope of doing so would seem to be to discover a record of the helmet when it was in its original position in the notes of some early antiquary or herald. In reply to my inquiries, Chris Brooks of the Devon Nineteenth-Century Churches Project, Exeter University, kindly wrote as follows on August 30, 1986:

The three major possibilities were Jeremiah Milles' *Parochial Collections* of c. 1770, John Davidson's 19th century *Church Notes*, and Beatrix Cresswell's early 20th century *Devon Parish Churches*, all still in MS. Milles, who was collecting material for a county history in the 1770s, has an entry for Crediton which describes both the Tuckfield and Periam monuments, but mentions no funerary achievements. Davidson, who visited every church in the county between the late 1820s and 1850, dates his account of Crediton 29 July, 1843: he was a particularly thorough antiquarian and records all monuments, epitaphs and armorials in the church, but again without mentioning any helmet. Cresswell didn't get to Crediton until 1918 and her account adds nothing relevant to the present purpose. I also checked 19th century newspapers as far as I could, but no results. For my own purposes, I have been through the Crediton church records deposited in the Devon Record Office: I'm fairly sure that I would have noted any significant references to the fate of funerary achievements but, as far as I can see, there aren't any. The problem with the Crediton records in DRO, however, is that they are very incomplete: most are still in the hands of the Crediton Church Governors. . . .

I am grateful also to M. Maguire of the Exeter Central Library and to G. D. Dickinson of the Devon Record Office, Exeter, to whom I had written previously, for also searching the Davidson and Cresswell notes and for the information that the latter mention that the helmet was "traditionally asserted to have been worn at Crecy [1346] by Sir John de Sully . . .[but is] of the 15th century."

55 Kienbusch 1963, p. 68, no. 82, pl. XLVI.

56 Laking 1920–22, vol. 4, pp. 134–38.

57 See note 66.

58 For accounts of the Negroli family and their work, see Bruno Thomas and Ortwin Gamber, "L'Arte milanese dell'armatura," *Storia di Milano*, vol. 11 (1958), pp. 734–35, 760–76; Lionello G. Boccia and E. T. Coelho, *L'Arte dell'armatura in Italia* (Milan, 1967), pls. 239–53, 255–59, 261–74.

59 Since this was written, the helmet has been described as being in the manner of Filippo Negroli by Mario Scalini, in *Armature all' Eroica dei Negroli* (Florence, 1987), pp. 14, 17.

60 For accounts of Modrone and his work, see Thomas and Gamber 1958, pp. 757–60; Boccia and Coelho 1967, pl. 254; Claude Blair, *The James A. de Rothschild Collection at Waddesdon Manor. Arms, Armour, and Base-Metalwork* (London and Fribourg, 1974), pp. 22–27; John F. Hayward, "Filippo Orso, Designer, and Caremolo Modrone, Armourer, of Mantua," *Waffen-und Kostümkunde*, vol. 24 (1982), pp. 1–16, 87–102.

61 Blair 1974, p. 50.

62 See Thomas and Gamber 1958; Boccia and Coelho 1967; Sir James G. Mann, *Wallace Collection Catalogues. European Arms and Armour. Volume I. Armour* (London, 1962), pp. 112–13; Hayward 1982; Blair 1974; A.V.B. Norman, *Wallace Collection Catalogues: European Arms and Armour Supplement* (London, 1986), pp. 49–51.

63 It must be emphasized strongly that these comments and the ones immediately following are broad generalizations and not hard and fast rules. Examples of helmets that provide supporting evidence for them are to be found in most major armor collections.

64 Carl Otto von Kienbusch and Stephen V. Grancsay, *The Bashford Dean Collection of Arms and Armor* (Portland, Me., 1933), pp. 137–38, no. 53; John F. Hayward, "The Armours of the Family of d'Avalos, Marchese di Pescara e del Vasto," *Waffen- und Kostümkunde*, vol. 1 (1959), pp. 47–53, where the helmet is dated to the 1560s. Stuart W. Pyhrr, Curator of the Department of Arms and Armor at the Metropolitan Museum of Art, has given me cogent reasons for a date some ten or more years earlier than this. For other examples of German helmets with visors and upper-bevors of this form, see A. R. Dufty, ed., *European Armour in the Tower of London* (London, 1968), pl. XCI (IV.472); Oswald Graf Trapp, *The Armoury of the Castle of Churburg*, translated by James G. Mann (London, 1929), pl. LIX (nos. 97, 100). See also note 68.

65 A rare example of a sixteenth-century Italian helmet with a finial is A109 in the Wallace Collection, London.

66 The visors and upper-bevors of some helmets made in the Greenwich Armouries from the mid-sixteenth century onward have a generally similar outline to those on the Crediton helmet, especially the tilt-visors and brevors, though they do not have the dog's-leg lower edge. This is probably the explanation for C. R. Beard's Greenwich attribution in his letter to Cripps-Day quoted earlier in the text. The resemblance, however, is very superficial, and, as already pointed out, the helmet does not have any features that would justify accepting the attribution even tentatively. See the Tower of London Armouries, *Exhibition of Armour Made in the Royal Workshops at Greenwich* (London, 1951), nos. 9, 11, 21, 43; Dufty, ed. 1968, pls. XCIV (II.81), XCV (II.78, IV.43). A sixteenth-century field helmet of a type usually called English, used for funerary purposes on an unidentified monument in Carlisle Cathedral, Cumbria, is also fitted with a visor and lower-bevor of superficially similar outline.

67 See Claude Blair, "The Emperor Maximilian's Gift of Armour to King Henry VIII and the Silvered and Engraved Armour at the Tower of London," *Archaeologia*, vol. 99 (1965), pp. 35–36.

68 *Armour*, vol. 1 of *The Hever Castle Collection, the Property of Lord Astor*, Sotheby-Parke-Bernet, London, May 5, 1983, lot 44. The construction of the visor and upper-bevor and their fastenings are the same as that of the Crediton helmet, and the bevor also has a dog's-leg lower edge. The visor, however, has a stepped sight and is set well down inside the bevor, which curves up at the front in a high, prowlike point. This last feature is found on many helmets with French, Flemish, and English associations, and suggests that the armor was made in the French style. The same comment applies to the "Lion" armor in the Tower of London (II.89), which has been attributed to Giovan Battista Negroli and other members of his family, and of which the helmet has all the characteristics of construction and form found on the Crediton helmet, except for the dog's-leg edge to the upper-bevor. Here, however, there appears to be good reason for doubting the Negroli attribution. The extremely fine and precise embossed decoration on the armor is technically unlike anything on any of their firmly attributed work, and is much closer in style to that of the French royal workshop. See Dufty, ed. 1968, pl. XCVI; and Lionello G. Boccia, Francesco Rossi, and M. Morin, *Armi e Armature Lombarde* (Milan, 1980), p. 122.

69 See Jean-Pierre Reverseau, *Les armures des rois de France au Musée de l'Armée* (Saint-Julien-du-Sault, 1982), pp. 50–80, and the works cited by Blair 1974, p. 58.

ACKNOWLEDGMENTS

My thanks are due first and foremost to A. H. King Robinson, Clerk to the Governors of Crediton Church, for giving me permission in 1958 to examine and photograph the helmet in the church, and for subsequently searching the Governors' records for information about it and giving me every possible assistance with my research into its history. C. A. Ralegh Radford has very kindly provided information about his father, A. L. Radford, and has also permitted the publication of the account of his views on the circumstances leading to the substitution of the fake helmet for the original. Donald LaRocca, former Assistant Curator of the Kienbusch Collection at the Philadelphia Museum of Art, not only made the helmet then under his care available to me for examination but has since patiently answered questions about it and related matters, has read the typescript of this chapter and made a number of useful suggestions for its improvement, and also obtained a number of the accompanying photographs. Sarah Barter Bailey, Librarian of the Royal Armouries, Her Majesty's Tower of London, has, with her customary generosity, devoted much time to answering inquiries about manuscript material in her charge. A. R. Dufty helped with the initial examination of the helmet at Crediton in 1958 and subsequently discovered the vital 1908 Crossley photograph (fig. 111). A.V.B. Norman, Mr. Dufty's successor as Master of the Tower of London Armouries (now Royal Armouries), has read the article in manuscript and made helpful suggestions. Mr. M. Maguire of the Exeter Central Library, provided me with bibliographical information about Crediton Church. Stuart W. Pyhrr, Curator of the Department of Arms and Armor at the Metropolitan Museum of Art, New York, kindly supplied the photograph of the helmet reproduced as figure 115. The late Carl Otto von Kienbusch provided information, encouragement, and photographs in the early stages of my inquiries. I am very grateful to all of them, as well as to the following for help of various kinds not acknowledged in the main text or notes: Colin Davison, Editor, *Western Morning News*; I.D.D. Eaves, Keeper of Armour at the Royal Armouries, Her Majesty's Tower of London; A.R.E. North of the Department of Metalwork, Victoria and Albert Museum, London; P. K. Pratt of Chelsea Library and her staff; P. W. Thomas, Assistant Librarian of Exeter Cathedral Library; and the staff of the Local History Library, Plymouth, Devon. Finally, special thanks are due to Jane Watkins for her careful editorial work.

Sorting Out Simonin: Pattern Books for Decorated Firearms, 1684–1705

DONALD J. LAROCCA

Although the collection of Carl Otto von Kienbusch has been well known and appreciated by students of arms and armor for many years, it is perhaps less well known that Kienbusch also assembled an arms and armor research library with the same dedication and discernment that he applied to collecting. Kienbusch's interest in research was due, in part, to his training in art history at Princeton University and to the guidance of his friend and mentor, Bashford Dean. In a characteristic letter to Dean, written February 23, 1920, Kienbusch commented on his collecting activities: "As to the ruling passion—the only recent accessions are books. Among others—Complete File of Zeitschrift fur Historische Waffenkunde. Burgkmair—Turnierbuch von 1529. Forrer—Schwerter & Schwertknaufe, etc. What is home without these!"[1]

The Kienbusch Library, which came to the Philadelphia Museum of Art with the arms and armor collection in 1977, consists of more than two thousand books, periodicals, and auction catalogues dating from the seventeenth century to the present. Among the rarer items are two French pattern books for the decoration of luxury firearms: the 1695 and 1705 editions from a series engraved principally by the ornamentalist Claude Simonin. This series of pattern books was one of the principal means by which the French style of firearms decoration was disseminated throughout Europe. During the early seventeenth century, France had superseded Germany as the leading producer of both technically innovative and highly ornamental firearms. Louis XIII (reigned 1610–43) was an avid collector of firearms and a patron of French gunsmiths.[2] Gunmakers were granted *logement* in the Galeries du Louvre beginning in 1608, and official patronage continued to flourish through the reign of Louis XIV (ruled 1643–1715). As the effects of French art and culture spread to foreign courts, so, too, did French firearms and the ornamental style represented by Simonin.

The influence of the Simonin pattern books on firearm decoration may be gauged by the appearance of the pattern books in ten known editions—six in France and four pirated versions printed elsewhere—far more than any other comparable pattern book.[3] In addition, although comparatively few extant firearms bear designs that can be traced to other pattern books, many firearms do survive from the late seventeenth to the late eighteenth century with ornamentation derived from the various Simonin editions.[4] These albums of designs, along with surviving dated firearms, are the prime sources of information for tracing the evolution of luxury firearms from the late seventeenth through the eighteenth centuries.

Pattern books of this type were used by practicing gunmakers and, like much else in an active workshop, probably remained in use until they were worn out or replaced. Consequently, those few surviving copies are frequently incomplete or are composites of the remnants of various editions. It is understandable, therefore, that the Simonin albums have never been republished in full (although the combined French editions here proposed as original contain only twenty-five different plates) and that some errors and omissions have been made in the modern scholarly literature concerning them.

In sorting out the various editions of the Simonin albums, much is to be learned by a careful reading of the title pages. Beyond establishing the correct sequence of publication, the minor variations in wording, names, and dates from one title page to another testify to the ever-changing relationships among those who were responsible for creating the albums. One result is the identification proposed here of a second and significantly different 1705 edition, when previously only one was thought to have been published. It should also be noted that although the pattern books under discussion have been referred to under the name of Simonin, other individuals were intimately involved with their production. The general rubric "Simonin" is conveniently used because that name is the only one to appear on all six French editions.

The first recorded Simonin pattern book appeared in 1684 and consists of a title page and seven plates of designs numbered two through eight (figs. 116–123). Its full title (fig. 116) reads:

PLVSIEVRS PIECES ET ORNEMENTS/Darquebuzerie Les plus en Vsage Tire des/Ouurages de Laurent le Languedoc Arquebuziers/Du Roy et Dautres Ornement Inuenté et graué/Par Simonin et Se Vend Ledit Liure Chez ledit/Simonin a Lantree du faubour St Anthoine/A Paris Auec Priuilege du Roy/1684

[Several parts and ornaments most utilized in gunmaking, drawn from the works of Laurent le Languedoc, gunmaker to the king, and other ornament invented and engraved by Simonin, and the said book is sold at the house of the said Simonin at the entrance to the district Saint-Antoine in Paris with privilege of the king 1684].[5]

The 1684 album is extremely rare. However, a complete and homogeneous copy in pristine condition is in the Bibliothèque Nationale, Paris.[6] The individual prints of this copy are still on their original oversized sheets, having never been trimmed for binding and distribution. It may, in fact, be one of the proof copies acquired in accordance with the *dépôt legal*, by which one copy of each work granted royal privilege was to be deposited in the library of the chancellor, or keeper, of the seals (from 1638) and two in the royal library (from 1642).[7] Whether from this source or not, the excellent condition of the Paris copy is in stark contrast to the shopworn condition of most extant Simonin albums.

Two dissociated 1684 title pages are also known. One, formerly in the possession of Stephen V. Grancsay, was bequeathed as part of his personal library to the arms and armor department of the Metropolitan Museum of Art, New York. The other is found in the print collection of the Victoria and Albert Museum, London.[8]

Fig. 116. Title page, 1684 Simonin pattern book. Bibliothèque Nationale, Paris.

Fig. 117. Plate 2, 1684 edition. Bibliothèque Nationale, Paris.

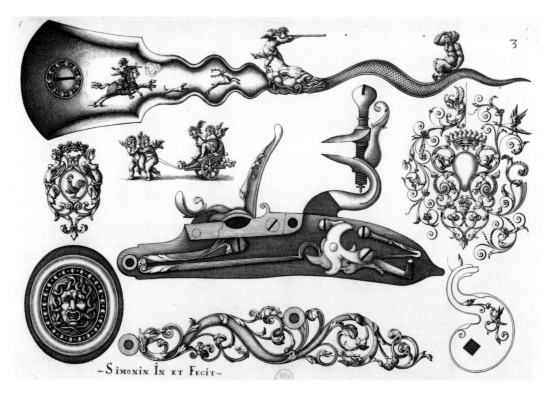

Fig. 118. Plate 3, 1684 edition. Bibliothèque Nationale, Paris.

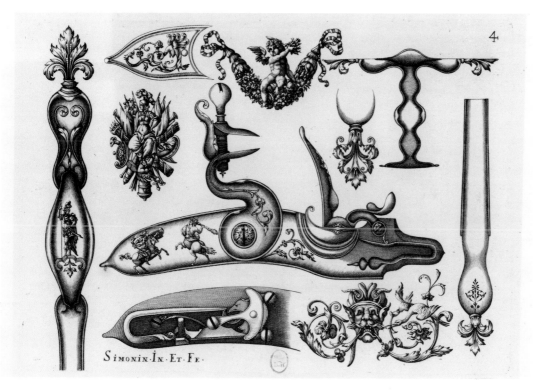

Fig. 119. Plate 4, 1684 edition. Bibliothèque Nationale, Paris.

Fig. 120. Plate 5, 1684 edition. Bibliothèque Nationale, Paris.

Fig. 121. Plate 6, 1684 edition. Bibliothèque Nationale, Paris.

Fig. 122. Plate 7, 1684 edition. Bibliothèque Nationale, Paris.

Fig. 123. Plate 8, 1684 edition. Bibliothèque Nationale, Paris.

Torsten Lenk, whose general discussion of pattern books remains the most reliable and comprehensive, believed the earliest Simonin album to have been that of 1685.[9] The 1685 edition, which is identical to that of 1684 save for the changed date on its title page, is known in at least one homogeneous copy, in the library of the Staatliche Museen, Preussischer Kulturbesitz, Berlin.[10] Lenk's oversight of the earlier edition may be attributed to the rarity of extant 1684 examples—the three previously cited copies being the only ones recorded thus far.

The misconception that the 1684 and 1685 editions consisted of twelve plates apparently originated in print with D. Guilmard in 1880. He was later joined in this assertion by Grancsay, who assembled and published a composite twelve-plate edition based on his 1684 title page and plates from other editions.[11] The composite Grancsay album, except for its rare title page, must therefore be disregarded as misleading.

Simonin's given name, Claude, is not actually encountered until the title page of the next pattern book, issued in 1693. There it is stated that the pattern book was being sold at the house of Claude Simonin's widow, "a l'entree du faubourg S. Anthoine," the same address given on the 1684 and 1685 title pages.[12] This suggests that the Simonin of the 1684/1685 pattern books is the same Claude Simonin of the 1693 edition, and that his death occurred sometime between 1685 and 1693. In light of this, it seems necessary to revise his death date, which is usually cited in the art historical literature as 1721, and to conclude that the Claude Simonin who did die in 1721 was not the same Simonin who was responsible for the pattern books.[13]

As we have seen, the 1684/1685 title pages cite firearms by "Laurent le Languedoc Arquebuziers Du Roy" as the models for some of Simonin's engravings. Languedoc's name appears again only on plate six (fig. 121; "Le Langvedoc A Paris"), also the only plate on which the legend simply reads "Simonin Fecit," as opposed to "Simonin In[venit] et fecit," an important distinction that I will discuss. Beyond Languedoc's involvement with the Simonin pattern books and extant firearms signed by him, little substantive information concerning him is available.[14] Many guns made by him carry the monogram JL and in some cases, possibly, JLL.[15] A "François" and a "Jean Laurent Le Languedoc" have been cited as recorded in documents for 1717 as royal gunmakers. It has been suggested that they represent the same person (Jean François Laurent le Languedoc).[16] Based on surviving firearms, Languedoc's greatest patron was the ducal house of Saxony, as evidenced by the thirty-one guns and six pairs of pistols by him still in the Historisches Museum, Dresden. These range in date from 1717 to 1733, the latter of which is also apparently the latest securely dated evidence of Languedoc's activity.[17] The earliest mention of Languedoc is on the title page of the 1684 pattern book, by which time he was already described as a royal gunmaker. Despite the appellation "Arquebuziers du Roy," there is apparently only one surviving Languedoc gun that has been identified as made for a member of the French royal family. This is a composite sporting gun in the Musée de l'Armée, Paris, which bears on its escutcheon plate the arms of

Louis Le Grand Dauphin (1661–1711).[18] Owing to the extended period of Languedoc's documented activity (1684–1733), it has long been speculated that there were two gunmakers named Languedoc, possibly father and son. A career of this length by a single gunmaker, however, is not without precedent.[19]

As a gunmaker, Languedoc's best works rank among the finest luxury arms of the period. If Languedoc had been, in fact, the source for the majority of Simonin's designs, rather than the recipient of them, then he would also have to be considered, in terms of ornament, one of the most widely influential gunmakers of the seventeenth and eighteenth centuries. It should be taken into account, however, that Simonin, rather than Languedoc, held the copyright to the designs included in the 1684/1685 albums, as indicated by the phrase "Auec Priuilege du Roy" in line seven of the 1684 title page (fig. 116). Print privileges were granted by the office of the Communauté des Librairies et Imprimeurs, which was empowered to judge an applicant's right to a given work. Such a privilege gave its holder legal copyright to a particular print or book for a specific number of years.[20] Languedoc's role may have been that of *éditeur*—responsible for the financing and organization of the publication—and he was probably responsible for the ornament on plate six (fig. 121), which bears his name. However, the terms "In[venit] et fecit," versions of which are found on the title page and six of the seven plates, were not used loosely by the close, well-regulated community of Parisian printmakers. The use of these terms to describe Simonin clearly identifies him as both the creator and engraver of the designs so inscribed. By also acting as the *marchand* (distributor/seller), Simonin united three functions in himself (*inventeur, graveur, marchand*) that were frequently handled by separate individuals in the print trade.[21] Given this, Simonin's role in the production of the pattern books appears to have been the dominant one.

The 1693/1695 Simonin pattern books are relatively unknown in comparison with the 1684/1685, and 1705 editions and have been given scant treatment in the modern literature.[22] They consist of a title page and eleven plates numbered two through twelve. The plates illustrated here (figs. 124–135) comprise the 1695 edition in the Kienbusch Library, which is identical to the 1693 edition with the exception of the altered date and the addition of an inscription across the top of the title page reading: "A present Ce liure Se Vend Ches Jaques Simonin graueur A Toulouse" [At present this book is sold at the house of Jacques Simonin engraver of Toulouse].[23] The full title reads:

PLVSIEVRS PIECES ET AVTRES/Ornements pour Les Arquebuziers et/Les brizures demonteé et Remonteé Le/tous designé et graué par Simonin/et des plus beaux Ouurages de paris/Ce Vend Chez la Veufüe a L'entreé du/faubourg St Anthoine A Paris A/l'enseigne du Cabinet a fleurs/AVEC PRIVILEGE/1695

[Several pieces and other ornament for gunmakers and pieceworkers, disassembled and reassembled, all designed and engraved by Simonin and from the most beautiful works of Paris, this is sold at the house of his widow at the entrance to the district Saint-Antoine in Paris at the sign of the flowered cabinet with privilege 1695].

Fig. 124. Title page, 1695 Simonin pattern book. Kienbusch Library, Philadelphia Museum of Art.

Fig. 125. Plate 2, 1695 edition. Kienbusch Library, Philadelphia Museum of Art.

Fig. 126. Plate 3, 1695 edition. Kienbusch Library, Philadelphia Museum of Art.

Fig. 127. Plate 4, 1695 edition. Kienbusch Library, Philadelphia Museum of Art.

SIMONIN PATTERN BOOKS

193

Fig. 128. Plate 5, 1695 edition. Kienbusch Library, Philadelphia Museum of Art.

Fig. 129. Plate 6, 1695 edition. Kienbusch Library, Philadelphia Museum of Art.

Fig. 130. Plate 7, 1695 edition. Kienbusch Library, Philadelphia Museum of Art.

Fig. 131. Plate 8, 1695 edition. Kienbusch Library, Philadelphia Museum of Art.

SIMONIN PATTERN BOOKS

Fig. 132. Plate 9, 1695 edition. Kienbusch Library, Philadelphia Museum of Art.

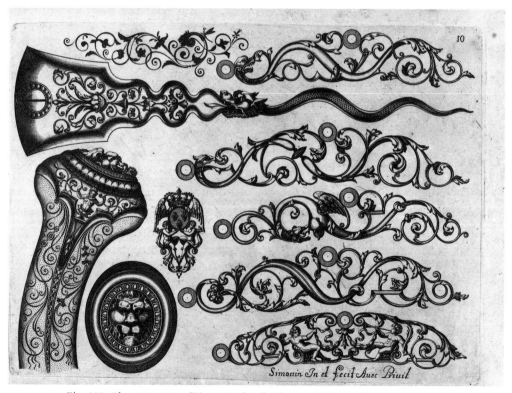

Fig. 133. Plate 10, 1695 edition. Kienbusch Library, Philadelphia Museum of Art.

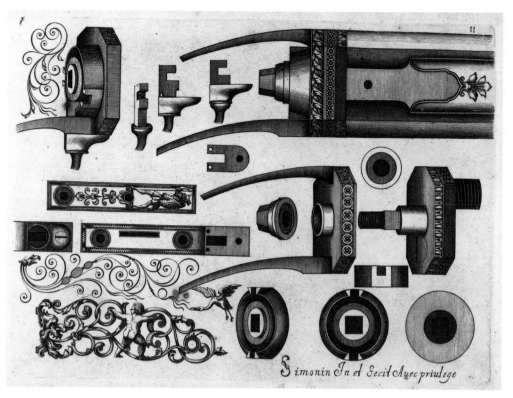

Fig. 134. Plate 11, 1695 edition. Kienbusch Library, Philadelphia Museum of Art.

Fig. 135. Plate 12, 1695 edition. Kienbusch Library, Philadelphia Museum of Art.

Beneath this is the line (found on both editions), "Le tout dessigné et graueé Par Claude Simonin et Jacques Simonin Son fils auec Priuilege du Roy" [All designed and engraved by Claude Simonin and Jacques Simonin his son with privilege of the king]. The mention of Simonin's shop sign, "l'enseigne du Cabinet a fleurs," is found only on the 1693 and 1695 albums.

In light of the preceding, it is apparent, contrary to what has been published in the arms literature, that the 1693/1695 pattern books are not simply reprints of the 1684/1685 editions, but are entirely different.[24] Languedoc's name appears neither on the title page nor on any of the plates in the 1693/1695 editions. A version of "Simonin In et Fecit" is found on each plate except one (plate six; fig. 129), which reads only "Simonin Fecit." "Auec Priuilege" (or a form thereof) follows "fecit" on seven of the twelve plates. A few individual design elements have been taken from the 1684/1685 albums;[25] otherwise, the designs are new.

Four important facts can be gleaned from a close reading of the title pages of the 1693/1695 albums: first, a *terminus ante quem* for the death of Claude Simonin; second, that Simonin, on this occasion, operated independently of Languedoc; third, that Claude had a son Jacques who was his co-worker; and fourth (from the 1695 edition), that Jacques was for a time established in Toulouse rather than Paris. Jacques's name has long appeared in the firearms literature but not in the general art historical literature.[26]

In 1705 two editions based on the 1684/1685 versions were published. The first, that generally cited, was a reprint of the eight-plate 1684/1685 albums, with only the date and the last two lines of the title altered. A copy of this, possibly a composite, is in the Kienbusch Library (fig. 136). Another copy considered to be homogeneous is in the library of the Livrustkammaren, Stockholm.[27] The full title reads:

PLVSIEVRS PIECES ET ORNEMENTS/Darquebuzerie Les plus en Vsage Tire des/Ouurages de Laurent le Languedoc Arquebuziers/Du Roy et Dautres Ornement Inuenté et graué/par Simonin et Se Vend Ledit Liure Chez ledit/Languedoc rue de bretagne aux marais/A Paris Auec Priuilege du Roy/1705

[Several parts and ornaments most utilized in gunmaking drawn from the works of Laurent le Languedoc, gunmaker to the king, and other ornament invented and engraved by Simonin, and the said book is sold at the house of the said Languedoc, rue de Bretagne aux Marais in Paris with privilege of the king 1705].

That Languedoc is here identified as the seller suggests that his affiliation with the Simonins had ceased and that the copperplates of the 1684/1685 albums were in his possession, perhaps acquired from Claude's heirs. Languedoc was soon affiliated, however, with two other engravers, as evidenced by the title and the signed plates of what is here proposed as a second, expanded 1705 edition (fig. 137, here referred to as the "long 1705 album").[28] The engravers, both enigmatic figures known only by their surnames, were Demarteau and DeLaCollombe. The full title of the long 1705 album is:

PLVSIEVRS PIECES ET ORNEMENTS/Darquebuzerie Les plus en Vsage Tire des/Ouurages de Laurent

Fig. 136. Title page, 1705 Simonin pattern book. Kienbusch Library, Philadelphia Museum of Art.

le Languedoc Arquebuziers/et Dautres Ornement Inuenté et graué/Par Simonin et Se Vend Ledit Liure Chez Ledit/Languedoc rue de bretagne aux marais/A Paris chez Demarteau Grav./Cloitre St Benoit N.º 350/1705

[Several parts and ornaments most utilized in gunmaking drawn from the works of Laurent le Languedoc, gunmaker, and other ornament invented and engraved by Simonin, and the said book is sold at the house of the said Languedoc, rue de Bretagne aux Marais in Paris at the house of Demarteau, engraver, Cloître St. Benoit No. 350/1705].

Perhaps the most interesting change in this title page, aside from the addition of Demarteau's name and address, is the removal of Languedoc's title as royal gunmaker; "Du Roy" has been erased from line four of the copperplate and its place filled with a calligraphic flourish. Moreover, the dolphin emblem and the fleur-de-lis, well-known insignias of the French royal house, have likewise been deleted from the title page. "Auec Priuilege" has also been removed from the last line of the title.[29] The implications are that Languedoc was no longer in royal service or, for whatever reason, was no longer allowed to describe himself as gunmaker to the king; and that the original print privilege or copyright granted to Simonin had ceased to apply.

The long 1705 album, then, consists of the title page, plates two to eight from the 1684/1685 albums, four plates signed by DeLaCollombe, numbered nine, ten, eleven, and thirteen (figs. 138–140, 142), and a panoramic engraving of a battle scene (plate twelve; fig. 141) signed by Simonin.[30] The existence of the numbered DeLaCollombe plates has long been known, but their connection, and that of the battle scene, with a Simonin pattern book was brought to light by James Lavin in 1967.[31]

That the names Demarteau and DeLaCollombe should be connected with one another as early as 1705 is also of interest. A later engraver with the same surname, Gilles Demarteau (1722–1776), is well known for his engravings after the works of François Boucher (1703–1740) and Fragonard (1732–1806), among others, and is credited with the invention or early use of the engraving technique *en manière de crayon*. Born in Liège, the son of a *gravier armurier*, he was trained as a goldsmith. At least one source described him as apprenticed to DeLaCollombe as a *graveur ciseleur* in 1739.[32] A working relationship of some kind between Gilles Demarteau and DeLaCollombe is verified by the title of a later (non-Simonin) pattern book, which reads:

Nouveaux Dessins/D'Arquebvseries/Dessiné & Gravé Par DeLaCollombe/Paris 1730/Se Vend Chez DeMarteau/Eleve de Fev M[c] DeLaCollombe

[New designs for gunmaking designed and engraved by DeLaCollombe, Paris, 1730, sold at the house of DeMarteau, student of the late M[c] DeLaCollombe].

There are two known plates signed by DeLaCollombe and dated 1730 that may have been part of this later pattern book. Its exact composition is unknown. There also exists a plate signed by DeLaCollombe and dated 1736. This suggests that in 1730, before his affiliation with Gilles, DeLaCollombe published or planned to publish a pattern book with the title as previously cited, except for the last line (which describes him as "the late" DeLaCollombe). Following DeLaCollombe's death, which must postdate the plate dated 1736, his pupil Gilles Demarteau presumably added the last line to the title page and published the pattern book, perhaps including sheets of his own dated 1743–45.[33]

The long 1705 album establishes that there was already a relationship between DeLaCollombe and another engraver named Demarteau in 1705—perhaps the father, Henri, or an uncle of the more famous Gilles Demarteau. This early relationship could explain why Gilles Demarteau and his brother Joseph were later apprenticed to DeLaCollombe. Soon after the death of Gilles in 1776, his nephew and co-worker Gilles-Anthoine moved his residence and business to 350, Cloître Saint-Benoit, the same address as that of the Demarteau cited on the title page of the long 1705 album.[34] Cloître Saint-Benoit was located on the rue Saint-Jacques, in the heart of the commercial district of Paris and, from the late-sixteenth century onward, the center of the print trade.[35] Given this information, it is safe to assume a direct familial relationship between the Demarteau cited in 1705 and Gilles and Gilles-Anthoine Demarteau.

Little is known about DeLaCollombe. Signed and dated designs indicate that he was active between 1702 and 1736.[36] The long 1705 album establishes an affiliation between

Fig. 137. Title page, long 1705 Simonin pattern book. Collection of James D. Lavin.

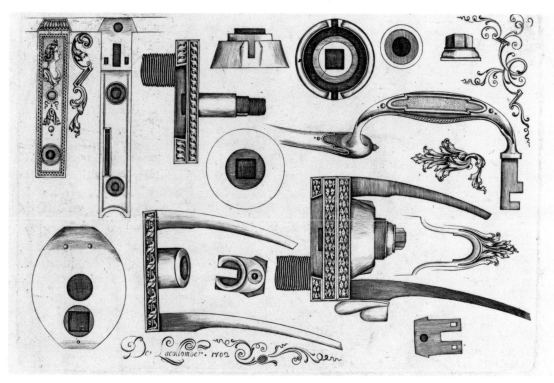

Fig. 138. Plate 9, long 1705 edition. Collection of James D. Lavin.

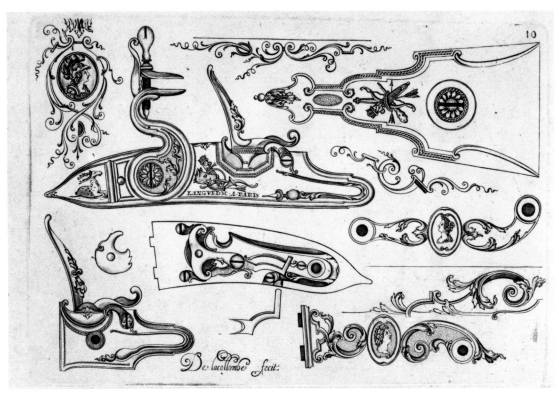

Fig. 139. Plate 10, long 1705 edition. Collection of James D. Lavin.

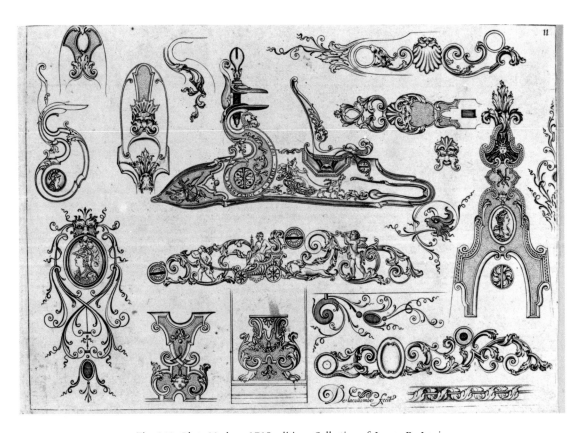

Fig. 140. Plate 11, long 1705 edition. Collection of James D. Lavin.

Fig. 141. Plate 12, long 1705 edition. Collection of James D. Lavin.

Fig. 142. Plate 13, long 1705 edition. Collection of James D. Lavin.

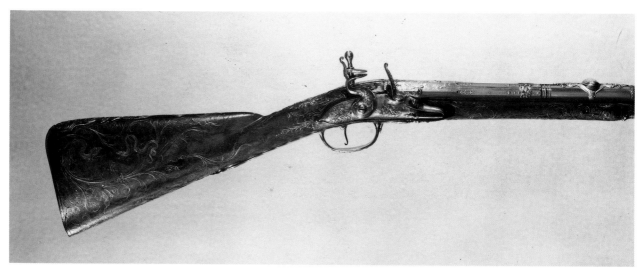

Languedoc and the senior Demarteau. Presumably, it was this link that led to the inclusion of four DeLaCollombe plates in the long 1705 album. Moreover, it can be assumed that the relationship with the Demarteaus lasted until perhaps as late as the 1740s.

In attempting to determine the respective influence of the Simonin and DeLaCollombe designs on the work of Languedoc, it should be remembered that the great majority of extant Languedoc firearms postdate Simonin's death. It is not surprising, therefore, that the decoration of the firearms shows far greater reliance on designs signed by DeLaCollombe, as opposed to those of Simonin. A pivotal piece—perhaps the finest surviving work by Languedoc—is a superb flintlock gun in the Historisches Museum, Dresden (figs. 143, 144),[37] containing a mix of designs from Simonin and DeLaCollombe that appears on no other Languedoc gun. It is noteworthy that the Simonin designs are mainly from the 1693/1695 albums, apparently the least utilized of all Simonin editions. This rare appearance of the 1693/1695 designs in conjunction with DeLaCollombe designs from the long 1705 album could be the result of a shift by Languedoc away from the Simonins (after Claude's death) to DeLaCollombe as his primary ornamentalist, perhaps about 1695 to 1700. These dates are consistent with the dating of the Dresden gun.

When considered as a whole, the texts of the six Simonin title pages reveal some easily overlooked facts, which have prompted the preceding suggestions concerning the relationships of Claude and Jacques Simonin, Laurent le Languedoc, DeLaCollombe, and the Demarteaus. This examination has also touched upon the complex question of who was originally responsible for the designs in these pattern books—gunmaker or engraver. In the case of the Simonin pattern-book designs, the facts as interpreted here suggest that the engraver/ornamentalist, not the gunmaker, was their primary creator.

Fig. 144. Detail of lockplate on flintlock gun (fig. 143).

NOTES

1 Correspondence file, Arms and Armor Department, The Metropolitan Museum of Art, New York; copy in the archives of the Kienbusch Collection of Armor and Arms, Philadelphia Museum of Art.

2 See Leonid Tarassuk, "The *Cabinet d'Armes* of Louis XIII: Some Firearms and Related Problems," *Metropolitan Museum Journal*, vol. 21 (1986), pp. 65–122.

3 Of the pirated versions, two were published in Amsterdam and two in Nuremberg. See Torsten Lenk, *The Flintlock: Its Origin and Development*, translated by G. A. Urquart, edited by John F. Hayward (London, 1965), pp. 148–49. Originally published as *Flintlåset, dess uppkomst och utveckling* (Stockholm, 1939); all citations here are to the English edition.

4 A late example is found on a pair of Italian pistols by Antonio Cameri, dated 1788 (Kienbusch Collection, 1977-167-854). The designs on the butt caps of a pseudoclassical warrior and a club-wielding centaur are taken directly from plate 4 of the 1684, 1685, and 1705 Simonin albums. The design of the side plates is taken from plate 11, signed by DeLaCollombe, of the 1705 Simonin album.

5 Translations are the author's.

6 Département des Estampes, Bibliothèque Nationale, Paris, no. Le 24 in-4, réserve, pp. 79–86 (no. P140777 to P140784). I am grateful to Maxime Preaud, Conservateur de la Reserve, Bibliothèque Nationale, and to his staff for facilitating my examination of the originals. What is apparently the earliest mention in the arms literature of the 1684 album appears in Wendelin Boeheim, "Die Luxusgewehr-Fabrication in Frankreich im XVII. and XVIII. Jahrhundert," pt. 1, *Blatter fur Kunstgewerbe*, vol. 15 (Vienna, 1886), p. 36. Boeheim, however, does not give the location of the Simonin album cited.

7 One copy was also required for the king's cabinet at the Louvre from 1686 onward. See Peter Fuhring, "The Print Privilege in Eighteenth-Century France," pt. 1 of 2, *Print Quarterly*, vol. 2, no. 3 (September 1985), p. 180. What may also be the proof copy of Jean Berain's pattern book of 1667 is in the Département des Estampes, Bibliothèque Nationale, bound in the same volume as the Simonin pattern book under discussion (see note 6, nos. P140767–P140775).

8 Victoria and Albert Museum, London, inv. no. 1230-1908.

9 Lenk 1965, p. 147.

10 The Berlin copy is cited in A. Lotz, *Katalog der Ornament-stichsammlung der Staatlichen Kunstbibliothek, Berlin* (Berlin, 1936–39), no. O.S.840:1. I am grateful to Christina Thon of the Kunstbibliothek, Berlin, for allowing me to examine this copy and for providing photographs.

11 D. Guilmard, *Les Maîtres ornemanistes, dessinateurs, peintres, architectes, sculpteurs, et graveurs: Ecoles francaise,—italienne,—allemande,—et des Pays-Bas (flamande & hollandaise) . . .* (Paris, 1880–81), p. 109, no. 61G. Lenk 1965, p. 147, implies that Guilmard cites the Bibliothèque Nationale's copy as having twelve sheets. Guilmard's entry, however, states only his belief that the 1684 pattern book should have twelve sheets, eight of which, he says, are to be found in the Bibliothèque Nationale. Guilmard apparently confused the 1684/85 editions with the 1693/95 editions, which he incorrectly considered to be identical. On the composition of the Grancsay version, see Stephen V. Grancsay, *Master French Gunsmiths' Designs of the XVII–XIX Centuries* (New York, 1970), p. 14; also Wallace B. Gusler and James D. Lavin, *Decorated Firearms, 1540–1870 from the Collection of Clay P. Bedford* (Williamsburg, Va., 1977), p. 152, n. 1.

12 For a description of the entrance to Faubourg Saint-

Antoine, see G. Brice, *Description de la ville de Paris*, 9th ed. (Paris, 1752), p. 243. Simonin's shop was presumably close to the entrance to Saint-Antoine, which was next to the Bastille and was the principal portal to the faubourg. Faubourg Saint-Antoine was one of the privileged quarters (*lieux privileges*), areas in which artisans could practice their crafts free from certain taxes, guild restrictions, and other regulations. It was a particularly popular quarter for woodworkers. See Jacques Hillairet, *Dictionnaire historique des rues de Paris*, vol. 1 (Paris, 1963), p. 496.

13 Regarding the 1721 date of death, see Ulrich Thieme and Felix Becker, eds., *Allgemeines Lexikon der Bildenden Kunstler von der Antike bis zur Gegenwart*, vol. 31 (Leipzig, 1937), p. 74; Marquis de Granges de Surgeres, *Les Artistes nantais . . . du moyen age a la revolution. Notes et documentes inedits* (1898), pp. 433–34; E. Benezit, *Dictionnaire critique et documentaire des peintres, sculpteurs, dessinateurs, et graveurs . . .*, vol. 9 (Paris, 1976), pp. 617–18; Simon Jervis, *Dictionary of Design and Designers* (Harmondsworth, 1984), p. 452. Certainly more than one engraver named Claude Simonin may have been active, as the documents cited in the previous sources attest. Note, however, that Lenk correctly gave the date of Claude Simonin's death as "not later than 1693" (1965, p. 147).

14 For the most concise summary of the available information on Languedoc, see entry 87 by Stuart W. Pyhrr in The Metropolitan Museum of Art, New York, *Liechtenstein: The Princely Collections* (New York, 1985), pp. 133–35 (exhibition, October 26, 1985–May 1, 1986). Languedoc's address is given on the 1705 title pages (see excerpts later in the text) as "rue de bretagne aux marais." Marais bordered Faubourg Saint-Antoine and housed a large community of *serruriers* (makers of decorative ironwork). See Catherine Prade, "Sur les traces des maitres serruriers," in *Le Marais: Mythe et realite* (Paris, 1987), pp. 209–12.

15 For instance, at least nineteen of the Languedoc pieces in the Historisches Museum, Dresden, bear a version of the JL monogram (see note 17). What may be the JLL monogram is found on Dresden guns nos. GG1279, 1280, and 1281. A Languedoc gun in the Clay Bedford Collection bears a rubbed monogram read as possibly JS by Gusler and Lavin (1977, p. 38).

16 See The Metropolitan Museum of Art 1985, with references to Pierre Jarlier, *Répertoire d'arquebusiers et de fourbisseurs français . . .* (Saint Julien du Sault, 1976; 1st suppl., 1978; 2nd suppl., 1981); and to Eugène Heer, *Der Neue Støckel . . .* (Schwäbisch Hall, 1978). Jarlier, unfortunately, does not list the specific documentary sources from which his information is drawn.

17 I am greatly indebted to Dieter Schaal, Director, Historisches Museum, Dresden, for his kind assistance in allowing me to examine these firearms. Of the thirty-one guns, six have barrels signed by Languedoc and locks signed by Johann Wirsling of Dresden (nos. GG1282, 1283, 1284, 1292, 1293, and 1294). In reference to the latest dated Languedoc guns, note that John F. Hayward (*The Art of the Gunmaker*, vol. 2 [London, 1963], p. 46) gave the date as 1722. Pyhrr (The Metropolitian Museum of Art 1985) cited a Languedoc gun dated 1733 in the Liechtenstein Collection (no. 3935). The Dresden example dated 1733 is an

over-and-under flintlock shotgun (no. GG1397). The 1738 date given in Max von Ehrenthal (*Fuhrer durch die Konigliche Gewehr-Galerie zu Dresden* [Dresden, 1900], p. 68) is apparently incorrect.

18 Composite sporting gun, Musée de l'Armée, Paris, inv. no. M21088. Sold at Hôtel Drouot, Paris, March 23, 1973, lot 107. I thank J.-P. Reverseau for photographs and information concerning this gun. It is composed of a barrel by the Spanish gunmaker Gaspar Fernandez (active c. 1626–c. 1657), which bears his mark and the inscription "Don Carlos Segundo" (King of Spain, 1665–1700), a lock inscribed "LE LANGUEDOC A PARIS," and a stock that appears to date from the second quarter of the eighteenth century.

19 The possibility of two Languedocs was suggested as early as 1886 by Wendelin Boeheim (1886, p. 38), when he included "Languedoc der Jünger" on his list of important eighteenth-century French gunmakers. In 1897 Boeheim stated that two famous masters were known under the name of Laurent le Languedoc (*Meister der Waffenschmiede-Kunst vom XIV. bis ins XVIII Jahrhundert* [Berlin, 1897], p. 111). In neither instance, however, did he cite documentary evidence or the reason behind the assertion. Regarding longevity, Languedoc's contemporary, the gunmaker Bertrand Piraube, held *brevet de logement* from 1660 to 1724. George Keiser (1647–1740), a Viennese court gunmaker, made weapons into his nineties (see Hayward 1963, pp. 43 and 120).

20 For an overall discussion, see Fuhring 1985, pt. 1, pp. 174–93, and pt. 2 (vol. 3, no. 1 [March, 1986]), pp. 19–33.

21 Regarding the use of these terms and the division of labor, see Marianne Grivel, *Le Commerce de l'estampe à Paris au XVIIᵉ siècle* (Paris, 1986), pp. 7ff.

22 Lenk 1965, pl. 121, 1 and 2, illustrating the 1693 title page, and pl. 10. The 1693 and, more seldom, the 1695 editions are mentioned elsewhere in the firearms literature but have not been discussed in detail (for instance, Boeheim 1897, p. 111; and Hayward 1963, pp. 294–96). Grancsay 1970, incorrectly illustrates plates 8, 9, 10, and 12 of the 1693/1695 album as part of his composite 1684 album (see note 24 below).

23 Based on a comparison of the Metropolitan Museum of Art's 1693 edition (20.36.2), the 1695 edition in the Kienbusch Collection Library, and an identical 1695 edition in the Kunstbibliothek, Berlin (no. OS840: 2; cited in Lotz 1936–39).

24 Grancsay, apparently again following Guilmard (see note 11), twice incorrectly published the 1693/1695 editions as identical to the 1684/1685 editions. See Grancsay 1970, p. 168, and his *Master French Gunsmiths' Designs of the Mid-Seventeenth Century* (New York, 1950), p. 20. In both he cited the number of the Metropolitan Museum of Art's 1693 edition incorrectly as 27.23.19–29. This number, in fact, belongs to an unbound composite Simonin album consisting of a 1695 title page, plates 2–8 of the 1684/1685 editions, and plates 9–12 of the long 1705 edition. Perhaps Grancsay overlooked or disregarded the Metropolitan Museum of Art's homogeneous 1693 edition, no. 20.36.2.

25 For instance, from the 1684/1685 albums a trigger

guard (plate 7; fig. 122) and interior views of two locks (plates 4 and 5; figs. 119, 120) appear in the 1693/1695 albums on plates 5 (fig. 128), 8 (fig. 131), and 9 (fig. 132), respectively.

26 There is no mention of a Jacques Simonin in the sources cited in note 13, although other sons of Claude are cited. Jarlier (1976, col. 252) cited Claude and Jacques as brothers who were responsible for pattern books in 1685 and 1693.

27 I am grateful to Lena Rangström and Enar Erikson of the Livrustkammaren, Stockholm, for information and reproductions of the Simonin album.

28 See James Duncan Lavin, ''The French Pattern Book of Nicholas Bis: Gunsmith to Felipe V of Spain,'' *Connoisseur*, vol. 165, no. 666 (August, 1967), pp. 274–79. The title page illustrated here (fig. 137) is the only extant copy known to me. It was apparently also unknown to Grancsay, Lenk, and other writers on the subject. I am also very grateful to Dr. Lavin for his advice throughout the preparation of this article.

29 The removal of the emblems and of ''Auec Priuilege'' was pointed out by Lavin in ibid., p. 276.

30 On a detached print of the battle scene in the Metropolitan Museum of Art (27.23.30), Simonin's signature is followed by ''AVEC PRVILE DV ROY.'' This has been deleted from the Lavin plate 12, probably for the same reason—the grant of privilege had expired—that ''Auec Priuilege'' was removed from the title page.

31 Lavin 1967, p. 276.

32 Marcel Roux, *Bibliothèque nationale, Département des estampes. Inventaire du fonds francais, graveurs du XVIIIᵉ siècle*, vol. 6 (Paris, 1949), p. 329, no. 1. See also Henri Bouchot, ''Les Graveurs Demarteau, Gilles, et Gilles-Anthoine (1722–1802), d'après des documents inédits,'' *La Revue de L'Art Ancien et Moderne*, no. 18 (July–December 1905), p. 98.

33 Examples of the 1730 title page, the DeLaCollombe sheets dated 1730 and 1736, and the Demarteau sheets dated 1743, 1744, and 1745 may be found in the Cooper-Hewitt Museum, New York, in a bound volume (inv. no. 1921-6-325). I am grateful to Elaine Evans Dee and Lillian Clagett of the Cooper-Hewitt. The composition of this pattern book is speculated upon by G. de Bellaigue and A.V.B. Norman in ''An Eighteenth-Century French Pattern Book: Its Sources and Uses,'' *Connoisseur*, vol. 157, no. 631 (September 1964), p. 16.

34 Regarding Gilles, Gilles-Anthoine, and Joseph Demarteau, see Roux 1949, pp. 327–29, 484, and 501; also the exhibition catalogue by the Baltimore Museum of Art and the Minneapolis Institute of Arts, *Regency to Empire: French Printmaking, 1715–1814* (Minneapolis, 1984), nos. 40 and 74, and p. 347. The short biography of Gilles on page 347 states that he joined his younger brother Joseph as an apprentice in DeLaCollombe's shop. See Bouchot 1905, pp. 109–10, where he states that Gilles-Anthoine purchased the Cloître Saint-Benoit property from the creditors of a former wine merchant named Percheron.

35 Grivel 1986, pp. 59ff.

36 The 1702 plate is found in the long 1705 album as plate 9. For DeLaCollombe, in addition to the references cited in notes 30 and 32, see Lenk 1965, pp. 153–55; Michèle Hébert and Yves Sjöberg, *Bibliothèque nationale, Département des estampes. Inventaire du fonds français, graveurs du XVIIIᵉ siècle*, vol. 12 (Paris, 1973), pp. 283–84, with references; and Heribert Seitz, ''DeLaCollombe as a Furbisher,'' *Livrustkammaren*, vol. 13, nos. 11–12 (1975), pp. 345–51.

37 Historisches Museum, Dresden, no. GG735. See Lenk 1965, pl. 81 and p. 153.